# THE RIGHT TO KEEP AND BEAR ARMS

# THE RIGHT TO KEEP AND BEAR ARMS

☆☆☆

*A Continuing American Dilemma*

*By*

**EARL R. KRUSCHKE, Ph.D.**

*Professor of Political Science*
*California State University, Chico*
*Chico, California*



**CHARLES C THOMAS • PUBLISHER**
*Springfield • Illinois • U.S.A.*

*Published and Distributed Throughout the World by*

CHARLES C THOMAS • PUBLISHER
2600 South First Street
Springfield, Illinois 62717



ISBN 0-398-05141-0

Library of Congress Catalog Card Number: 85-4760

*With* THOMAS BOOKS *careful attention is given to all details of manufacturing and design. It is the Publisher's desire to present books that are satisfactory as to their physical qualities and artistic possibilities and appropriate for their particular use.* THOMAS BOOKS *will be true to those laws of quality that assure a good name and good will.*

*Printed in the United States of America*
*Q-R-3*

**Library of Congress Cataloging in Publication Data**

Kruschke, Earl R. (Earl Roger), 1934-
The right to keep and bear arms.

Bibliography: p.
1. Firearms--Law and legislation--United States.
I. Title.
KF3941.K78 1985 344.73'0533 85-4760
ISBN 0-398-05141-0 347.304533

**TO MARILYN ANN KRUSCHKE**

# PREFACE

I HAVE BEEN interested in the subject of the Second Amendment—the "right to keep and bear arms"—for nearly 30 years. The issue of whether that amendment refers to a "collective" or to an "individual" right has lain relatively dormant for much of that time. During the last decade or so, however—and especially during the last five years—the controversy over the meaning and application of the amendment's provisions has received increasing attention. And with the relatively recent decisions in *Quilici v. Village of Morton Grove* and *Michael Kalodimos et al., Appellants v. The Village of Morton Grove, Appellee*, it seems almost certain that the issue will capture even more interest in the future and that the groundwork may very well have been laid for a review by the United States Supreme Court.

There exist by now in the legal and historical journals many excellent articles which attempt analysis of the meaning and origins of the Second Amendment. There are also a number of more or less polemical works on the subject. The bulk of the most scholarly work has appeared only relatively recently, however; and during especially the last three or four years, the work of scholars such as Kates and Malcolm—and particularly that of Halbrook—have provided the most definitive treatments of the subject.

But these are works of scholarship which are, unfortunately, not readily accessible to, or—again unfortunately—not likely to be read by a wide audience outside of the professional academic and legal communities. This book attempts to bridge this gap, at least in part. It attempts in an admittedly general and rudimentary way to set out the major dimensions of the controversy surrounding the Second Amendment for both students and interested laymen. It attempts to do this by:

(1) briefly introducing the reader to the historical context of the controversy surrounding the language of the Second Amendment;
(2) presenting an interpretation of the amendment by a writer on each side of the controversy (articles were chosen almost exclusively on the basis of brevity; there are many lengthy articles on the subject which constitute more complete expositions of the respective positions, but space limitations did not permit their use);
(3) presenting excerpts from court opinions representing both the collective and the individual views;
(4) presenting excerpts from the four United States Supreme Court opinions which have for the most part dealt only indirectly with the subject;
(5) summarizing the controversy and raising some issues—as presented in the literature—in the context of the so-called "gun problem" in the United States and by presenting a few alternative "solutions" suggested by some scholars of the subject;
(6) offering the student and layman two appendices containing information otherwise not readily available:
    (a) the provisions of state constitutions dealing with the right to keep and bear arms; and
    (b) a list of selected cases on the right to keep and bear arms, and on the bases for state and federal regulation; and
(7) presenting a Selected Bibliography which will serve as a sound introduction for future study of the subject.

Engaging in research and writing in a university which does not have a major research library nor which readily provides money or free time to produce scholarly work presents many obtacles which cannot be easily overcome without the help of others. I wish especially to acknowledge the assistance and encouragement of Joel Leonard and Henrietta Lo, the university's law and social science reference librarians; Bill Stuve, government publications and map librarian, and Gloria Cancello, library assistant, for their extraordinary ability to locate almost instantly those arcane government documents which seem otherwise virtually inaccessible; Sylvia Jones and Lorraine Mosley, of the university's inter-library loan department, whose efforts to locate books and periodicals over many months have been nothing but outstanding; the staff of the State Law Library in Sacramento, California, for their expertise and unstinting willingness to assist in any way necessary; the staff of the Butte County, California, Law Library, for putting their resources at my disposal; Carl Borgquist, my former student and assistant during the very early phases of this project; and the hundreds of writers and scholars, only some of whose works are cited in the Selected Bibliography, whose publications were consulted during the completion of this volume. Finally, to my wife, Marilyn Ann Kruschke, who endured a not inconsiderable number of inconveniences while this book was being completed, I owe, as always, my greatest debt.

For any errors of commission or omission, I alone assume responsibility.

Earl R. Kruschke
Chico, California

# CONTENTS

# THE RIGHT TO KEEP AND BEAR ARMS

# Chapter I

# "TO KEEP AND BEAR ARMS": INTRODUCTION TO A DILEMMA

THE SECOND AMENDMENT to the Constitution of the United States provides:

"A well regulated Militia, being necessary to the security of a free State, the right of the people to keep and bear arms shall not be infringed."

These few words, the meaning and interpretation of which may appear obvious to the casual reader, remain the subject of intense controversy among jurists, scholars, and laymen alike. Indeed, since the decision in *Quilici v. Village of Morton Grove*[1]—a decision which banned (with some exceptions) the possession of all operable handguns in the Village of Morton Grove, Illinois—the debate over the meaning of the words of the Second Amendment seems destined to reach epic proportions. The fact that the decision in *Quilici* has withstood challenges in the federal courts, and that it has only recently been upheld by the Illinois Supreme Court,[2] has hardly quelled the debate, but has probably added only further grist to the scholarly and judicial mill.

It is not the intention here to develop a full examination of the evolution of the right to keep and bear arms. The literature on this

[1] *Quilici v. Village of Morton Grove*, 532 F. Supp. 1169 (N.D. Ill. 1981), affd. 695 F.2d 261 (7th Circ. 1982), cert. den. 104 S. Ct. 194 (1983).

[2] *Michael Kalodimos et al., Appellants, v. The Village of Morton Grove, Appellee*, Filed October 19, 1984.

subject is already rich and extensive.[3] Here we shall attempt only to introduce the reader to the historical setting of the controversy. Implications and ramifications of these comments will be reserved for the last part of the book.

To state that man has kept and borne arms since prehistoric times is undoubtedly to state a truism. Whether with stick, club, tree branch, rock, or the jawbone of a subdued beast, the brute which was to evolve into modern man went forth, drawing upon the experience stored in the dim recesses of his underdeveloped brain, to attack, to hunt, or to defend. Prehistoric man was probably born into an environment in which weapons were fundamental instruments of existence. This fact lays the foundation, of course, for those who argue that the use of weapons was evolved in the original state of nature and that, therefore, the right to keep and bear arms—particularly in defense of one's self, one's family, and one's property—is a "natural right."

Awareness of this natural rights philosophy was surely a part of the intellectual, philosophical, and political foundation on which the framers of the Constitution and the writers of the Second Amendment based their thinking. These were enlightened and informed men. To them, the study of history and philosophy was considered both a noble and a practical undertaking. Indeed, to the colonists in general, "books were the high road to history. . . ."[4]

More specifically, that they had read and been influenced by literature warning of the baleful effects of standing armies and of mercenaries, and of the advantages of an individually-armed citizenry for the maintenance of both personal and public liberty is likewise evident. Although the framers might have been eclectic in their reading, as a group they were exposed to the work of Plato, Aristotle, Livy, Cicero, Grotius, Vattel, Pufendorf, Galen, Hobbes, Rousseau, Beccaria, Machiavelli, Montesquieu, Hume, Bodin, Locke, Harrington, Sydney, Voltaire, Burgh, Trenchard, Gordon, Macaulay, Smith,

---

[3]The reader is referred to the Selected Bibliography at the end of this volume for references which will serve as a good introduction to the subject. The best book currently available is Stephen P. Halbrook, *That Every Man Be Armed: The Evolution of a Constitutional Right* (Albuquerque: University of New Mexico Press, 1984). See also Joyce Lee Malcolm, "The Right of the People to Keep and Bear Arms: The Common Law Tradition," *Hastings Constitutional Law Quarterly*, Volume 10, 1983.

[4]H. Trevor Colbourn, *The Lamp of Experience: Whig History and the Intellectual Origins of the American Revolution* (Chapel Hill: University of North Carolina Press, 1965), p. 9.

Coke, and Blackstone, among others, all of whom had made observations of one type or another about the role of an armed citizenry and the bearing of weapons. In the words of Bailyn,

> To judge simply from an enumeration of the colonists' citations, they had at their finger tips, and made use of, a large portion of the inheritance of western culture, from Aristotle to Moliere, from Cicero to 'Philoleuterus Lipiensis' [Richard Bentley], from Virgil to Shakespeare, Ramus, Pufendorf, Swift, and Rousseau. They liked to display authorities for their arguments, citing and quoting from them freely; at times their writings become almost submerged in annotation. . . .[5]

Thus, in Plato they would have read about the early concept of a people's militia:

> . . . citizens ought to practise war—not in time of war, but rather while they are at peace. And every city which has any sense, should take the field at least one day in every month, and for more if the magistrates think fit, having no regard to winter cold or summer heat; and they should go out *en masse*, including their wives and children . . . and they should have tournaments, imitating in as lively a manner as they can real battles.[6]

In Cicero, they would have read of the natural law of self defense:

> . . . gentlemen, there exists a law, not written down anywhere but inborn in our hearts; a law which comes to us not by training or custom or reading but by itself; a law which has come to us not from theory but from practice, not by instruction but by natural intuition. I refer to the law which lays it down that, if our lives are endangered by plots of violence or armed robbers or enemies, any and every method of protecting ourselves is morally right. When weapons reduce them to silence, the laws no longer expect one to await their pronouncements. For people who decide to wait for these will have to wait for justice, too. . . . Indeed, even the wisdom of the law itself, by a sort of tacit implication, permits self-defense, because it does not actually forbid men to kill; what it does, instead, is to forbid the bearing of a weapon with the inten-

[5]Bernard Bailyn, *The Ideological Origins of the American Revolution* (Cambridge: The Belknap Press of Harvard University Press, 1967), p. 23.

[6]Plato, *Laws*, Book VIII, Jowett translation, in *Great Books of the Western World* (Chicago: Encyclopedia Britannica, Inc., 1952), Volume 7, p. 732.

tention to kill.[7]

From Adam Smith they would have gleaned the following about standing armies: "Men of republican principles have been jealous of a standing army as dangerous to liberty. . . . The standing army of Caesar destroyed the Roman republic. The standing army of Cromwell turned the Long Parliament out of doors."[8]

From Rousseau they would have been counseled about the dangers of mercenaries and standing armies as follows:

> . . . for all the victories of the early Romans . . . had been won by brave citizens, who were ready, at need, to give their blood in the service of their country, but would never sell it. Only at the siege of Veii did the practice of paying the Roman infantry begin. . . . As they were given over to blind obedience, their swords were always at the throats of their fellow-citizens, and they were prepared for general butchery at the first sign. It would not be difficult to show that this was one of the principal causes of the ruin of the Roman Empire.[9]

And, in Machiavelli, they would have read that ". . . the ruin of Italy has been caused by nothing else than by resting all her hopes for many years on mercenaries. . . ."[10]

In summary, the framers of the constitution worked in an intellectual universe of classical and seventeenth century republican thought. And, "Among the strands of thought most commonly discussed as central to this persuasion two are immediately relevant to understanding the Second Amendment. These are the fear of standing armies and the exaltation of militias composed of ordinary citizens."[11] Republican thought rested largely on Florentine tradition as represented especially by Machiavelli, who ". . . idealized the citizen-warrior as the staunchest bulwark of a republic. . . . From this developed a

---

[7]*Selected Political Speeches of Cicero*, translated with an Introduction by Michael Grant (Baltimore: Penguin Books, 1969), p. 222.

[8]Adam Smith, *An Inquiry Into the Nature and Causes of the Wealth of Nations*, in *Great Books of the Western World* (Chicago: Encyclopedia Britannica, Inc., 1952), Volume 39, p. 308.

[9]Jean Jacques Rousseau, *A Discourse on Political Economy*, in *Great Books of the Western World* (Chicago: Encyclopedia Britannica, Inc., 1952), Volume 38, p. 380.

[10]Nicolo Machiavelli, *The Prince*, in *Great Books of the Western World* (Chicago: Encyclopedia Britannica, Inc., 1952), Volume 23, p. 18.

[11]Robert E. Shalhope, "The Ideological Origins of the Second Amendment," *The Journal of American History*, Volume 69, No. 3, December, 1982, p. 601.

sociology of liberty that rested upon the role of arms in society: political conditions must allow the arming of all citizens. . . ."[12]

Of more immediate and direct influence on the framers, however, was the tradition of the English common law, with which all of them were familiar. It must be emphasized, in other words, that the right to keep and bear arms was not established by the Second Amendment. It has its foundation in English jurisprudence. Indeed,

> None of the rights found in the Bill of Rights is granted or created by that document. Rather, the Bill of Rights protects against infringement or abridgement those fundamental human rights which the framers viewed as naturally belonging to each individual human being. It would be a grotesque perversion of the framers' understanding of the concept of rights to suggest that any of the rights found in the Bill of Rights, particularly the few substantive rights of the first and second amendments, were created by that document.[13]

That Englishmen were armed as early as 602 or 603 is evident from charters and the early laws of England. At that time, for example, Ethelbert, King of Kent, issued a decree limiting their use (thus, in effect, recognizing a prior right to keep and bear them). He proclaimed, "If anyone provides a man with weapons, when a quarrel has arisen, and [yet] no injury results, he is to pay six shillings compensation."[14] Similar edicts were proclaimed by Hlothhere and Eadric in the 600s,[15] Alfred in the 800s,[16] and Cnut in 1020-1023, whose secular laws include, for example, "If anyone illegally disarms a man, he is to compensate him. . . ."[17]

The right—and obligation—of every Englishman to be armed can be traced approximately to the year 870, however, when Alfred estab-

[12] *Ibid.* See also Stephen P. Halbrook, "The Second Amendment as a Phenomenon of Classical Political Philosophy," in Don B. Kates, ed., *Firearms and Violence: Issues of Public Policy* (San Francisco: Pacific Institute for Public Policy Research and Ballinger, 1984), and J. G. A. Pocock, *The Machiavellian Moment* (Princeton: Princeton University Press, 1975).

[13] See Richard E. Gardiner, "To Preserve Liberty—A Look at the Right to Keep and Bear Arms," *Northern Kentucky Law Review*, Volume 10, No. 1, 1982, p. 64, n. 3

[14] See Dorothy Whitelock, ed., *English Historical Documents c. 500-1042* (New York: Oxford University Press, 1955), Volume I, p. 358.

[15] *Ibid.*, p. 361.

[16] *Ibid.*, p. 379.

[17] *Ibid.*, p. 427.

lished a military organization known as the fyrd. The fyrd was composed of three units: the king's personal troops, known as house guards; the select fyrd, made up of individuals who trained more or less regularly and who were paid out of the treasury; and the general fyrd, comparable to the French *arrière-ban*, made up of all able males in the kingdom, each of whom was required to arm himself at his own expense, and be prepared to defend the nation.

Later, such statutes as the Assize of Arms of Henry II (1181), the Statute of Winchester of Edward I, and the Statute of Northhampton of Edward III, carried further the legal requirement that all persons keep arms for the purpose of defending the nation. The Statute of Winchester, for example, is particularly instructive. Enacted during a time when brigandry and bands of armed marauders were commonplace, ". . . it brought up-to-date the list of weapons and armour which every male between 16 and 60 was to keep in instant readiness at his house, for service in the militia. According to a nicely graded scale of wealth these ranged from a simple bow and arrows to 'a hauberke and helme of iron, a sword, a knife, and a horse'."[18] By 1511, moreover, Henry VII had ordered that all Englishmen under 40 years of age regularly train with the long bow, which at the time was probably the deadliest weapon known.

Thus, the absence of a standing army and the nonexistence of a police force necessitated an armed population. Citizens were organized into so-called "trained bands," usually under the leadership of influential members of the town or community, for purposes of providing protection.[19] Attempts were made to equip these citizen-soldiers and to train them in appropriate military tactics of the time.

In addition, it was expected that all able-bodied males would be available for service in the *posse comitatus*, called up by the sheriff to pursue law-breakers or to deal with other disturbances to the public order. Citizens were expected to maintain suitable weapons for such service. The role of the citizenry in police work is also reflected in the fact that when they had witnessed a crime, they were expected to raise a "hue and cry" and were expected to summon their neighbors for

[18] T. A. Critchley, *The Conquest of Violence* (New York: Schocken Books, 1970), p. 35.

[19] A good discussion of "trained bands" is found, for example, in Lindsay Boynton, *The Elizabethan Militia 1558-1638* (London:. Routledge & Kegan Paul, 1967), pp. 90-125.

pursuit of the law-breaker. In addition, it was the obligation of citizens to keep watch and ward. At night, when a town or city "closed down," the responsibility for preserving the public peace and alerting others to public danger was rotated among the citizens. Similar duties were required during the daytime. "Widows, disabled men, and other townsmen unable to carry out the task had to hire substitutes to serve in their stead."[20] For all of these activities, then, individual citizens were expected to have private arms.

William Blackstone, one of the most authoritative commentators on the common law as it had developed in eighteenth-century England, clearly set forth the absolute rights of individuals. He regarded these rights as fundamental to man; they were rights which grew out of the state of nature and were part of every man's entitlement. It is worth quoting Blackstone at some length on this issue:

> . . . we have taken a short view of the principal absolute rights which appertain to every Englishman. But in vain would these rights be declared, ascertained, and protected by the dead letter of the laws, if the constitution had provided no other method to secure their actual enjoyment. It has therefore established certain other auxiliary subordinate rights of the subject, which serve principally as outworks or barriers to protect and maintain inviolate the three great and primary rights, of personal security, personal liberty, and private property. These are:
>
> 1. The constitution, powers, and privileges of parliament; . . .
> 2. The limitation of the king's prerogative. . . .
> 3. . . . applying to the courts of justice for redress of injuries. . .
> 4. . . . the right of petitioning the king, or either house of parliament, for the redress of grievances. . . .
> 5. The fifth and last auxiliary right of the subject, that I shall at present mention, is that of having arms for their defence, suitable to their condition and degree, and such as are allowed by law. Which is also declared by the same statute . . . and is indeed a public allowance, under due restrictions, of the natural right of resistance and self-preservation, when the sanctions of society and laws are found insufficient to restrain the violence of oppression.[21]

[20]Joyce Lee Malcolm, "The Right of the People to Keep and Bear Arms: The Common Law Tradition," *Hastings Constitutional Law Quarterly*, Volume 10, 1983, p. 292.

[21]William Blackstone, *Commentaries on the Laws of England*, pp. 141-144, George Chase ed. (New York: Banks & Brothers, 1884), pp. 81-84.

Other commentators, such as Hawkins and Coke, for example, supported Blackstone in his view. Eventually, the right to bear arms was written into the English Bill of Rights of 1689. Thus, "As an article of the English Bill of Rights, the right to have arms was part and parcel of that bundle of rights and privileges that Englishmen carried with them to America and which they later fought to preserve."[22]

Only a few final observations need be made in this brief introduction. One has to do with the meaning of the word "militia" in the eighteenth century context of revolutionary America. Clearly, given the colonists' English background, it was intended to mean every able-bodied white male between what was considered the age of majority and some ultimate maximum age. The obligation to keep arms applied to every household. Even the Congress, after the passage of the Second Amendment, ". . . defined the militia to include the entire able-bodied military-age male citizenry of the United States and required each of them to own his own firearm."[23]

Subsequently, Thomas M. Cooley, one of the great commentators on American jurisprudence, wrote:

> The Right is General.—It might be supposed from the phraseology of this provision that the right to keep and bear arms was only guaranteed to the militia; but this would be an interpretation not warranted by the intent. The militia . . . consists of those persons who, under the law, are liable to the performance of military duty, and are officered and enrolled for service when called upon. . . . The meaning of the provision undoubtedly is, that the people, from whom the militia must be taken, shall have the right to keep and bear arms; and they need no permission or regulation of law for the purpose.[24]

Finally, even the Supreme Court, in one of the rare instances in which it has confronted a Second Amendment issue, has defined the militia to mean all citizens or all males capable of bearing arms. It also stated that "ordinarily when called for service these men were ex-

---

[22]Joyce Lee Malcolm, "The Right of the People to Keep and Bear Arms: The Common Law Tradition," *Hastings Constitutional Law Quarterly*, Volume 10, 1983, pp.305-306.

[23]Don B. Kates, Jr., "Handgun Prohibition and the Original Meaning of the Second Amendment," *Michigan Law Review*, Volume 82, No. 2, November, 1983, p. 216.

[24]Thomas M. Cooley, *The General Principles of Constitutional Law in the United States of America* (Boston: Little, Brown, and Company, 1880), p. 271,

pected to appear bearing arms supplied by themselves and of the kind in common use at the time."[25]

A second observation has to do with the meaning of the word "people." When referring to the "right of the people" in the Second Amendment, did they have in mind a collectivity or were they referring to individuals? Undoubtedly, given the framers' experience with English tradition and the context in which the Amendment is located, they had an individual right in mind. This was not a blanket endorsement, inasmuch as English and colonial tradition had likewise excluded certain classes from weapons ownership, e.g., lunatics, idiots, infants, and felons. But given the fact that the amendment is part of the Bill of Rights, and that the first, fourth, ninth, and tenth amendments have been construed to refer to individuals rather than to a collectivity, it would seem bizarre to assume that they did not have individuals in mind when they wrote the second. To rationalize a collective view, one would have to assume that the framers referred to individuals in the first amendment, to the states in the second, to individuals in the fourth, to individuals in the ninth, and then separated the states and the people in the tenth amendment, even though this was inconsistent with the wording of the second. In the words of Don B. Kates, Jr., "Any one of these textual incongruities demanded by an exclusively state's rights position dooms it. Cumulatively they present a truly grotesque reading of the Bill of Rights."[26] Indeed, in an extraordinarily useful linguistic analysis of the Second Amendment, Stephen P. Halbrook reaches the same conclusion: ". . . the syntax of the proposition that makes up the Second Amendment necessitates the construction that the right to keep and bear arms is absolute and is not dependent on the needs of the militia; the contrary view . . . commits the fallacy of denying the antecedent and is therefore a misconstruction."[27]

In short, the best evidence points toward the assertion of an individual right. Had the framers had in mind a collective right, they

---

[25]*U.S. v. Miller*, 307 U.S. 174, 179 (1939).

[26]Don B. Kates, Jr., "Handgun Prohibition and the Original Meaning of the Second Amendment," *Michigan Law Review*, Volume *2, No. 2, November, 1983, p. 218.

[27]Stephen P. Halbrook, *That Every Man Be Armed: The Evolution of a Constitutional Right* (Albuquerque: University of New Mexico Press, 1984), p. 86.

probably would have said ". . . the right of *the militia* to keep and bear arms shall not be infringed."[28]

This, in brief, provides the historical context of the contemporary controversy over the role of the Second Amendment in resolving legal and philosophical issues raised by decisions like that of *Quilici*. Scholars, lawyers, and judges, using essentially the same body of evidence, have reached diametrically opposed conclusions on the meaning and application of the language of the Second Amendment. The collective, or state's rights, view, embraces the idea that the writers of the Second Amendment were responding to fears that the national government might attempt to disarm the state militias. Those who embrace the collective view also assert that the Second Amendment was a response to the fear of large standing armies. In short, the "people" referred to are—according to this view—to be considered those who were intended to serve in the militias. The proponents of the individual view, on the other hand, argue that the Amendment does not create a state right but instead protects a preexisting individual right. It was through an attempt to protect the individual that protection of the militia was achieved. The "people" referred to in the Amendment are, therefore, to be viewed as the same people referred to in the first, fourth, ninth, and tenth amendments—namely, individuals.

In the next section of the book, a representative viewpoint from both "individual" and "collective" positions is presented. Then in Chapter III, excerpts from legal opinions illustrative of both individual and collective positions are reproduced from leading cases, together with excerpts from the four Supreme Court cases which have touched to some extent upon Second Amendment issues.

[28]James E. Edwards, *Myths About Guns* (Coral Springs: Peninsula Press, 1978), p. 88.

# Chapter II

# "THE RIGHT TO KEEP AND BEAR ARMS": "COLLECTIVE" v. "INDIVIDUAL" INTERPRETATION

## A. COLLECTIVE INTERPRETATION

### THE RIGHT TO BEAR ARMS: THE DEVELOPMENT OF THE AMERICAN EXPERIENCE*

JOHN LEVIN

#### I. Introduction

AS THE crime rate in the United States grows and pressures mount for laws restricting the use of firearms, the need for an understanding of the development of the "right to bear arms" has increased. Perhaps more than any other "right" enumerated in the federal and state constitutions, the "right" to bear arms was directed to maintaining a balance of power within our society. The "right to bear arms" developed at a time when a well-armed population was necessary for defense, and when the social and political structure was kept in balance by a balance of armed power.

While the American "right to bear arms" developed at the time of

*Source: John Levin, "The Right to Bear Arms: The Development of the American Experience," *Chicago-Kent Law Review*, Fall-Winter, 1971, pp. 110-129. Footnotes and references have been deleted. Reprinted with permission.

the Revolution, it grew out of the duty imposed on the early colonists to keep arms for the defense of their isolated and endangered communities. The definition of "bearing arms" as the phrase was used in legal instruments up to revolutionary times was "serving in an organized armed force." It did not imply any personal right to possess weapons. For example, when Parliament in drafting the English Bill of Rights or Blackstone in his *Commentaries on the Laws of England* intended to convey the meaning of a personal right to possess arms, they spoke of the right to *have* arms, not of the right to *bear* arms.

## II. EARLY HISTORY

### A. *The Colonial Period*

The earliest colonial statutes requiring that the colonists arm themselves were Virginia statutes of 1623 stating that "no man go or send abroad without a sufficient party will [sic] armed," and that "men go not to worke in the ground without their arms (and a centinell upon them)." In 1658 Virginia required that "every man able to beare armes have in his house a fixt gunn." The colony, being unable to afford to arm its militia or troops, required them to arm themselves. If the militia, however, found itself under-armed, the county courts could levy on the population for the provision of arms and distribute them to those not provided—the distributees then paying for the arms at a reasonable rate.

Massachusetts in 1632 required each person to "have . . . a sufficient musket or other serviceable peece for war . . . for himself and each man servant he keeps able to beare arms." In the Code of 1672 men were to provide their own arms, but arms would be supplied to those unable to obtain them. In New York, each town was to keep a stock of arms, and each man between 16 and 60 was to have arms. Even those not obligated to serve in the militia were required to keep arms and ammunition in their houses. The militia provisions of the Connecticut Code of 1650 said, "All persons . . . shall beare arms . . .; and every male person . . . shall have in continuall readiness, a good muskitt or other gunn, fitt for service." South Carolina had similar codes.

This duty to keep and bear arms was limited by the interest of colonial governments in preventing the use of firearms for harmful ends. In order to prevent civil disturbances the colonial governments strove to keep arms from falling into the "wrong hands." To provide against Negro insurrections, Virginia forbade Negroes from carrying arms without their masters' certificate. Pennsylvania had a similar provision by 1700, and South Carolina even required that the master keep all arms not in use safely locked up in his house. Virginia forbade the sale of arms or ammunition to Indians, and Massachusetts required that Indians possess a license to carry a gun within certain areas of the colony.

In times of civil disturbance the colonies controlled arms to protect the security of orderly government. For example, in 1692 the Massachusetts Assembly felt it necessary to arrest "such as shall ride or go armed offensively before any of their majesties' justices or other of their officers or ministers doing their office or elsewhere by night or by day, in fear or affray of their majesties' people."

In addition to those laws preventing arms from falling into the hands of those groups openly hostile to colonial society, statutes regulated the conditions under which arms could be used. As the settlements grew crowded, shooting was restricted in order to protect people and livestock. By 1678 Massachusetts forbade shooting "so near or into any House, Barn, Garden, Orchards or High-Wayes in any town or towns of this Jurisdiction, whereby any person or persons shall be or may be killed, wounded or otherwise damaged." In order to prevent fires caused by gunfire, Pennsylvania in 1721 forbade firing a gun within the city of Philadelphia without a special license from the governor. Pennsylvania also forbade hunting by anyone on improved lands without the permission of the owner, and forbade those not qualified to vote from hunting on unimproved lands without the permission of the owner.

Colonial statutes established a duty to keep and bear arms for the defense of the colonies and regulated the use of the arms in circulation. The American Revolution in turn provided fertile ground for the growth of the concept of the right of revolution and the related right to bear arms.

### B. *The Revolutionary Period*

During the revolutionary period the issue of arms and the bearing of arms developed along two distinct lines. One line of development related to the balance of military power between the people and their respective governments. The people feared that if the state or federal government became too powerful, that government would abridge the liberties of the people and impose its will by force. The other line of development related to the balance of military power between the governmental bodies of the union. The state governments feared that if they entrusted too much power in the hands of the central government, that government would destroy the political and military independence of the states. Both lines of development concened the creation of a military balance within the political structure which would result in the maintenance of liberty of the constituent parts—whether personal liberty under a government or state liberty in a union; and both lines of development resulted in the creation of a "right to bear arms" in order to insure the liberty of those constituent parts.

The colonists, fearful of oppression by governmental power, and being aware of the events of 17th century England, believed that liberty was guaranteed by giving the rulers as little power as possible and by balancing governmental power with popular power. The foremost factor in this balance of power was the existence of a standing army. Standing armies had been used by the English crown and by continental monarchs to impose their will on their subjects, and royal forces had been used by the English crown to intimidate and control the colonies. In 1774 the Continental Congress declared that keeping a "standing army in these colonies, in time of peace, without the consent of the legislature of that colony, in which such army is kept, is against law." In 1775 the draftsmen of the Declaration of the Causes and Necessity of Taking up Arms gave the presence of royal troops a prominent role in that declaration, and several sections of the Declaration of Independence were given to the issue. Colonial mistrust of standing armies extended even to colonial troops. In 1776 Sam Adams wrote:

> [A] standing army, however necessary it be at some times, is always dangerous to the liberties of the people. Soldiers are apt to consider themselves as a body distinct from the rest of the citizens. They have their arms always in their hands. Their rules and their discipline is severe. They soon become attached to their officers and disposed to yield implicit obedience to their commands. Such a power should be watched with a jealous eye.

## III. Constitutional Provisions

The state constitutions framed during the War for Independence reflected the fears of a standing army. The framers felt that such an army would create an overbearing force at the disposal of the state governments. All the states included provisions regarding standing armies and militia in their bills of rights. Several had provisions similar to Virginia's:

> That a well-regulated militia, composed of the body of the people, trained to arms, is the proper, natural, and safe defense of a Free State; that standing armies, in time of peace, should be avoided, as dangerous to liberty; and that in all cases the military should be under strict subordination to, and governed by, the civil power.

Several others were similar to that of Maryland:

> XXV. That a well-regulated militia is the proper and natural defense of a free government.
>
> XXVI. That standing armies are dangerous to liberty, and ought not to be raised or kept up, without the consent of the Legislature.
>
> XXVII. That in all cases, and at all times, the military ought to be under strict subordination to and control of the civil power.
>
> XXVIII. That no soldier ought to be quartered in any house, in time of peace, without the consent of the owner; and in time of war, in such manner only, as the Legislature directs.
>
> XXIX. That no person, except regular soldiers, mariners, and Marines in the service of this state, or militia when in actual service, ought in any case to be subject to or punishable by martial law.

Some specifically mentioned a "right to bear arms," such as Pennsylvania's:

> That the people have a right to bear arms for the defense of themselves and the State; and as standing armies in the time of peace are dangerous to liberty, they ought not to be kept up. And that the military should be kept under strict subordination to, and governed by, the civil power.

North Carolina included a "right to bear arms" for the "defense of the

State," and Massachusetts included such a right for "the common defense." Widespread copying by the draftsmen of state constitutions created, in part, the similarity between provisions. These provisions were to be the basis of the militia provisions in the federal Constitution and Bill of Rights.

When the draftsmen of the majority of the state bills of rights wrote of replacing the standing army with a popular militia, they believed it would remove a source of arbitrary military power from the hands of the state governments and replace it with a military less likely to oppress the people. They attempted to structure the political and military balance in the new states by making the governments less powerful and the citizens more powerful. The "right to bear arms" was a more extreme and revolutionary manifestation of this restructuring. By having a right to "bear arms," *i.e.*, to serve in the armed forces of the state, the people would have far greater military power than if the militia were merely the preferred defense, for the state governments would be unable to maintain a narrowly-based standing army against the interests of the people. Rather the people would rely on their "right" to bear arms and demand that the defense force be broadly based.

The "right to *have* arms" was an adjunct to the right of revolution. The right of revolution is the natural right of a people to overthrow their government when that government no longer serves the purpose for which it was formed. By the middle of the 18th century, Blackstone had recognized that the primary rights of Englighment—"personal security, personal liberty, and private property"—could not be maintained solely by law, for "in vain would these rights be declared, ascertained, and protected by the dead letter of the laws, if the constitution had provided no other method to secure their actual enjoyment." There were auxiliary rights in order to enable the subject to preserve the primary rights, and,

> The fifth and last auxiliary right of the subject . . . is that of having arms for their defense, suitable to their condition and degree, and such as are allowed by law. Which . . . is indeed a public allowance, under due restrictions, of the natural right of resistance and self-preservation when the sanctions of society and laws are found insufficient to restrain the violence of oppression.

The provisions in the state constitutions granting a "right to bear arms" were not intended to permit a public allowance of the right of revolution. In the first place, the phrase "to *bear* arms" only meant serving in an organized armed force. In the second place, the right of revolution, or at least a statement of the principle of that right, was specifically contained in other sections of most state constitutions. In the third place, the guaranty of the "right to bear arms" or similar statements of preference for the militia was contained in that section of the constitutions directly concerned with controlling the military power of the state and not in the section recognizing the right of revolution.

When the Constitutional Convention met on May 14, 1787, it was faced with some issues quite dissimilar to those which had troubled the states. In the years during and immediately following the Revolution, the doctrine of the natural right of revolution was an accepted part of colonial political theory. After the Revolution, however, the need for stable and orderly government grew, and the philosophy of rebellion withered. The fundamental problem facing the convention was not to support and nourish a revolutionary situation, but to create a viable federal government out of the jealous and independent states. One of the major aspects of this problem was the creation of a national army. The delegates to the convention feared that if the new federal government could obtain sufficient military power, it could then impose its will on the states and on the people.

The delegates, however, did not consider the new federal standing army to be a danger to the states or the people since Congress would have strict control over the appropriations for troops, and most delegates assumed that the standing army would be small. The Articles of Confederation had left complete control of land forces in the hands of the states which raised them, and by 1788 the Army of the Confederation consisted of only 679 officers and men. The question of the balance of military power between the states and the federal government was raised rather on the issue of federal control over the state militia.

On August 18, 1787, a motion was made in the convention to give Congress the power "to make laws for the regulation and discipline of the Militia of the several States reserving to the States the appointments of Officers." Here the military power of the states was at stake. John Dickinson exclaimed that "we are come now to a most important matter, that of the sword. . . . The states never would or ought to give up all authority over the Militia." Oliver Ellsworth believed that "the whole authority over the Militia ought by no means to be taken away from the States whose consequence would pine away to nothing after such a sacrifice of power." Supporters of the motion recalled how ineffectual the militia was during the Revolution. They stressed the need for an effective and centralized military.

When the debate continued on August 23rd, Edmund Randolph felt that the militia could be trusted to look after the liberties of the people. He asked, "What dangers there could be that the Militia could be brought into the field and made to commit suicide on themselves. This is a power that cannot from its nature be abused, unless indeed the whole mass should be corrupted." Elbridge Gerry stated, when a motion was made to allow the federal government to appoint the general officers, that "as the States are not to be abolished, he wondered at the attempts that were made to give powers inconsistent with their existence." James Madison replied: "As the greatest danger is that of disunion of the States it is necessary to guard against it by sufficient powers to the Common Government and as the greatest danger to the liberty is from large standing armies, it is best to prevent them by an effectual provision for a good Militia."

A compromise was reached whereby the federal government would maintain a standing army plus have the authority to regulate and call out the militia, and the states would have authority over the militia except when it was called into federal service. The results of the compromise appear in article I, section 8 of the United States Constitution declaring that Congress shall have power:

> To make Rules for the Government and Regulation of the land and naval Forces;
>
> To raise and support Armies, but no Appropriation of Money to that Use shall be for a longer term than two Years;
>
> To provide for calling forth the Militia to execute the Laws of the Union, suppress Insurrections and repel Invasions;
>
> To provide for organizing, arming, and disciplining the Militia, and for governing such Part of them as may be employed in the Service of the United States, reserving to the States respectively, the Appointment of the Officers, and the Authority of training the Militia according to the discipline prescribed by Congress;

Thus, a tentative military balance was achieved between the federal government and the states.

Before the Constitution was ratified, however, its provisions were debated before the legislatures and in the press. The militia provisions were again argued in terms of the balance of military power between the states and the federal government. Charles Pinckney argued for a federalized militia to give the federal government the power to impose its will on the states:

> The exclusive right of establishing regulations for the Government of the Militia of the United States ought certainly to be vested in the Federal Councils. As standing Armies are contrary to the Constitutions of most of the States, and the nature of our Government, the only immediate aid and support that we can look up to, in case of necessity, is the Militia . . . Independent of our being obliged to rely on the Militia as a security against Foreign Invasions or Democratic Convulsions, they are in fact the only adequate force the Union possesses, if any should be requisite to coerce a refractory or negligent Member, and to carry the Ordinances and Decrees of Congress into execution. This, as well as the cases I have alluded to, will sometimes make it proper to order the Militia of one State into another. At present the United States possesses no power of directing the Militia, and must depend upon the States to carry their Recommendations upon this subject into execution . . . To place before a necessary and Constitutional power of defense and coercion in the hands of the Federal authority, and to render our Militia uniform and national, I am decidedly in opinion they should have exclusive right of establishing regulations for their Government and Discipline, which the States should be bound to comply with, as well as with their Regulations for any number of Militia, whose march into another State, the Public safety or benefit should require.

Luther Martin, speaking before the Maryland legislature, argued against the federalized militia as it would give the federal government so great a power that it could destroy the integrity of the states:

> [Through] this extraordinary provision by which the Militia, the only defense and protection which the State can have for the security of their rights against arbitrary encroachments of the general government, is taken entirely out of the power of their respective States, and placed under the power of Congress. . . . It was argued at the Constitutional convention that, if after having retained to the general government the great power already granted, and among

> those, that of raising and keeping up regular troops, without limitations, the power over the Militia should be taken away from the States, and also given to the general governments, it ought to be considered as the last *coup de grace* to the State governments; that it must be the most convincing proof, the advocates of this system design the destruction of the State governments, and that no professions to the contrary ought to be trusted: and that every State in the Union ought to reject such a system with indignation, since, if the general government should attempt to oppress and enslave them, they could not have any possible means of self-defense. . . .

Superimposed upon this debate over the balance of power between the states and the federal government was the issue of the balance of power between the people themselves and the new government. To assuage fears that the new federal government would infringe upon the rights of the people, the authors of *The Federalist* raised the factors of militia, arms, and the right of revolution in describing how the new government could be controlled. Federalist Number 28 mentioned the right of revolution:

> If the representatives of the people betray their constituents, there is then no recourse left but in the exertion of that original right of self-defense which is paramount to all positive forms of government.

And the military power of the states:

> When will the time arrive that the fedeal government can raise and maintain an army capable of erecting a despotism over the great body of the people of an immense empire, who are in a situation, through the medium of their States governments, to take measure for their own defense, with all the celerity, regularity and system of independent nations?

The 46th Federalist by Madison discussed the armed population and its relationship to the militia and the central government:

> Besides the advantage of being armed, which the Americans possess over the people of almost every other nation, the existence of subordinate governments to which the people are attached, and by which the Militia officers are appointed, forms a barrier against the enterprises of ambition, more insurmountable than any which a simple government of any form can admit. Notwithstanding the military establishments in the several kingdoms of Europe, which are carried as far as the public resources will bear, the governments

are afraid to trust the people with arms.

Though the Constitution was ratified, the issue of the federal militia was not resolved until adoption of the second amendment. Several of the states had suggested during their ratifying conventions that a bill of rights be added to the United States Constitution. When such a bill of rights was debated in the First Congress, the militia amendment was first reported out of committee of the House of Representatives reading:

> A well-regulated Militia, composed of the body of the people, being the best security of a free State, the right of the people to keep and bear arms shall not be infringed: but no person religiously scrupulous shall be compelled to bear arms.

Several of the representatives objected to the provision excusing those people "religiously scrupulous" from bearing arms. Elbridge Gerry stated that as the purpose of the militia "is to prevent the establishment of a standing army" it was "evident, that under this provision, together with their own powers, Congress could take such measures with respect to a Militia, as to make a standing army necessary." This could be accomplished by Congress using "a discretionary power to exclude those from the Militia who have religious scruples." In such event, so many citizens would attempt to avoid Militia duty on religious grounds that a standing army would be necessary for national defense.

In any event the religious exemption from the Militia was dropped and the amendment in its final form read:

> A well-regulated Militia, being necessary to the security of a free State, the right of the people to keep and bear Arms, shall not be infringed.

From the debates it seems that the intent of Congress in passing the Second Amendment was to prevent the federal government from destroying the state militia. Pinckney would keep a defense force uniform and at the disposal of the federal government. Martin was assured that the federal government would not emasculate the states and leave them at the mercy of federal troops. The "right to bear arms" was a corporate right used to insure that a desired balance between liberty and authority within the union would be maintained.

Attempts were made to include a personal right to have arms in the Bill of Rights. Sam Adams introduced a bill in the Massachusetts legislature that the state support an amendment holding that the "Constitution be never construed to authorize Congress to . . . prevent the people of the United States, who are peaceable citizens from keeping their own arms." New Hampshire supported a provision that "Congress shall never disarm any citizen unless such as are or have been in Actual Rebellion." Though these provisions were never adopted, they indicate that there has never been any absolute "American" philosophy on the right to bear arms. This confusion arises from America's situation of being a frontier nation created out of revolution and espousing a belief in revolution but which also desires and needs to create an orderly social and political structure.

The result has been the use of the concept of the right to bear arms to support several different, and often contradictory, theories of the relation of armed citizens to the government. The judicial opinions of the courts of the various jurisdictions in the United States best exemplify this situation.

## IV. RELEVANT COURT DECISIONS

### A. *State Courts*

The first pronouncement on the right to bear arms was by a Kentucky court in *Bliss v. Commonwealth*. The court held that "the right of the citizens to bear arms in defense of themselves and the State must be preserved entire," and all legislative acts "which diminish or impair it as it existed when the Constitution was framed are void." Thus an act prohibiting the wearing of concealed arms was declared void. This point of view which considers the right to bear arms as absolute, unabridgable, and personal is rare. Most cases follow the reasoning of a Texas court which asked "How far personal liberty may be restrained for the prevention of crime."

A few states adopted the thinking of the early Tennessee case of *Aymette v. State* which held that the right to bear arms was a right of the people to enable them to rise up and defend their rights against an oppressive government. This concept was similar to Blackstone's presentation of the right to bear arms as a public allowance of the right of revolution. Courts holding this theory consider that, as the right is by public allowance, the state can regulate the use of arms to insure the public peace and welfare. This position was well presented by the Arkansas court in *Haile v. State*:

> The constitutional provision sprung from the former tyrannical practice on the part of governments, of disarming the subjects, so as to render them powerless against oppression. It is not intended to afford citizens the means of prosecuting, more successfully, their private broils in a free government. It would be a perversion of its object, to make it a protection to the citizen, in going, with convenience to himself, and after his own fashion, prepared all times to inflict death upon his fellow citizens, upon the occasion of any real or imaginary wrongs.

While most courts have not attempted to counter the assertion of the right of revolution, an earlier Arkansas court had stated in *State v. Buzzard* that such a right was unnecessary under a free, republican government which could be changed at the will of the people.

The *Aymette* line of cases is perhaps truest to the intention of the draftsmen of the state bills of rights. The right to bear arms was a means of preserving the liberty of the people by balancing the military power in the hand of the state by military power in the hands of the people. The desire to maintain such a balance has had a long history dating from feudal times, through the English revolution to the present day. Such thinking, however, is rare in judicial opinions. Similarly rare is the unitary concept of society and government expressed by the Kansas court in *City of Salina v. Blakesly*.

> The provision . . . that 'the people have the right to bear arms for their defense and security' refers to the people as a collective body. It was the safety and security of society that was being considered when this provision was put into our Constitution. . . . The provision in question applies only to the right to bear arms as a member of the State Militia, or some other military organization provided for by the law.

Such thinking indicates belief that there is no need to provide for a military balance within the political and social structure when that structure is responsive to the people.

Most state courts have never spoken of the right to bear arms in the sophisticated terms of political balance, but rather treated the right as synonymous with the right of self-defense. In 1950 an Illinois court warned in the construction of an arms control statute "that it is aimed at persons of criminal instincts, and for the prevention of crime, and not against use in the protection of person or property." In *Andrews v. State*, a dissenting judge found that "the right exists only for the purpose of defense: and this is a right which no constitutional or legislative enactment can destroy." The dissent in the Oklahoma case of *Pierce v. State* proclaimed—"From time immemorial, the home, be it ever so humble, has been sacred—the castle of the occupant—with the right to repell [sic] invasion or any trespass."

Answers to such claims vary from the flat declaration in *Buzzard* that individuals have surrendered the right of self-defense to the society as a whole, to the more moderate holding in *Andrews* that "every good citizen is bound to yield his preference as the means to be used, to the demands of the public good." A Michigan court put forth a novel answer saying that the state's power is "subject to the limitation that its exercise be reasonable [and does not result] in the prohibition of those arms which, by the common opinion and usage of law-abiding people, are [to be kept for] protection of person and property.

These debates over the issue of the right of self-defense, though of primary interest today, have little relation to the intent of the draftsmen of the Bill of Rights. The right of self-defense has had a long history; but its history was parallel to, not connected with, the right to bear arms. The use of the right of self-defense to support a right to bear arms is of modern usage. Nevertheless, its modernity does not affect its relevance. The concept is the supreme law in several states of the union, and is a concept to be considered by any legislature hoping to pass restrictive arms legislation.

The confusion in the state courts over the right to bear arms is partly due to the judicial process itself. A court generally does not base its decision on political theory but considers the facts of the particular case before it. If a court feels a particular restrictive arms statute to be necessary and fair, and if the facts of the case before it are favorable, then the court will uphold the statute using whatever language and doctrine is required to so hold. If the statute appears unfair, if the times are unfavorable, or if the factual situation is difficult, then the court will use the language and doctrine necessary to overturn the statute. For example, a Florida court stated in 1912 that the right to bear arms "was intended to give the people the means of protecting themselves against oppression and public outrage, and was not designed as a shield for the individual man." Fifty years later the court declared that "doubtless the guarantee was intended to secure to the people the right to carry weapons for their protection." Similar situations have occurred in several states. The development of federal doctrine, however, has followed a more constant and evolutionary course.

## B. *Federal Courts*

Cases concerning the Second Amendment arose in the federal courts only after the Civil War. The first of such cases, *U.S. v. Cruickshank*, implied that there was a *personal* right to bear arms upon which Congress could not infringe. The central point of the opinion, however, was to state the Second Amendment did not apply to state governments, and such governments could pass whatever legislation they desired without fear of federal sanction.

*Cruickshank* was not directly concerned with the right to bear arms or the militia, but with civil rights legislation. The first federal case to be directly concerned with arms was *Presser v. Illinois*. Presser was convicted for leading a military parade in violation of an Illinois statute which forbade such parades by any group but the state militia. Presser claimed that the Illinois statute was in violation of the Second Amendment. The court relied on *Cruickshank* in stating that the "amendment is a limitation only upon the power of Congress and the National Government, and not upon that of the States," but added a restriction upon the State's power:

> It is undoubtedly true that all citizens capable of bearing arms constitute the reserved military force or reserve Militia of the United States as well as of the States; and, in view of this prerogative of the General Government, as well as of its general powers, the States cannot, even laying the constitutional provision in question out of view, prohibit the people from keeping and bearing arms, so as to deprive the United States of their rightful resource for maintaining the public security, and disable the people from performing their duty to the General Government.

This principle harkens back to the citizen army of Saxon times and had little relevance in 1886. It was understandable, however, that only twenty years after the Civil War, the Supreme Court would be concerned with state attempts to weaken the central government by withholding arms and troops from national service. Nevertheless, the restriction is a complete reversal from the aims of the draftsmen of the Constitution and Bill of Rights which was to restrict the military power of the central government and give the state more leverage.

On one subject *Presser* was quite clear—there was no right to band together in paramilitary organizations:

> Military organization and military drill and parade under arms are subjects especially under the control of the goverment of every country. They cannot be claimed as a right independent of law. Under our political system they are subject to the regulation and control of the State and Federal Governments, acting in due regard to their respective prerogatives and powers.

Thus, whatever right to bear arms was recognized, that right was limited to arms and organizations that did not threaten the security of the government. The court did not approve of an armed population as a balance to governmental power.

For many years after *Presser* the issue of the Second Amendment appeared in federal courts only in reaffirming the *Cruickshank* holding that the Second Amendment did not apply to the states. In the 1930s Congress passed two laws, the Federal Firearms Act and the National Firearms Act, to control commerce in certain types of dangerous weapons. Both acts were attacked in court for being in violation of the Second Amendment. In upholding the National Firearms Act, the district court held in *United States v. Adams* that the Second Amendment "refers to the Militia, a protective force of government; to the collective body and not individual rights." This language was quoted verbatim by another district court in *United States v. Tot* in upholding the Federal Firearms Act. Neither court went into the problem of the extent to which the collective right could be regulated, but both made clear that no personal right to own arms existed under the federal Constitution.

The issue of regulating the collective right arose in *United States v. Miller* in which the Supreme Court held that as long as the weapon regulated did not have a direct relationship to the arms used in maintaining a well-regulated militia, they could be controlled:

> In the absence of any evidence tending to show that possession or use of a 'shotgun having a barrel of less than eighteen inches in length' at this time has some reasonable relationship to the preservation or efficiency of a well-regulated Militia, we cannot say that

> the Second Amendment guarantees the right to keep and bear such an instrument.

The difficulty with such an interpretation is that were a weapon to have such a "reasonable relationship" it would be a protected weapon under the "Second Amendment. The circuit court in *Cases v. United States* recognized this problem saying: "But to hold that the Second Amendment limits the federal government to regulations concerning only weapons which can be classed as antiques or curiosities, — almost any other might bear some reasonable relationship to the preservation or efficiency of a well-regulated militia unit of the present day, — is in effect to hold that the limitation of the Second Amendment is absolute." The court also recognized that such an interpretation would prohibit the federal goverment from prohibiting private ownership of heavy weapons "even though under the circumstances of such possession or use it would be inconceivable that a private person could have any legitimate reason for having such a weapon." The court then decided it would be impossible to formulate any general test to determine the limits of the Second Amendment and each case would have to be decided on its individual merits.

The federal courts have interpreted the right to bear arms contained in the Second Amendment very narrowly. The right exists only to the extent that the arms are required for a well-regulated militia. Since *Presser*, however, the Second Amendment has been interpreted as a source of federal power and not as a protection of state power. The need for the old military balance between state and national governments had disappeared, and the federal courts no longer recognized its existence.

Similarly, the federal courts no longer recognized the need for a military balance between the population and its government. Rather, the courts have held that the interests of order and stability must be balanced against the need for revolution, and such interests may outweigh any need for the right of revolution. Thus, there could also be restrictions on other, subsidiary natural rights such as the right to bear arms. As Justice Vinson said in *Dennis v. United States* in upholding the Smith Act:

> That it is within the *power* of the Congress to protect the government of the United States from armed rebellion is a proposition which requires little discussion. Whatever theoretical merit there

> may be to the argument that there is a "right" to rebellion against dictatorial government is without force where the existing structure of the government provides for peaceful and orderly change. We reject any principle of governmental helplessness in the face of preparations for revolution, which principle, carried to its logical conclusion, must lead to anarchy.

Even though the right of revolution has never been recognized by the courts of the United States, armed rebellion has been—and still is—an important part of the American political tradition. From the early Republic to the present day, dissident elements who have not been able to achieve their goals within the political structure have resorted to arms as a final resort. In many instances, such elements have been punished as rebellious or treasonable, but in others the use of threat of violence has forced the political structure to compromise with the dissidents. Though not protected by the Constitution, this use of arms is the most important and relevant use of arms today.

## V. CONCLUSION

Regardless of the long history of violence and assassination in the United States, the right to bear arms has remained closely and jealously guarded. This right appears to provide the individual with the means of protecting himself against other individuals and of protecting himself against his government. The maintenance of a military balance within the political structure was the genesis of this right, and the desire to continue such a balance will promote its continuation. The right to bear arms supports man in his fear of being defenseless in the face of personal danger or oppression.

The possibility, however, of maintaining a military balance within a political structure has become smaller as society has become more complex and warfare more destructive. In the words of Roscoe Pound:

> In the urban industrial society of today a general right to bear efficient arms so as to be enabled to resist oppression by the government would mean that gangs could exercise an extra-legal rule which could defeat the whole Bill of Rights.

Thus, after over three centuries, the right to bear arms is becoming anachronistic. As the policing of society becomes more efficient, the need for arms for personal self-defense becomes more irrelevant;

and as the society itself becomes more complex, and the government itself more responsive, the right to bear arms becomes more futile, meaningless and dangerous.

## B. INDIVIDUAL INTERPRETATION

### HISTORY: SECOND AMENDMENT RIGHT TO "KEEP AND BEAR ARMS"*

The right to keep and bear arms as a part of English and American law antedates not only the Constitution, but also the discovery of firearms. Under the laws of Alfred the Great, whose reign began in 872 A.D., all English citizens from the nobility to the peasants were obliged to privately purchase weapons and be available for military duty. This was in sharp contrast to the feudal system as it evolved in Europe, under which armament and military duties were concentrated in the nobility. The body of armed citizens were known as the "fyrd."

While a great many of the Saxon rights were abridged following the Norman conquest, the right and duty of arms possession was retained. Under the Assize of Arms of 1181, "the whole community of freemen" between the ages of 15 and 40 were required by law to possess certain arms, which were arranged in proportion to their possessions. They were required twice a year to demonstrate to Royal officials that they were appropriately armed. In 1253, another Assize of Arms expanded the duty of armament to include not only freemen, but also villeins, who were the English equivalent of serfs. Now all "citizens, burgesses, free tenants, villeins and others from 15 to 60 years of age" were obliged to be armed. While on the Continent the villeins were regarded as little more than animals hungering for rebellion, the English legal system not only permitted, but affirmatively required them, to be armed.

---

*Source: *The Right to Keep and Bear Arms*. Report of the Subcommittee on the Constitution of the Committee of the Judiciary, United States Senate, 97th Congress, 2d Session. Washington: U.S. Government Printing Office, 1982, pp. 1-13. Footnotes and references have been deleted. Reprinted with permission.

The thirteenth century saw further definitions of this right as the long bow, a formidable armor-piercing weapon, became increasingly the mainstay of British national policy. In 1285, Edward I commanded that all persons comply with the earlier Assizes and added that "anyone else who can afford them shall keep bows and arrows." The right of armament was subject only to narrow limitations. In 1279, it was ordered that those appearing in Parliament or other public assemblies "shall come without all force and armor, well and peaceably." In 1328, the statute of Northampton ordered that no one use their arms in "affray of the peace, nor to go nor ride armed by day or by night in fairs, markets, nor in the presence of the justices or other ministers." English courts construed this ban consistently with the general right of private armament as applying only to wearing of arms "accompanied with such circumstances as are apt to terrify the people." In 1369, the King ordered that the sheriffs of London require all citizens "at leisure time on holidays" to use in their recreation bowes and arrows" and to stop all other games which might distract them from this practice.

The Tudor kings experimented with limits upon specialized weapons—mainly crossbows and the then-new firearms. These measures were not intended to disarm the citizenry, but on the contrary, to prevent their being diverted from longbow practice by sport with other weapons which were considered less effective. Even these narrow measures were shortlived. In 1503, Henry VII limited shooting (but not possession) of crossbows to those with land worth 200 marks annual rental, but provided an exception for those who "shote owt of a howse for the lawefull defense of the same." In 1511, Henry VIII increased the property requirement to 300 marks. He also expanded the requirement of longbow ownership, requiring all citizens to "use and exercyse shootyng in longbowes, and also have a bowe and arrowes contynually" in the house. Fathers were required by law to purchase bows and arrows for their sons between the age of 7 and 14 and to train them in longbow use.

In 1514 the ban on crossbows was extended to include firearms. But in 1533, Henry reduced the property qualification to 100 pounds per year; in 1541 he limited it to possession of small firearms ("of the length of one hole yard" for some firearms and "thre quarters of a yarde" for others) and eventually he repealed the entire statute by proclamation. The later Tudor monarchs continued the system and Elizabeth added to it by creating what came to be known as "train bands," selected portions of the citizenry chosen for special training. These trained bands were distinguished from the "militia," which term was first used during the Spanish Armada crisis to designate the entire of the armed citizenry.

The militia continued to be a pivotal force in the English political system. The British historian Charles Oman considers the existence of the armed citizenry to be a major reason for the moderation of monarchical rule in Great Britain; "More than once he [Henry VIII] had to restrain himself, when he discovered that the general feeling of his subjects was against him. . . . His 'gentlemen pensioners' and his yeomen of the guard were but a handful, and bills or bows were in every farm and cottage."

When civil war broke out in 1642, the critical issue was whether the King or Parliament had the right to control the militia. The aftermath of the civil war saw England in temporary control of a military government, which repeatedly dissolved Parliament and authorized its officers to "search for, and seize all arms" owned by Catholics, opponents of the government, "or any other person whom the commissioners had judged dangerous to the peace of this Commonwealth."

The military government ended with the restoration of Charles II. Charles in turn opened his reign with a variety of repressive legislation, expanding the definition of treason, establishing press censorship and ordering his supporters to form their own troops, "the officers to be numerous, disaffected persons watched and not allowed to assemble, and their arms seized." In 1662, a Militia Act was enacted empowering officials "to search for and seize all arms in the custody or possession of any person or persons whom the said lieutenants or any two or more of their deputies shall judge dangerous to the peace of the kingdom." Gunsmiths were ordered to deliver to the government lists of all purchasers. These confiscations were continued under James II, who directed them particularly against the Irish population. "Although the country was infested by predatory bands, a Protestant gentleman could scarcely obtain permission to keep a brace of pistols."

In 1688, the government of James was overturned in a peaceful uprising which came to be known as "The Glorious Revolution." Parliament resolved that James had abdicated and promulgated a Declaration of Rights, later enacted as the Bill of Rights. Before coronation, his successor William of Orange, was required to swear to respect these rights. The debates in the House of Commons over this Declaration of Rights focused largely upon the disarmament under the 1662 Militia Act. One member complained that "an act of Parliament was made to disarm all Englishmen, who the lieutenant should suspect, by day or night, by force or otherwise—this was done in Ireland for the sake of putting arms into Irish hands." The speech of another is summarized as "militia bill—power to disarm all England—now done in Ireland." A third complained "Arbitrary power exercised by the ministry. . . . Militia—imprisoning without reason; disarming—himself disarmed." Yet another summarized his complaints "Militia Act—an abominable thing to disarm the nation. . . ."

The Bill of Rights, as drafted in the House of Commons simply provided that "the acts concerning the militia are grievous to the subject" and that "it is necessary for the public Safety that the Subjects, which are Protestants, should provide and keep arms for the common defense; And that the Arms which have been seized, and taken from them, be restored." The House of Lords changed this to make it a more positive declaration of an individual right under English law: "That the subjects which are Protestant may have arms for their defense suitable to their conditions and as allowed by law." The only limitation was on ownership by Catholics, who at that time composed only a few percent of the British population and were subject to a wide variety of punitive legislation. The Parliament subsequently made clear what it meant by "suitable to their conditions and as allowed by law." The poorer citizens had been restricted from owning firearms, as well as traps and other commodities useful for hunting, by the 1671 Game Act. Following the Bill of Rights, Parliament reenacted that statute, leaving its operative parts unchanged with one exception—which removed the word "Guns" from the list of items forbidden to the poorer citizens. The right to keep and bear arms would henceforth belong to all English subjects, rich and poor alike.

In the colonies, availability of hunting and need for defense led to armament statutes comparable to those of the early Saxon times. In 1623, Virginia forbade its colonists to travel unless they were "well armed"; in 1631 it required colonists to engage in target practice on Sunday and to "bring their peeces to church." In 1658 it required every householder to have a functioning firearm within his house and in 1673 its laws provided that a citizen who claimed he was too poor to purchase a firearm would have one purchased for him by the government, which would then require him to pay a reasonable price when able to do so. In Massachusetts, the first session of the legislature ordered that not only freemen, but also indentured servants own firearms, and in 1644 it imposed a stern 6 shilling fine upon any citizen who was not armed.

When the British government began to increase its military presence in the colonies in the mid-eighteenth century, Massachusetts responded by calling upon its citizens to arm themselves in defense. One colonial newspaper argued that it was impossible to complain that his act was illegal since they were "British subjects, to whom the privilege of possessing arms is expressly recognized by the Bill of Rights" while another argued that this "is a natural right which the people have reserved to themselves, confirmed by the Bill of Rights, to keep arms for their own defense." The newspaper cited Blackstone's commentaries on the laws of England, which had listed the "having and using arms for self preservation and defense" among the "absolute rights of individuals." The colonists felt they had an absolute right at common law to own firearms.

Together with freedom of the press, the right to keep and bear arms became one of the individual rights most prized by the colonists. When British troops seized a militia arsenal in September, 1774, and incorrect rumors that colonists had been killed spread through Massachusetts, 60,000 citizens took up arms. A few months later, when Patrick Henry delivered his famed "Give me liberty or give me death" speech, he spoke in support of a proposition "that a well regulated militia, composed of gentlemen and freemen, is the natural strength and only security of a free government. . . ." Throughout the following revolution, formal and informal units of armed citizens obstructed British communication, cut off foraging parties, and harassed the thinly stretched regular forces. When seven states adopted state "bills of rights" following the Declaration of Independence, each of those bills of rights provided either for protection of the concept of a militia or for an express right to keep and bear arms.

Following the revolution but previous to the adoption of the Constitution, debates over militia proposals occuped a large part of the political scene. A variety of plans were put forth by figures ranging from George Washington to Baron von Steuben. All of the proposals called for a general duty of all citizens to be armed, although some proposals (most notably von Steuben's) also emphasized a "select militia" which would be paid for its services and given special training. In this respect, this "select militia" was the successor of the "trained bands" and the predecessor of what is today the "national guard." In the debates over the Constitution, von Steuben's proposals were criticized as undemocratic. In Connecticut one writer complained of a proposal that "this looks too much like Baron von Steuben's militia, by which a standing army was meant and intended." In Pennsylvania, a delegate argued "Congress may give us a select militia which will, in fact, be a standing army—or Congress, afraid of a general militia, may say there will be no militia at all. When a select militia is formed, the people in general may be disarmed." Richard Henry Lee, in his widely read pamphlet "Letters from the Federal Farmer to the Republican" worried that the people might be disarmed "by modeling the militia. Should one fifth or one eighth part of the people capable of bearing arms be made into a select militia, as has been proposed, and those the young and ardent parts of the community, possessed of little or no property, the former will answer all the purposes of an army, while the latter will be defenseless." He proposed that "the Constitution ought to secure a genuine, and guard against a select militia," adding that "to preserve liberty, it is essential that the whole body of the people always possess arms and be taught alike, especially when young, how to use them."

The suspicion of select militia units expressed in these passages is a clear indication that the framers of the Constitution did not seek to guarantee a State right to maintain formed groups similar to the National Guard, but rather to protect the right of individual citizens to keep and bear arms. Lee, in particular, sat in the Senate which approved the Bill of Rights. He would hardly have meant the Second Amendment to apply only to the select militias he so feared and disliked.

Other figures of the period were of like mind. In the Virginia convention, George Mason, drafter of the Virginia Bill of Rights, accused the British of having plotted "to disarm the people—that was the best and most effective way to enslave them," while Patrick Henry observed that "The great object is that every man be armed" and "everyone who is able may have a gun."

Nor were the antifederalists, to whom we owe credit for a Bill of Rights, alone on this account. Federalist arguments also provide a source of support for an individual rights view. Their arguments in favor of the proposed Constitution also relied heavily upon universal armament. The proposed Constitution had been heavily criticized for its failure to ban or even limit standing armies. Unable to deny this omission, the Constitution's supporters frequently argued to the people that the universal armament of Americans made such limitations unnecessary. A pamphlet written by Noah Webster, aimed at swaying Pennsylvania toward ratification, observed

> Before a standing army can rule, the people must be disarmed; as they are in almost every kingdom in Europe. The supreme power in American cannot enforce unjust laws by the sword, because the whole body of the people are armed, and constitute a force superior to any band of regular troops that can be, on any pretense, raised in the United States.

In the Massachusetts convention, Sedgwick echoed the same thought, rhetorically asking if an oppressive army could be formed or "if raised, whether they could subdue a Nation of freemen, who know how to prize liberty, and who have arms in their hands?" In Federalist Paper 46, Madison, later author of the Second Amendment, mentioned "The advantage of being armed, which the Americans possess over the people of other countries" and that "notwithstanding the military establishments in the several kingdoms of Europe, which are carried as far as the public resources will bear, the governments are afraid to trust the people with arms."

A third and even more compelling case for an individual rights perspective on the Second Amendment comes from the State demands for a bill of rights. Numerous state ratifications called for adoption of a Bill of Rights as a part of the Constitution. The first such call came from a group of Pennsylvania delegates. Their proposals, which were not adopted but had a critical effect on future debates, proposed among other rights that "the people have a right to bear arms for the defense of themselves and their own state, or the United States, or for the purpose of killing game; and no law shall be passed for disarming the people or any of them, unless for crimes committed, or a real danger of public injury from individuals." In Massachusetts, Sam Adams unsuccessfully pushed for a ratification conditioned on adoption of a Bill of Rights, beginning with a guarantee "That the said Constitution shall never be construed to authorize Congress to infringe the just liberty of the press or the rights of conscience; or to prevent the people of the United States who are peaceable citizens from keeping their own arms. . . ." When New Hampshire gave the Constitution the ninth vote needed for its passing into effect, it called for adoption of a Bill of Rights which included the provision that "Congress shall never disarm any citizen unless such as are or have been in actual rebellion." Virginia and North Carolina thereafter called for a provision "that the people have the right to keep and bear arms; that a well regulated militia composed of the body of the people trained to arms is the proper, natural and safe defense of a free state."

When the first Congress convened for the purpose of drafting a Bill of Rights, it delegated the task to James Madison. Madison did not write upon a blank tablet. Instead, he obtained a pamphlet listing the State proposals for a Bill of Rights and sought to produce a briefer version incorporating all the vital proposals of these. His purpose was to incorporate, not distinguish by technical changes, proposals such as that of the Pennsylvania minority, Sam Adams, and the New Hampshire delegates. Madison proposed among other rights that:

> "The right of the people to keep and bear arms shall not be infringed; a well armed and well regulated militia being the best security of a free country; but no person religiously scrupulous of bearing arms shall be compelled to render military service in person."

In the House, this was initially modified so that the militia clause came before the proposal recognizing the right. The proposals for the Bill of Rights were then trimmed in the interests of brevity. The conscientious objector clause was removed following objections by Elbridge Gerry, who complained that future Congresses might abuse the exemption for the scrupulous to excuse everyone from militia service.

The proposal finally passed the House in its present form: "A well regulated militia, being necessary to the security of a free state, the right of the people to keep and bear arms, shall not be infringed." In this form it was submitted into the Senate, which passed it the following day. The Senate in the process indicated its intent that the right be an individual one, for private purposes, by rejecting an amendment which would have limited the keeping and bearing of arms to bearing "for the common defense."

The earliest American constitutional commentators concurred in giving this broad reading to the amendment. When St. George Tucker, later Chief Justice of the Virginia Supreme Court, in 1803 published an edition of Blackstone annotated to American law, he followed Blackstone's citation of the right of the subject "of having arms suitable to their condition and degree, and such as are allowed by law" with a citation to the Second Amendment, "And this without any qualification as to their condition or degree, as is the case in the British government." William Rawle's "View of the Constitution" published in Philadelphia in 1825 noted that under the Second Amendment.

> The prohibition is general. No clause in the Constitution could by a rule of construction be conceived to give to Congress a power to disarm the people. Such a flagitious attempt could only be made under some general pretense by a state legislature. But if in blind pursuit of inordinate power, either should attempt it, this amendment may be appealed to as a restraint on both."

The Jefferson papers in the Library of Congress show that both Tucker and Rawle were friends of, and corresponded with Thomas Jefferson. This suggests that their assessment, as contemporaries of the Constitution's drafters, should be afforded special consideration.

Later commentators agreed with Tucker and Rawle. For instance, Joseph Story in his "Commentaries on the Constitution" considered the right to keep and bear arms as "the palladium of the liberties of the republic," which deterred tyranny and enabled the citizenry at large to overthrow it should it come to pass.

Subsequent legislation in the Second Congress likewise supports the interpretation of the second amendment that creates an individual right. In the Militia Act of 1792, the second Congress defined "militia of the United States" to include almost every free adult male in the United States. These persons were obligated by law to possess a firearm and a minimum supply of ammunition and military equipment. This statute, incidentally, remained in effect into the early years of the present century as a legal requirement of gun ownership for most of the population of the United States. There can be little doubt from this that when the Congress and the people spoke of a "militia," they had reference to the traditional concept of the entire populace capable of bearing arms, and not to any formal group such as what is today called the National Guard. The purpose was to create an armed citizenry, such as the political theorists at the time considered essential to ward off tyranny. From this militia, appropriate measures might create a "well regulated militia" of individuals trained in their duties and responsibilities as citizens and owners of firearms.

The Second Amendment as such was rarely litigated prior to the passage of the Fourteenth Amendment. Prior to that time, most courts accepted that the commands of the federal Bill of Rights did not apply to the states. Since there was no federal firearms legislation at this time, there was no legislation which was directly subject to the Second Amendment, if the accepted intepretations were followed. However, a broad variety of state legislation was struck down under state guarantees of the right to keep and bear arms and even in a few cases, under the Second Amendment, when it came before courts which considered the federal protections applicable to the states. Kentucky, in 1813, enacted the first carrying concealed weapon statute in the United States; in 1822, the Kentucky Court of Appeals struck down the law as a violation of the state constitutional protection of the right to keep and bear arms; "And can there be entertained a reasonable doubt but the provisions of that act import a restraint on the right of the citizen to bear arms? The court apprehends it not. The right existed at the adoption of the Constitution; it then had no limit short of the moral power of the citizens to exercise it, and in fact consisted of nothing else but the liberty of the citizen to bear arms." On the other hand, a similar measure was sustained in Indiana, not upon the grounds that a right to keep and bear arms did not apply, but rather upon the notion that a statute banning only concealed carrying still permitted the carrying of arms and merely regulated one possible way of carrying them. A few years later, the Supreme Court of Alabama upheld a similar statute but added "We do not desire to be understood as maintaining, that in regulating the manner of wearing arms, the legislature has no other limit than its own discretion. A statute which, under the pretense of regulation, amounts to a destruction of that right, or which requires arms to be so borne as to render them wholly useless for the purpose of defense, would be clearly unconstitutional." When the Arkansas Supreme Court, in 1842, upheld a carrying concealed weapons statute, the chief justice explained that the statute woud not "detract anything from the power of the people to defend their free state and the established institutions of the country. It prohibits only the wearing of certain arms concealed. This is simply a regulation as to the manner of bearing such arms as are specified," while the dissenting justice proclaimed "I deny that any just or free government upon earth has the power to disarm its citizens."

Sometimes courts went farther. When in 1837, Georgia totally banned the sale of pistols (excepting the larger pistols "known and used as horsemen's pistols") and other weapons, the Georgia Supreme Court in *Nunn* v. *State* held the statute unconstitutional under the Second Amendment to the federal Constitution. The court held that the Bill of Rights protected natural rights which were fully as capable of infringement by states as by the federal government and that the Second Amendment provided "the right of the whole people, old and young, men, women, and boys, and not militia only, to keep and bear arms of every description, and not merely such as are used by the militia, shall not be infringed, curtailed, or broken in on, in the slightest degree; and all this for the important end to be attained: the rearing up and qualifying of a well regulated militia, so vitally necessary to the security of a free state." Prior to the Civil War, the Supreme Court of the United States likewise indicated that the privileges of citizenship included the individual right to own and carry firearms. In the notorious *Dred Scott* case, the court held that black Americans were not citizens and could not be made such by any state. This decision, which by striking down the Missouri Compromise did so much to bring on the Civil War, listed what the Supreme Court considered the rights of American citizens by way of illustrating what rights would have to be given to black Americans if the Court were to recognize them as full fledged citizens:

> It would give to persons of the Negro race, who are recognized as citizens in any one state of the Union, the right to enter every other state, whenever they pleased . . . and it would give them full liberty of speech in public and in private upon all subjects upon which its own citizens might meet; to hold public meetings upon political affairs, and to keep and carry arms wherever they went.

Following the Civil War, the legislative efforts which gave us three amendments to the Constitution and our earliest civil rights acts likewise recognized the right to keep and bear arms as an existing constitutional right of the individual citizen and as a right specifically singled out as one protected by the civil rights acts and by the Fourteenth Amendment to the Constitution, against infringement by state authorities. Much of the reconstruction effort in the South had been hinged upon the creation of "black militias" composed of the armed and newly freed blacks, officered largely by black veterans of the Union Army. In the months after the Civil War, the existing southern governments struck at these units with the enactment of "black codes" which either outlawed gun ownership by blacks entirely, or imposed permit systems for them, and permitted the confiscation of firearms owned by blacks. When the Civil Rights Act of 1866 was debated members both of the Senate and House referred to the disarmament of blacks as a major consideration. Senator Trumbull cited provisions outlawing ownership of arms by blacks as among those which the Civil Rights Act would prevent; Senator Sulsbury complained on the other hand that if the act were to be passed it would prevent his own state from enforcing a law banning gun ownership by individual free blacks. Similar arguments were advanced during the debates over the "anti-KKK act"; its sponsor at one point explained that a section making it a federal crime to deprive a person of "arms or weapons he may have in his house or possession for the defense of his person, family or property" was "intended to endorse the well-known constitutional provisions guaranteeing the right of the citizen to 'keep and bear arms'." Likewise, the debates over the Fourteenth Amendment Congress frequently referred to the Second Amendment as one of the rights which it intended to guarantee against state action.

Following adoption of the Fourteenth Amendment, however, the Supreme Court held that that Amendment's prohibition against states depriving any persons of their federal "privileges and immunities" was to be given a narrow construction. In particular, the "privileges and immunities" under the Constitution would refer only to those rights which were not felt to exist as a process of natural right, but which were created solely by the Constitution. These might refer to rights such as voting in federal elections and of the existence of a federal government and which could not be said to be "natural rights." This paradoxically meant that the rights which most persons would accept as the most important—those flowing from concepts of natural justice—

were devalued at the expense of more technical rights. Thus when individuals were charged with having deprived black citizens of their right to freedom of assembly and to keep and bear arms, by violently breaking up a peaceable assembly of black citizens, the Supreme Court in *United States* v. *Cruickshank* held that no indictment could be properly brought since the right "of bearing arms for a lawful purpose" is "not a right granted by the Constitution. Neither is it in any manner dependent upon that instrument for its existence." Nor, in the view of the Court, was the right to peacefully assemble a right protected by the Fourteenth Amendment: "The right of the people peaceably to assemble for lawful purposes existed long before the adoption of the Constitution of the United States. In fact, it is and has always been one of the attributes of citizenship under a free government. . . . It was not, therefore, a right granted to the people by the Constitution." Thus the very importance of the rights protected by the First and Second Amendments was used as the basis for the argument that they did not apply to the states under the Fourteenth Amendment. In later opinions, chiefly *Presser* v. *Illinois* and *Miller* v. *Texas*, the Supreme Court adhered to the view. *Cruikshank* has clearly been superseded by twentieth century opinions which hold that portions of the Bill of Rights—and in particular the right to assembly with which *Cruikshank* dealt in addition to the Second Amendment—are binding upon the state governments. Given the legislative history of the Civil Rights Acts and the Fourteenth Amendment, and the more expanded views of incorporation which have become accepted in our own century, it is clear that the right to keep and bear arms was meant to be and should be protected under the civil rights statutes and the Fourteenth Amendment against infringement by officials acting under color of state law.

Within our own century, the only occasion upon which the Second Amendment has reached the Supreme Court came in *United States* v. *Miller*. There, a prosecution for carrying a sawed-off shotgun was dismissed before trial on Second Amendment grounds. In doing so, the court took no evidence as to the nature of the firearm or indeed any other factual matter. The Supreme Court reversed on procedural grounds, holding that the trial court could not take judicial notice of the relationship between a firearm and the Second Amendment, but must receive some manner of evidence. It did not formulate a test nor state precisely what relationship might be required. The court's statement that the amendment was adopted "to assure the continuation and render possible the effectiveness of such [militia] forces" and "must be interpreted and applied with that end in view," when combined with the court's statement that all constitutional sources "show plainly enough that the militia comprised all males physically capable of acting in concert for the common defense. . . . these men were expected to appear bearing arms supplied by themselves and of the kind in common use at the time," suggests that at the very least private ownership by a person capable of self-defense and using an ordinary privately owned firearm must be protected by the Second Amendment. What the Court did not do in Miller is even more striking: It did not suggest that the lower court take evidence on whether Miller belonged to the National Guard or a similar group. The hearing was to be on the nature of the firearm, not on the nature of its use; nor is there a single suggestion that National Guard status is relevant to the case.

The Second Amendment right to keep and bear arms therefore is a right of the individual citizen to privately possess and carry in a peaceful manner firearms and similar arms. Such an "individual rights" interpretation is in full accord with the history of the right to keep and bear arms, as previously discussed. It is moreover in accord with contemporaneous statements and formulations of the right by such founders of this nation as Thomas Jefferson and Samuel Adams, and accurately reflects the majority of the proposals which led up to the Bill of Rights itself. A number of state constitutions, adopted prior to or contemporaneously with the federal Constitution and Bill of Rights, similarly provided for a right of the people to keep and bear arms. If in fact this language creates a right protecting the states only, there might be a reason for it to be inserted in state constitutions. State bills of rights necessarily protect only against action by the state, and by definition a state cannot infringe its own rights; to attempt to protect a right belonging to the state by inserting it in a limitation of the state's own powers would create an absurdity. The fact that the contemporaries of the framers did insert these words into several state constitutions would indicate clearly that they viewed the right as belonging to the individual citizen, thereby making it a right which could be infringed either by state or federal government and which must be protected against infringement by both.

Finally, the individual rights interpretation gives full meaning to the words chosen by the first Congress to reflect the right to keep and bear arms. The framers of the Bill of Rights consistently used the words "right of the people" to reflect individual rights—as when these words were used to recognize the "right of the people" to peaceably assemble, and the "right of the people" against unreasonable searches and seizures. They distinguished between the rights of the people and of the state in the Tenth Amendment. As discussed earlier, the "militia" itself referred to a concept of a universally armed people, not to any specifically organized unit. When the framers referred to the equivalent of our National Guard, they uniformly used the term "select militia" and distinguished this from "militia." Indeed, the debates over the Constitution constantly referred to organized militia units as a threat to such organized units did not constitute, and indeed were philosophically opposed to, the concept of a militia.

That the National Guard is not the "Militia" referred to in the second amendment is even clearer today. Congress has organized the National Guard under its power to "raise and support armies" and not its power to "Provide for organizing, arming and disciplining the Militia." This Congress chose to do in the interests of organizing reserve military units which were not limited in deployment by the strictures of our power over the constitutional militia, which can be called forth only "to execute the laws of the Union, suppress insurrections and repel invasions." The modern National Guard was specifically intended to avoid status as the constitutional militia, a distinction recognized by 10 U.S.C. §311(a).

The conclusion is thus inescapable that the history, concept, and wording of the Second Amendment to the Constitution of the United States, as well as its interpretation by every major commentator and court in the first half-century after its ratification, indicates that what is protected is an individual right of a private citizen to own and carry firearms in a peaceful manner.

# Chapter III

# "THE RIGHT TO KEEP AND BEAR ARMS": ILLUSTRATIVE COURT OPINIONS

## A. OPINIONS ILLUSTRATING THE "COLLECTIVE" VIEW*

### City of Salina v. Blaksley
### 83 P. 619, 72 Kan. 230 (1905)

JAMES BLAKSLEY was convicted in the police court of the city of Salina . . . of carrying a revolving pistol within the city while under the influence of intoxicating liquor. He appealed to the district court, where he was again convicted, and this proceeding is prosecuted to reverse the judgment of the latter court. The question presented is the constitutionality of section 1003 of the General Statutes of 1901, which reads: "The council may prohibit and punish the carrying of firearms or other deadly weapons, concealed or otherwise, and may arrest and imprison, fine or set at work all vagrants and persons found in said city without visible means of support, or some legitimate business."

Section 4 of the bill of rights is as follows: "The people have the right to bear arms for their defense and security; but standing armies, in time of peace, are dangerous to liberty, and shall not be tolerated,

*Cases in this and succeeding sections have been heavily edited. Footnotes, references, case citations, and other materials have been deleted. In most instances, these deletions have been indicated with ellipses. The reader is directed to the appropriate court record for a complete opinion.

and the military shall be in strict subordination to the civil power."

The contention is that this section of the bill of rights is a constitutional inhibition upon the power of the legislature to prohibit the individual from having and carrying arms, and that section 1003 of the General Statutes of 1901 is an attempt to deprive him of the right guaranteed by the bill of rights, and, is therefore, unconstitutional and void. . . . In view of the disagreements in the reasonings of the different courts by which they reached conflicting conclusions, we prefer to treat the question as an original one. The provision in section 4 of the Bill of Rights that "the people have the right to bear arms for their defense and security" refers to the people as a collective body. It was the safety and security of society that were being considered when this provision was put into our Constitution. It is followed immediately by the declaration that standing armies in time of peace are dangerous to liberty and should not be tolerated, and that "the military shall be in strict subordination to the civil power." It deals exclusively with the military; individual rights are not considered in this section. The manner in which the people shall exercise this right of bearing arms for the defense and security of the people is found in article 8 of the constitution, which authorizes the organizing, equipping, and disciplining of the militia, which shall be composed of "all able-bodied male citizens between the ages of twenty-one and forty-five years." The militia is essentially the people's army, and their defense and security in time of peace. There are no other provisions made for the military protection and security of the people in time of peace. In the absence of constitutional or legislative authority no person has the right to assume such duty.

In some of the states where it has been held, under similar provisions, that the citizen has the right preserved by the Constitution to carry such arms as are ordinarily used in civilized warfare, it is placed on the ground that it was intended that the people would thereby become accustomed to handling and using such arms, so that in case of an emergency they would be more or less prepared for the duties of a soldier. The weakness of this argument lies in the fact that in nearly every state in the Union there are provisions for organizing and drilling state militia in sufficient numbers to meet any such emergency.

That the provision in question applies only to the right to bear arms as a member of the state militia, or some other military organization provided for by law, is also apparent from the Second Amendment to the federal Constitution, which says: "A well-regulated militia being necessary to the security of a free state, the right of the people to keep and bear arms shall not be infringed." Here also the right of the people to keep and bear arms for their security is preserved, and the manner of bearing them for such purpose is clearly indicated to be as a member of a well-regulated militia, or some other military organization provided for by law. . . .

The defendant was not a member of an organized militia, nor of any other military organization provided for by law, and was therefore not within the provision of the bill of rights and was not protected by its terms. The judgment is affirmed.

**Strickland v. State**
**72 S.E. 260 (1911)**

The first question propounded by the Court of Appeals is whether . . . "An act to prohibit any person from having or carrying about his person, in any county in the state of Georgia, any pistol or revolver without first having obtained a license from the ordinary of the county of said state, in which the party resides, and to provide how said license may be obtained and a penalty prescribed for a violation of the same, and for other purposes," is violative . . . of the Constitution of this state, which provides that "the right of the people to keep and bear arms shall not be infringed, but the General Assembly shall have power to prescribe the manner in which arms may be borne. . . ."

An examination of the various decisions whether dealing with laws against carrying concealed weapons, or with regulations as to the manner of carrying certain weapons, or the prohibition against carrying weapons of a particular character, will show that two general lines of reasoning have been employed in upholding such statutes: First, that such provisions are to be construed in the light of the origin of the constitutional declarations, of their connection with words declaratory of the necessity for an efficient militia or for the common defense, or the like, where they are used, and in view of the general public purpose which such provisions were intended to subserve; and, second, that the right to bear arms, like other rights of person and property, is to be construed in connection with the general police power of the state, and as subject to legitimate regulation thereunder. Where a state constitution in terms provides, in connection with the right to bear arms, that the state may regulate this right, or may regulate the manner of bearing arms, these words expressly recognize the police power in direct connection with the constitutional declaration as to the right. But even where such expressions do not occur, it has been held that the different provisions of the Constitution must be construed together, and that the declaration or preservation of certain rights is not to be segregated and treated as arbitrary, but in connection with the general police power of the state, unless the language of the instrument itself should exclude such a construction. Thus, if the right to bear arms includes deadly weapons of every character, and is absolute and arbitrary in its nature, it might well be argued, as it was in earlier days, that the citizen was guaranteed the right to carry weapons or arms, in the broadest meaning of that term, whenever, wherever, and however he pleased, and that any regulation, unless expressly provided for in the Constitution, was an infringement of that right. The ruling that the Legislature may prohibit the carrying of concealed weapons essentially concedes the police power of regulation to some extent. If this be conceded, the question then becomes one as to whether the particular regulation involved is legitimate and reasonably within the police power, or whether it is arbitrary, and, under the name of regulation, amounts in effect, to a deprivation of the constitutional right. . . .

It was argued that the requirement of a license to carry the weapons named in the act, and the fixing of a fee of 50 cents, were obnoxious to the constitutional provision. If this argument be sound, then practically the whole licensing system would be destroyed on the ground that to require a license is not a regulation but a prohibition. Many persons are required to obtain a license before engaging in certain businesses or performing certain acts; where a legitimate exercise of the police power of the state, it has never been thought that this was a violation of any constitutional right as to person or property. It was contended also that a requirement of a bond of $100, conditioned upon a proper and legitimate use of the weapons, rendered the act obnoxious to the Constitution. It was said that this might deprive some persons who could not give a bond of the right to carry the weapon. There are many cases in which a person may exercise a certain right by giving a bond. Numerous public officers are required to furnish bond before taking charge of the office, but this has not been thought to be unconstitutional because some citizens might desire to hold the office who could not give the bond. The right to appeal to the courts is guaranteed by the Constitution. In order to obtain a writ of attachment, the plaintiff must give bond. It would hardly be said that, because he could not give the bond required by the statute, he was unconstitutionally excluded from appealing to the court in that manner. Illustrations might be multiplied. We think, upon consideration, that the regulatory provisions of the act of 1910 are not so arbitrary or unreasonable as to amount, in effect, to a prohibition of the right to bear arms, or an infringement of that right as protected by the Constitution. . . .

The second question propounded by the Court of Appeals is whether the act of 1910 is in violation of the right of a citizen, under article 8, § 2, of the Constitution of the United States, which provides: "A well regulated militia being necessary to the security of a free state, the right of the people to keep and bear arms shall not be infringed." What has been said above answers this question in the negative. It is not contended that anything contained in this act affects, or was intended to affect, any federal law passed in pursuance of the Constitution of the United States in regard to the regulation of militia. . . .

## United States v. Tot
## 131 F.2d 261 (1942)

The defendant, Frank Tot, was convicted and sentenced for violation of the statute known as the Federal Firearms Act, . . . by which it is made unlawful for any person who has been convicted of a crime of violence "to receive any firearm or ammunition which has been shipped or transported in interstate or foreign commerce . . . ." That defendant had been previously convicted of a crime of violence, as defined in the Act, is undisputed. He was arrested by federal officers at his home in Newark, New Jersey, on a warrant charging theft of cigarettes from an interstate shipment. A .32 caliber Colt Automatic pistol was found in his place of residence at the time of the arrest. . . .

The Second Amendment to the Constitution of the United States provides: "A well regulated Militia, being necessary to the security of a free State, the right of the people to keep and bear Arms, shall not be infringed."

The appellant's contention is that if the statute under which this prosecution was brought is to be applied to a weapon of the type he had in his possession, then the statute violates the Second Amendment.

It is abundantly clear both from the discussions of this amendment contemporaneous with its proposal and adoption and those of learned writers since that this amendment, unlike those providing for protection of free speech and freedom of religion, was not adopted with individual rights in mind, but as a protection for the States in the maintenance of their militia organizations against possible encroachments by the federal power. The experiences in England under James II of an armed royal force quartered upon a defenseless citizenry was fresh in the minds of the Colonists. They wanted no repetition of that experience in their newly-formed government. The almost uniform course of decision in this country, where provisions similar in language are found in many of the State Constitutions, bears out this concept of the constitutional guarantee. A notable instance is the refusal to extend its application to weapons thought incapable of military use.

The contention of the appellant in this case could, we think, be denied without more under the authority of United States v. Miller. . . . This was a prosecution under the National Firearms Act of 1934 and the weapon, the possession of which had occasioned the prosecution of the accused, was a shotgun of less than 18-inch barrel. The Court said that in the absence of evidence tending to show that possession of such a gun at the time has some reasonable relationship to the preservation or efficiency of a well regulated militia, it could not be said that the Second Amendment guarantees the right to keep such an instrument. The appellant here having failed to show such a relationship, the same thing may be said as applied to the pistol found in his possession. It is not material on this point that the 1934 statute was bottomed on the taxing power while the statute in question here was based on a regulation of interstate commerce.

But, further, the same result is definitely indicated on a broader ground and on this we should prefer to rest the matter. Weapon bearing was never treated as anything like an absolute right by the common law. It was regulated by statute as to time and place as far back as the Statute of Northampton in 1328 and on many occasions since. The decisions under the State Constitutions show the upholding of regulations prohibiting the carrying of concealed weapons, prohibiting persons from going armed in certain public places and other restrictions, in the nature of police regulations, but which do not go so far as substantially to interfere with the public interest protected by the constitutional mandates. The federal statute here involved is one of that general type. One could hardly argue seriously that a limitation upon the privilege of possessing weapons was unconstitutional when applied to a mental patient of the maniac type. The same would be true if the possessor were a child of immature years. In the situation at bar Congress has prohibited the receipt of weapons from interstate transactions by persons who have previously, by due process of law, been shown to be aggressors against society. Such a classification is entirely reasonable and does not infringe upon the preservation of the well regulated militia protected by the Second Amendment. . . .

The social end sought to be achieved by this legislation, the protection of society against violent men armed with dangerous weapons, all would concede to be fundamental in organized government. The entry of the federal authority in the field to help accomplish this purpose has not been challenged. It has been taken for granted by both sides in the discussion of this case. We also think it may be assumed. In accomplishing the admittedly constitutional object we do not think the means taken by this statute, while stringent, have become so oppressive and arbitrary that we are entitled to say that Congress has exceeded its authority in acting without due process of law.

The judgment is affirmed.

## Cases v. United States
## 131 F.2d 916 (1942)

This is an appeal from a judgment of the District Court of the United States for Puerto Rico sentencing the defendant to a term of imprisonment after he had been found guilty by a jury on all four counts of an indictment charging him with violating . . . the Federal Firearms Act, . . . by transporting and receiving a firearm and ammunition. . . .

The defendant contends that the Federal Firearms Act is unconstitutional because (a) it is an ex post facto law; (b) it violates the Second Amendment by infringing the right of the people to keep and bear arms; (c) it is an undue extension of the commerce clause; (d) it creates an unreasonable presumption of guilt; and (e) it denies equal protection of the laws. In our view none of these contentions are sound. . . .

The Federal Firearms Act undoubtedly curtails to some extent the right of individuals to keep and bear arms but it does not follow from this as a necessary consequence that it is bad under the Second Amendment. . . .

The right to keep and bear arms is not a right conferred upon the people by the federal constitution. Whatever rights in this respect the people may have depend upon local legislation; the only function of the Second Amendment being to prevent the federal government and the federal government only from infringing that right. . . . But the Supreme Court in a dictum in Robertson v. Baldwin, . . . indicated that the limitation imposed upon the federal government by the Second Amendment was not absolute and this dictum received the sanction of the court in the recent case of United States v. Miller.

In the case last cited, the Supreme Court, after discussing the history of militia organizations in the United States, upheld the validity under the Second Amendment of the National Firearms Act in so far as it imposed limitations upon the use of a shotgun having a barrel less than eighteen inches long. It stated the reason for its result . . . as follows: "In the absence of any evidence tending to show that possession or use of a 'shotgun having a barrel of less than eighteen inches in length' at this time has some reasonable relationship to the preservation or efficiency of a well regulated militia, we cannot say that the Second Amendment guarantees the right to keep and bear such an instrument. Certainly it is not within judicial notice that this weapon is any part of the ordinary military equipment or that its use could contribute to the common defense."

Apparently, then, under the Second Amendment, the federal government can limit the keeping and bearing of arms by a single individual as well as by a group of individuals, but it cannot prohibit the possession or use of any weapon which has any reasonable relationship to the preservation or efficiency of a well regulated militia. However, we do not feel that the Supreme Court in this case was attempting to formulate a general rule applicable to all cases. The rule which it laid down was adequate to dispose of the case before it and that we think was as far as the Supreme Court intended to go. At any rate, the rule of the Miller case, if intended to be comprehensive and complete would seem to be already outdated, in spite of the fact that it was formulated only three and a half years ago, because of the well known fact that in the so-called "Commando Units" some sort of military use seems to have been found for almost any modern lethal weapon. In view of this, if the rule of the Miller case is general and complete, the result would follow that, under present day conditions, the federal government would be empowered only to regulate the possession or use of weapons such as a flintlock musket or a matchlock harquebus. But to hold that the Second Amendment limits the federal government to regulations concerning only weapons which can be classed as antiques or curiosities—almost any other might bear some reasonable relationship to the preservation or efficiency of a well regulated militia unit of the present day—is in effect to hold that the limitation of the Second Amendment is absolute. Another objection to the rule of the Miller case as a full and general statement is that according to it Congress would be prevented by the Second Amendment from regulating the possession or use by private persons not present or prospective members of any military unit, of distinctly military arms, such as machine guns, trench mortars, anti-tank or anti-aircraft guns, even though under the circumstances surrounding such possession or use it would be inconceivable that a private person could have any legitimate reason for having such a weapon. It seems to us unlikely that the framers of the Amendment intended any such result. Considering the many variable factors bearing upon the question it seems to us impossible to formulate any general test by which to determine the limits imposed by the Second Amendment but that each case under it, like cases under the due process clause, must be decided on its own facts and the line between what is and what is not a valid federal restriction pricked out by decided cases falling on one side or the other of the line.

We therefore turn to the record in the case at bar. From it it appears that on or about August 27, 1941, the appellant received into his possession and carried away ten rounds of ammunition, and that on the evening of August 30 of the same year he went to Annadale's Beach Club on Isla Verde in the municipality of Carolina, Puerto Rico, equipped with a .38 caliber Colt type revolver of Spanish make which, when someone turned out the lights, he used, apparently not wholly without effect, upon another patron of the place who in some way seems to have incurred his displeasure. While the weapon may be capable of military use, or while at least familiarity with it might be regarded as of value in training a person to use a comparable weapon of military type and caliber, still there is no evidence that the appellant was or ever had been a member of any military organization or that his use of the weapon under the circumstanes disclosed was in preparation for a military career. In fact, the only inference possible is that the appellant at the time charged in the indictment was in possession of, transporting, and using the firearm and ammunition purely and simply on a frolic of his own and without any thought or intention of contributing to the efficiency of the well regulated militia which the Second Amendment was designed to foster as necessary to the security of a free state. We are of the view that, as applied to the appellant, the Federal Firearms Act does not conflict with the Second Amendment to the Constitution of the United States.

**Harris v. State**
**432 P.2d 929 (1967)**

This is an appeal from the conviction of Edward Mark Harris for the possession of a tear gas weapon. . . .

On July 27, 1966 Harris entered a super market in Reno and was observed by store personnel to be shoplifting several cartons of cigarettes. A police officer was summoned. The officer placed him under arrest and searched him. The search produced a tear gas pen. He was convicted of possession of a tear gas device in violation of the statute. This appeal followed. We affirm.

As his first assignment of error Harris challenges the constitutionality of NRS 202.380 as an infringement of the Second Amendment of the U.S. Constitution. . . .

That amendment applies only to the Federal Government and does not restrict state action. . . . The right to bear arms does not apply to private citizens as an individual right.

In the absence of state or federal constitutional restraints authority of the states to regulate weapons comes from their police powers. . . . Tear gas pens are a proper subject for state regulation.

**Burton v. Sills**
**248 A.2d 521 (1968)**

The Law Division upheld the constitutionality of New Jersey's recently enacted "Gun Control Law" . . . and dismissed the plaintiff's complaint attacking it. The Appellate Division affirmed . . . and the plaintiffs appealed to this court as of right. . . .

The plaintiffs are three individuals associated with sportsmen's clubs in New Jersey, two gun dealers, and a corporation organized to promote the sports of shooting and marksmanship. They filed a complaint . . . naming the Attorney General and the Superintendent of State Police as defendants and seeking (1) a declaration that Chapter 60 of the Laws of 1966 is unconstitutional and (2) an injunction against its enforcement. Chapter 60 amended previous regulatory provisions governing firearms and provided, *inter alia*, for the licensing of manufacturers, wholesalers, and retail dealers, and for the issuance of permits and identification cards to purchasers. . . .

We find no merit in the plaintiff's first point and deal now with their next point under which they urge that Chapter 60 is violative of the second amendment of the United States Constitution. . . . Its history and purpose have been detailed elsewhere and need only be summarized here. . . .

The common law did not recognize any absolute right to keep and bear arms; that much is conceded by the plaintiffs who cite the Statute of Northampton, 2 Edw. III, c. 3 (1328), which declared that no man should "go nor ride armed by night or by day in fairs, markets, nor in the presence of the justices or other ministers" etc. . . . And though the English Bill of Rights of 1689 was aimed at certain abuses which included the disarming of Protestants while others remained armed, its history and terms make it clear that its reference to the right of Protestants to have arms was "a class right rather than an individual right" and that "individual self-defense was not within its protective purpose." . . . Indeed the right of Protestants to have arms was expressed to be "as allowed by law" and current English statutes place very stringent controls on the availability of arms. . . .

During the American colonial days there was great fear of military rule; the colonists believed that standing armies were acceptable only in extraordinary circumstances and under control of civil authorities, and that the Militia was the proper organ for defense of the individual States. When the Constitution was adopted, it expressly granted to Congress the power to provide for calling forth the Militia to execute the laws, suppress insurrections and repel invasions, along with the power to provide for organizing the Militia and for governing such part as may be employed in the service of the United States, "reserving to the States respectively, the Appointment of the Officers, and the Authority of training the Militia according to the discipline prescribed by Congress." . . . With their historic distrust of standing armies and the desire that the Militia be protected from federal encroachment, the States quickly obtained the adoption of the Second Amendment. As the language of the amendment itself indicates, it was not framed with individual rights in mind. Thus it refers to the collective right "of the people" to keep and bear arms in connection with "a well-regulated militia." Most students of the subject would undoubtedly express agreement with the substance of the currently expressed view that "the term well-regulated militia" must be taken to mean the active, organized militia of each state, which today is characterized as the state National Guard." . . .

The plaintiffs acknowledge that . . . federal cases which they cite are generally opposed to their contention that Chapter 60 is invalid under the Second Amendment, but they urge that "a reinterpretation of the effect of the Second Amendment upon the States is due to be made and the time is now with the New Jersey Statute to be the basis for reinterpretation." . . .

In *Cruikshank* the defendants were convicted in a lower federal court of conspiring to deprive certain freedmen of their right to bear arms, allegedly guaranteed them under the second amendment. In reversing, the Supreme Court noted that the right to bear arms was not one created by or dependent upon the federal constitution and that the second amendment meant "no more than it shall not be infringed by Congress." . . . In *Presser* the defendant was convicted under a state statute which provided that it shall be unlawful for any body of men, other than the state's "regular organized volunteer militia" and the troops of the United States, to associate themselves as a military organization or drill with arms, without the license of the Governor. The conviction was sustained in an opinion which expressed the view that the statute did not "infringe the right of the people to keep and bear arms" and which reaffirmed the holding of *Cruickshank* to the effect that the second amendment was inapplicable because it related only to congressional action. . . . In Miller v. Texas the defendant contended that a state statute which prohibited the carrying of a dangerous weapon on the person, infringed his rights as a citizen and was violative of the second amendment. The Supreme Court found no infringement of his rights and cited *Cruikshank* with full approval. . . .

In United States v. Miller the defendant was convicted of the interstate transportation of a shotgun having a barrel of less than eighteen inches, in violation of the National Firearms Act of 1934. In upholding the conviction, the Supreme Court rejected a defense under the second amendment, noting that there was no evidence indicating that possession of such a shotgun had "reasonable relationship to the preservation or efficiency of a well regulated militia." . . . It is sufficient here to suggest that under *Miller*, Congress, though admittedly governed by the second amendment, may regulate interstate firearms so long as the regulation does not impair the maintenance of the active, organized militias of the states.

In United States v. Tot . . . Judge Goodrich pointed out that, unlike the First Amendment which provides for protection of free speech and freedom of religion, the Second Amendment "was not adopted with individual rights in mind, but as a protection for the States in the maintenance of their militia organizations against possible encroachments by the federal power"; in upholding the federal regulation against the interstate shipment of firearms to persons convicted of crimes of violence, he had this to say on behalf of himself and his colleagues:

> Weapon bearing was never treated as anything like an absolute right by the common law. It was regulated by statute as to time and place as far back as the Statute of Northampton in 1328 and on many occasions since. The decisions under the State Constitutions show the upholding of regulations prohibiting the carrying of concealed weapons, prohibiting persons from going armed in certain public places and other restrictions, in the nature of police regulations, but which do not go so far as substantially to interfere with the public interest protected by the constitutional mandates. The Federal statute here involved is one of that general type. One could hardly argue seriously that a limitation upon a privilege of possessing weapons was unconstitutional when applied to a mental patient of the maniac type. The same would be true if the possessor were a child of immature years. In the situation at bar Congress has prohibited the receipt of weapons from interstate transactions by persons who have previously, by due process of law, been shown to be aggressors against society. Such a classification is entirely reasonable and does not infringe upon the preservation of the well regulated militia protected by the Second Amendment. . . .

The plaintiffs venture the prediction that, notwithstanding all of the foregoing, the Supreme Court will hereafter "extend the restrictions of the Second Amendment to all of the States" as it has done with some other amendments in the Bill of Rights. Enough has been said to differentiate the Second Amendment from those which protect individual rights and, as such, have been carried over into the Fourteenth Amendment. . . the matter need not be pursued, for as the decisions indicate, regulation (such as New Jersey's Gun Control Law) which does not impair the maintenance of the State's active, organized militia . . . is not at all in violation of either the terms or purposes of the Second Amendment or Art. 1, § 8, clauses 15 and 16. . . .

Long before the enactment of its recent Law . . ., New Jersey had many statutory provisions imposing restrictions not only on the carrying but also on the possession and sale of designated firearms. . . . To the extent they were challenged they were readily sustained. See, e.g., State v. Angelo, . . . where the court, in upholding a concealed weapon conviction, stated that, in the exercise of its police power the State could impose "such conditions precedent to the right to carry concealed weapons as the safety and welfare of the people of the state in its judgment require." . . . There are comparable decisions in other jurisdictions which, like New Jersey, have no express state constitutional provisions dealing with the right to bear arms. . . . Even in those jurisdictions which have such express state consitutional provisions, the courts have found little difficulty in upholding varying and extensive statutory firearms regulations. . . . We have no hesitancy in rejecting the plaintiff's point grounded on the Second Amendment. . . .

## Commonwealth v. Davis
## Mass., 343 N.E.2d 847 (1976)

In connection with a search under warrant of an apartment for narcotic drugs, the police found firearms and ammunition evidently in the possession of the defendant, Hubert Davis. The defendant was indicted . . . for illegal possession on January 4, 1974, of a shotgun with a barrel less than eighteen inches long, and he was found guilty of this crime after trial by a judge of the Superior Court sitting without a jury. On motion for a new trial, the defendant contended that the statute defining and punishing the offense violated his constitutionally guaranteed right to keep and bear arms, and he assigned error accordingly to the denial of his motion. Appeal having been lodged in the Appeals Court, we took the matter on our own initiative for direct review. . . .

Article 17 of our Declaration of Rights declares: "The people have a right to keep and to bear arms for the common defence. And as, in time of peace, armies are dangerous to liberty, they ought not to be maintained without the consent of the legislature; and the military power shall always be held in an exact subordination to the civil authority, and be governed by it."

The meaning of such provisions is to be gathered from their history, which is reasonably well known and need not be reviewed here in detail. . . . The colonists distrusted standing armies and preferred to look to a militia—"civilians primarily, soldiers on occasion"—for protection. Article 17 expresses the distrust in its second sentence. It refers to the preference in the first: the declared right to keep and bear arms is that of the people, the aggregate of citizens; the right is related to the common defense; and that in turn points to service in a broadly-based, organized militia. Provisions like art. 17 were not directed to guaranteeing individual ownership or possession of weapons. . . . This generalization is perhaps subject to a qualification: Militiamen customarily furnished their own equipment and indeed might be under legal obligation to do so. . . . a Law forbidding the keeping by individuals of arms that were used in the militia service might then have interfered with the effectiveness of the militia and thus offended the art. 17 right. But that situation no longer exists; our militia, of which the backbone is the National Guard, is now equipped and supported by public funds. . . . Moreover, the statute at bar is part of a large regulatory scheme to promote the public safety, and there is nothing to suggest that, even in early times, due regulation of possession or carrying of firearms, short of some sweeping prohibition, would have been thought to be an improper curtailment of individual liberty or to undercut the militia system. Very generally it has been held that such regulation is compatible with State constitutional provisions on the subject of the right to bear arms. . . .

If art. 17 does not help the defendant, then he is reduced, as far as State law is concerned, to a claim that the statute is beyond the police power. But that would involve an examination, in context, of the regulatory scheme and of the particular statute as a part of the scheme. The record is barren of any of this, as is the defendant's brief. Presumptively the statute is valid as a police measure; indeed a sawed-off shotgun seems a most plausible subject of regulation as it may be readily concealed and is especially dangerous because of the wide and nearly indiscriminate scattering of its shot. A Legislature might be justified in concluding that such weapons are associated with violent crime and call for strict licensing if not suppression.

The Second Amendment to the Constitution of the United States declares: "A well regulated Militia, being necessary to the security of a free State, the right of the people to keep and bear Arms, shall not be infringed." This was adopted to quiet the fears of those who thought that the Congressional powers under article I, § 8, clauses 15 and 16, with regard to the state militias might have the effect of enervating or destroying those forces. The amendment is to be read as an assurance that the national government shall not so reduce the militias. . . . Decisions of the courts have not retreated from the view that the amendment inhibits only the national government, not the States. . . . So the amendment is irrelevant to the present case. The chances appear remote that this amendment will ultimately be read to control the states, for unlike some other provisions of the Bill of Rights, this is not directed to guaranteeing the rights of individuals, but rather, as we have said, to assuring some freedom of state forces from national interference. Apart from such interference, Congress is not inhibited by the amendment from regulating firearms by exercise of its interstate commerce or other powers, and it has done so on a considerable scale with judicial approval. . . . Should the amendment perchance be held in the future to restrain the states in some fashion, one would suppose that the states' regulatory authority would remain.

We affirm the denial of the motion for a new trial. We also affirm the judgment of conviction, from which an appeal was taken, but not pressed.

**United States v. Warin**
**530 F.2d 103 (1976)**

This case requires a determination of whether certain provisions of the National Firearms Act as amended by the Gun Control Act of 1968, are an invalid infringement on the right to keep and bear arms guaranteed by the Second Amendment to the Constitution. . . .

At trial before the court, the following facts were stipulated to be true: That . . . Francis J. Warin willfully and knowingly possessed a firearm, that is, a 9-millimeter prototype submachine gun measuring approximately twenty-one inches overall length, with a barrel length of approximately seven and one-half inches, which had not been registered to him in the National Firearms Registration and Transfer Record, . . . that submachine guns are used by the armed forces of the United States, and that submachine guns contribute to the efficient operation of the armed forces of the United States in their function of defending the country. . . . [T]hat the weapon involved in this case is a submachine gun. . . . [T]hat 9-millimeter submachine guns have been used by at least one Special Forces Unit of the Army in Vietnam, . . . although they are not in general use. 9-millimeter submachine guns have been used by the military forces of the United States on at least one occasion during the Vietnam war. . . . [T]hat submachine guns are part of the military equipment of the United States military— . . . and that firearms of this general type, that is, submachine guns, do bear some relationship, some reasonable relationship, to the preservation or efficiency of the military forces.

The district court found that the defendant, as an adult male resident and citizen of Ohio, is a member of the "sedentary militia" of the State. It was not contended that Warin was a member of the active militia. The court also found that the defendant was an engineer and designer of firearms whose employer develops weapons for the government and— . . . that the defendant had made the weapon in question, which is indeed a firearm as described in the Act. It is also clear from the evidence that the weapon was of a type which is standard for military use, and fires the ammunition which is in common military use for the weapons used by individual soldiers in combat. The defendant testified that he had designed and built the weapon for the purpose of testing and refining it so that it could be offered to the Government as an improvement on the militiary weapons presently in use. The weapon was not registered to him as required by law. These findings are not disputed.

In *United States* v. *Miller*, . . . the Supreme Court held that the National Firearms Act of 1934 did not violate the Second Amendment. . . .

Warin argues . . . that a member of the "sedentary militia" may possess any weapon having military capability and that application of 26 U.S.C. § 5861(d) to such a person violates the Second Amendment. We disagree. In *Miller* the Supreme Court did not reach the question of the extent to which a weapon which is "part of the ordinary military equipment" or whose "use could contribute to the common defense" may be regulated. In holding that the absence of evidence placing the weapon involved in the charges against Miller in one of these categories precluded the trial court from quashing the indictment on Second Amendment grounds, the Court did not hold the converse—that the Second Amendment is an absolute prohibition against all regulation of the manufacture, transfer and possession of any instrument capable of being used in military action.

Within a few years after *Miller v. United States* was announced the First Circuit dealt with arguments similar to those made by Warin in the present case. In *Cases v. United States*, . . . the court held that the Supreme Court did not intend to formulate a general rule in *Miller*, but merely dealt with the facts of that case. The court of appeals noted the development of new weaponry during the early years of World War II and concluded that it was not the intention of the Supreme Court to hold that the Second Amendment prohibits Congress from regulating any weapons except antiques "such as a flintlock musket or a matchlock harquebus." . . . If the logical extension of the defendant's argument for the holding of *Miller* was inconceivable in 1942, it is completely irrational in this time of nuclear weapons.

Agreeing as we do with the conclusion in *Cases v. United States*, . . . that the Supreme Court did not lay down a general rule in *Miller*, we consider the present case on its own facts and in light of applicable authoritative decisions. It is clear that the Second Amendment guarantees a collective rather than an individual right. In *Stevens v. United States*, . . . this court held, in a case challenging the constitutionality of 18 U.S.C. App. § 1202(a)(1): Since the Second Amendment right "to keep and bear Arms" applies only to the right of the state to maintain a militia and not to the individual's right to bear arms, there can be no serious claim to any express constitutional right of an individual to possess a firearm. . . .

It is also established that the collective right of the militia is limited to keeping and bearing arms, the possession or use of which "at this time has some reasonable relationship to the preservation or efficiency of a well-regulated militia, . . . ."

The fact that the defendant Warin, in common with all adult residents and citizens of Ohio, is subject to enrollment in the militia of the state confers upon him no right to possess the submachine gun in question. By statute the State of Ohio exempts "members of . . . the *organized* militia of this or any other state, . . ." from the provision, "No person shall knowingly acquire, have, carry, or use any dangerous ordnance." . . . "Dangerous ordnance" is defined to include any automatic firearm. . . . There is no such exemption for members of the "sedentary militia." Furthermore, there is absolutely no evidence that a submachine gun in the hand of an individual "sedentary militia" member would have any, much less a "reasonable relationship to the preservation or efficiency of a well-regulated militia." . . . Thus we conclude that the defendant has no private right to keep and bear arms under the Second Amendment which would bar his prosecution and conviction for violating 26 U.S.C. § 5861(d).

Even where the Second Amendment is applicable, it does not constitute an absolute barrier to the congressional regulation of firearms. After considering several arguments the Third Circuit in *United States v. Tot*, . . . stated that it decided the case on the "broader ground" that "[w]eapon bearing was never treated as anything like an absolute right by the common law. It was regulated by statute as to time and place as far back as the Statute of Northampton in 1328 and on many occasions since." . . . In *Stevens v. United States*, . . . this court discussed the broad power of Congress in relying on the commerce clause of the Constitution to deal with the changing needs of the nation. . . . The congressional history of the National Firearms Act Amendments of 1968 and its predecessor statutes clearly sets out facts sufficient for Congress to have determined that the provisions of 26 U.S.C. § 5801 et seq., as amended in 1968, are within both the taxing power, . . . and the commerce power of Congress.

Warin argues that to uphold a tax on firearms transactions by one entitled to Second Amendment protection "would be to *sanction a tax on an activity which is constitutionally guaranteed and protected*." . . . He cites First Amendment cases . . . for the proposition that a person cannot be compelled to pay a license or tax in order to exercise a privilege granted by the Constitution. First Amendment rights occupy a "preferred position" among those guaranteed by the Bill of Rights, . . . a position never accorded to Second Amendment rights. . . .

As the legislative history of the Act under consideration clearly shows, Congress was dealing with problems which threaten the maintenance of public order. There can be no question that an organized society which fails to regulate the importation, manufacture and transfer of the highly sophisticated lethal weapons in existence today does so at its peril. The requirement that no one may possess a submachine gun which is not registered to him in the National Firearms Registration and Transfer Record is a reasonable regulation for the maintenance of public order.

The defendant appears to concede that some regulation of firearms is permitted. He argues that the taxes imposed upon the making and transfer of such weapons are not appropriate revenue measures, but that their imposition constitutes an indirect attempt to suppress the constitutional right to keep arms. Again, this argument assumes that the Second Amendment granted private rights to individuals, a position which we have rejected. Nevertheless it should be noted that the Act imposes no tax or license on the keeping and bearing of arms, the only rights referred to in the Second Amendment. The taxes are imposed on specific transactions involving firearms. Since the Act does not attempt to tax the right to keep and bear arms, its taxing provisions do not, under any set of circumstances, apply to rights protected by the Second Amendment. . . .

It would unduly extend this opinion to attempt to deal with every argument made by defendant and *amicus curiae*, Second Amendment Foundation, all of which are based on the erroneous supposition that the Second Amendment is concerned with the rights of individuals rather than those of the States or that defendant's automatic membership in the "sedentary militia" of Ohio brings him within the reach of its guarantees.

The judgment of the district court is affirmed.

## Application of Atkinson
## Minn., 291 N.W.2d 396 (1980)

On June 1, 1978, plaintiff Berton Atkinson filed an application with the Chief of Police of the City of Bloomington for a permit to carry a pistol, . . . His application was denied for failure to demonstrate a "personal safety hazard," as required by the statute, . . . The Hennepin County Municipal Court affirmed the denial. A three-judge panel of the district court affirmed the municipal court's order, and plaintiff appealed by leave of this court. We affirm.

Appellant Atkinson, a law-abiding citizen, seeks a handgun permit to continue his pre-1975 practice of carrying a loaded pistol in the glove compartment of his automobile "while traveling appreciable distances away from [his] home on public roads and highways."

In 1975, the Minnesota Legislature enacted legislation which requires that, in order for a person to carry or possess a pistol in a public place, he or she must first obtain a permit from the local police chief or county sheriff. . . . In order to obtain such a permit, an individual must establish that he has "an occupation or personal safety hazard requiring a permit to carry." . . .

No permit is required of a person who wishes to keep a pistol at home or at work, to carry the pistol between work and home or between home and the repair shop, or to carry a pistol in the woods, fields, or on water for hunting or target shooting. . . . Nor is a permit required for transporting a pistol anywhere, as long as it is unloaded and encased. . . . Plaintiff here seeks to carry a loaded pistol, uncased, in his automobile for travel other than between home and work or between home and the repair shop.

Two issues are raised by this appeal:

1. Is there an absolute constitutional or common-law right to carry a loaded gun on public highways?

2. Does travel for appreciable distances on the public roads constitute a "personal safety hazard" within the meaning of the statute?

We are asked to recognize an absolute right to carry weapons abroad—in this case, to carry a loaded pistol in an automobile absent any showing of particular need for such a weapon. Plaintiff argues that the common law has long recognized an individual right to carry weapons for self-defense. Although he recognizes that the Minnesota Constitution, unlike that of other states, contains no express reference to the right to bear arms for self-defense, he urges that this right, like other "organic" rights, is preserved in Article I, Section 16, which provides: "The enumeration of rights in this constitution shall not be construed to deny or impair others retained by and inherent in the people." He argues further that the U.S. Constitution's guarantee to the states of a "republican form of goverment" requires that state constitutions be interpreted consistent with historical republican principles—among them the recognition of a natural common-law right to bear arms for self-defense. Courts and legal scholars, considering the same historical documents that appellant uses to support his common-law right to carry weapons for self-defense, have reached the conclusion that any such right was not absolute. "Weapon bearing was never treated as anything like an absolute right by the common law. It was regulated by statute as to time and place as far back as the Statute of Northampton in 1328 and on many occasions since." . . .

There being no absolute common-law constitutional right to carry weapons abroad for individual self-defense, the state may reasonably exercise its police power to regulate the carrying of weapons by individuals in the interest of public safety. Exercise of the state's police power must be upheld unless it bears no relation to public health, safety, morals, or general welfare. The burden is on the person challenging the state's exercise of its police power to establish that no reasonable relationship exists. . . .

On two occasions we have articulated the purpose of the handgun permit statute. In *Blore v. Mossey*, . . . we rejected plaintiff's argument that because, when carrying a pistol under circumstances where no permit is necessary, he was always subject to the "hazard" that a police officer might doubt his word and arrest him, he had a "personal safety hazard" justifying the grant of a permit. Under that logic, everyone would be entitled to a permit, the wrong result because "[t]he obvious intent of [the 'personal safety hazard' requirement] is to restrict the class of persons entitled to permits." . . .

The following year, in *State v. Paige*, . . . we identified the sound public policy reason behind that restriction:

> "[T]he statute is intended to prevent the possession of firearms in places where they are most likely to cause harm in the wrong hands, i.e., in public places where their discharge may injure or kill intended or unintended victims. The only exception to this rule is for persons who have demonstrated a need or purpose for carrying firearms and have shown their responsibility to the police in obtaining a permit."

. . . The court characterized the effect of the gun control legislation as a general prohibition against carrying pistols in certain places. A particular need for carrying a pistol must be demonstrated before the permit will be granted. The requirement of a showing of particularized need and responsibility for carrying a loaded weapon other than between home and work or the repair shop is well founded on a policy of preserving human life and maintaining peace. . . .

Plaintiff urges this court to follow the Washington County District Court Appeals Panel decision in *Application of Vruno*, . . . where two judges reversed a denial of a pistol permit to a law-abiding citizen who sought the permit for no more pressing reason than plaintiff's here: in order to continue his past practice of carrying a loaded pistol in his glove compartment when traveling appreciable distances on the public highways. That decision rested on the language of the preamble to the gun control law, which expresses the legislature's intent not to "restrict the use of pistols by law-abiding citizens." . . . This decision, as appellant knows, is not binding on this court. . . .

The legislative intention to require an applicant to demonstrate a "personal safety hazard" which entitles him to a pistol permit is not unusual. A requirement that an individual seeking to carry a handgun make a showing of particularized need has been upheld and construed narrowly in a number of cases. . . .

In the instant case, plaintiff Atkinson seeks to carry a loaded gun in his car while traveling "appreciable distances" on the public highways. We find it difficult to believe that such travel was intended by the legislature to be a personal safety hazard. To accept plaintiff's argument would "gut" the statute; virtually every person could get a permit to carry a loaded pistol in the glove compartment of his or her car. The hazard plaintiff has identified is vague, general, and speculative. He has not made the showing of real and immediate danger which the statute requires in order to justify issuance of a handgun permit. The permit was properly denied.

Affirmed.

### Quilici v. Village of Morton Grove
### 532 F. Supp. 1169 (N. D. Ill. 1981)

This is a civil action challenging the constitutionality of a gun control ordinance passed by the Trustees of the Village of Morton Grove. . . . In part, the ordinance provides that "no person shall possess, in the Village of Morton Grove . . . [a]ny handgun, unless the same has been rendered permanently inoperative." The ordinance specifies various limited exceptions for certain individuals, such as peace officers, prison officials, and members of the armed forces and national guard. The ordinance also exempts licensed gun collectors and provides that handgun owners are free to retain their operative handguns for recreational use, as long as the guns are kept and used on the premises of licensed gun clubs and certain other rules are met. . . .

The plaintiffs have alleged that the enforcement of the ordinance, which has been stayed ending this court's ruling on its validity, would violate both the Illinois and United States constitutions. Both sides have moved for summary judgment on the issue of whether the ordinance, on its face, violates article 1, section 22 of the Illinois Constitution, or the Second, Fifth, Ninth or Fourteenth Amendments to the United States Constitution. . . .

In 1970, a right to arms clause was included in the Illinois Constitution for the first time. Article 1, section 22 provides:

> *Right to Arms*
> Subject only to the police power, the right of the individual ciizen to keep and bear arms shall not be infringed.

The plaintiffs have contended that Morton Grove's ordinance impermissibly infringes upon that right, while the defendant claims that its action represents a valid exercise of the police power. Central to the court's resolution of this controversy is a determination of the meaning of section 22, itself.

Section 22, on its face, requires a reconciliation of two competing notions of individual right and legislative prerogative. On one hand, it clearly recognizes the constitutional right of the individual "to keep and bear arms," and provides that the right "shall not be infringed." Yet, at the same time, the section expressly sanctions "constitutional infringements" of the right pursuant to the "police power," which is generally understood to mean the power of state and local goverments to regulate *and even prohibit* conduct which is perceived to be inimical to the safety, health and welfare of society. . . .

The plaintiffs have advocated a broad and liberal interpretation of the individual right to keep and bear arms, and a restrictive view of the scope of the police power. That power, they insist, must not be interpreted in a manner which would allow it to circumscribe the individual right contained in section 22. The defendant disagrees. Morton Grove argues that since the individual right in section 22 is made expressly subject to the broad power of the legislature, that right should be construed narrowly, and the police power should be interpreted according to its usual and customary meaning, free from artificially-imposed restrictions. Because the language contained in section 22 itself offers no clue as to the proper reconciliation of these two competing concepts, the court finds it necessary to examine the provision's constitutional history, the source traditionally relied upon for the clarification of ambiguous constitutional provisions. . . .

While it is true that there are several sources upon which one might draw in reviewing the constitutional history of a provision, "the practice of consulting the debates of the members of the convention . . . has long been indulged in by courts as adding to a true understanding of the meaning of provisions that are thought to be doubtful." . . . In this case, the court has found the delegates' debate on section 22 helpful to a meaningful reconciliation of the individual's right to arms and the state's broad police powers.

Prior to the delegates' floor debate on section 22, the Bill of Rights Committee voted twelve to three to include the following right to arms provision in the new constitution:

> "Subject only to the police power of the State, the right of the individual citizen to keep and bear arms shall not be infringed." . . .

Leonard Foster, the spokesman for the majority of the committee, was responsible for explaining the provision to the delegates. Although his explanation necessitated a narrow construction of the individual's right to arms, Foster suggested a resolution of the apparent tension between the section's terms. According to Foster, section 22 stood only for the limited right of the individual citizen to keep and bear "some form" of firearm; and as long as the government, in the exercise of its police power, did not totally prohibit the possession of *all* firearms, the right provided for in section 22 was not violated. . . .

Although the right to arms described by delegate Foster might have appeared on its face to be evanescent, Foster told the convention that under the 1870 Illinois Constitution, which contained no right to arms provision at all, a total prohibition of firearms was possible, and that the proposed section was designed to do no more than eliminate that possibility:

> "It could be argued that, in theory, the legislature now has the right to ban all firearms in the state as far as individual citizens owning them is concerned. That is the power which we wanted to restrict — an absolute ban on all firearms. Nothing further." . . .

During the debate, several of the delegates questioned Foster specifically with respect to the meaning of the terms "police power" in the context of section 22, and any limitations which section 22 might impose upon the legislature. Foster was unequivocal: Section 22 would restrain no exercise of the legislature's power short of an absolute ban on all firearms. . . . Clearly, section 22 was presented to the delegates as recognizing a narrow individual right which was subject to substantial legislative control. . . .

The plaintiffs, in urging the court to reject a narrow construction of the right to arms, have sharply criticized any significant reliance on the constitutional debates. First, they argue that emphasis on the debates is misplaced because the true inquiry in resolving constitutional ambiguities is to determine "the understanding . . . by the voters who, by their vote, have given life to the product of the convention." . . . To determine the voters' understanding, the plaintiffs have requested the court to consider such additional sources as: (1) The Official Explanation of section 22 which was provided to the voters prior to ratification of the constitution; (2) Newspaper articles written at around the time of the ratification vote discussing the right to arms provisions; and (3) The "plain meaning" which ordinary voters might have attributed to the term "police power." None of those sources, however, meaningfully addresses the reconciliation of individual right and legislative power which section 22 requires.

The "Official Text of the Proposed 1970 Illinois Constitution with Explanation" provides:

> Section 22 *Right to Arms*
> Subject only to the police power, the right of the individual citizen to keep and bear arms shall not be infringed.
> *Explanation*
> This new section states that the right of the citizen to keep and bear arms cannot be infringed, except as the exercise of this right may be regulated by appropriate laws to safeguard the welfare of the community.

Even taking the "Official Explanation" into consideration, the court is unconvinced of the plaintiffs' position. Far from reconciling the tension between the exercise of the individual right and the exercise of the police power, the above explanation begs the question. Like the text of the section itself, the explanation offers no clue as to the limits on the police power.

Similarly, the court can find no meaningful reconciliation of the two concepts in the Chicago Tribune article of December 13, 1970, which referred to the new right only sketchily as a "new right . . . to keep and bear arms," and summarized section 22 as providing "a guarantee of the individual's right to own firearms." No attention at all is devoted to the critical issue of interpretation as to the limit on the police power.

Finally, the suggestion that the right to arms warrants a liberal reading because that is how "the people" would read it must be rejected. According to this argument, the voters did not understand the full import of the term "police power"when they ratified the constitution. Instead, they most likely thought that they were ratifying a broad right to arms, one which would not tolerate a total handgun ban. Therefore, the plaintiffs argue that the court should give effect to the public's perception of the right rather than its actual meaning. The court cannot agree. Section 22 says explicitly that the individual right is subject to the police power. . . .

The plaintiffs' final attack on the debates concerns the conflict between certain language in the Bill of Rights Committee majority report on section 22 and the position taken by the committee on the floor of the convention. The plaintiffs refer the court to the following language in the report:

> The substance of the right [contained in Section 22] is that a citizen has the right to possess and make reasonable use of arms that law-abiding persons commonly employ for purposes of recreation or the protection of person and property. Laws that attempted to ban all possession or use of such arms, or laws that subjected possession or use of such arms to regulations or taxes so onerous that all possession or use was effectively banned, would be invalid." . . .

The plaintiffs argue first that those cases, decided under other states' constitutions, support their conclusion that the police power should be read restrictively. Second, they argue that the mere fact that those cases were included in the committee report serves as an indication of the delegates' intent that the police power should be narrowly construed, contrary to the intent expressed on the convention floor. The court rejects both of these arguments. . . .

After carefully reviewing the constitutional history of section 22, including the actual language used in the provision, the text of the convention debates, the committee report, and the other sources . . . the court concludes that the right to arms in Illinois is so limited by the police power that a ban on handguns does not violate that right. On at least five occasions, the convention debates indicated that such a ban would not be unconstitutional, . . . and the court agrees with that assessment. Furthermore, the court concludes that as long as a law does not totally ban all firearms, it must only qualify as a valid exercise of the police power in order to survive constitutional challenge under section 22. . . .

Certainly, there can be no question that the Morton Grove ordinance is oriented to those interests which are proper aims of any exercise of the state's police power. The preamble to the ordinance demonstrates that the public health and safety were uppermost in the minds of the Trustees of Morton Grove. . . .

Morton Grove defends its ordinance as a reasonable legislative response to the very serious problem of handguns in our society, and disputes the characterization of its ordinance as a total prohibition of firearms, or even handguns. By its terms, the ordinance (1) excludes "long guns" such as shot guns and rifles from its proscriptions; (2) exempts certain individuals, such as peace officers, members of the armed forces, and licensed gun collectors, from many of the ordinance's restrictions; and (3) allows the continued recreational use of handguns under certain conditions, at licensed gun clubs. The inclusion of those exceptions, the Village argues, indicates that the Trustees attempted to construct an ordinance broad enough to effectuate its objective of protecting public safety without unnecessarily restricting the possession and use of firearms. . . .

A prediction that the present ordinance may not be a panacea for all of the problems arising from the possession and use of handguns would not prove the plaintiffs' contention that this ordinance is arbitrary and simplistic. If the present ordinance was adopted on the expectation of the Trustees that it would serve to inch the Morton Grove community one step further to becoming peaceable and safe, this would justify the use of the police power. Many social experiments have only small beginnings. . . .

In addition to claiming that Morton Grove's exercise of its police power is "arbitrary and simplistic," plaintiffs also argue that the ordinance is invalid because it is a prohibition of the possession of handguns, rather than a regulation of their use. . . .

That argument by the plaintiffs misstates current Illinois law. As stated above, the police power does include the power to prohibit. "In the exercise of its inherent police power, the legislature may enact laws regulating, restraining *or prohibiting* anything harmful to the welfare of the people, even though such regulation, restraint *or prohibition* interferes with the liberty or property of an individual." . . .

Given that the Morton Grove ordinance is a reasonable response to the problems seen by the Trustees, it is not automatically invalid because it is a prohibition rather than a regulation.

In sum, this court concludes that the Morton Grove ordinance has as its basis the proper goals of protecting the safety and health of the people. In addition, the court finds that the ordinance does not represent a complete ban on firearms, and is reasonable and neither arbitrary nor simplistic. The ordinance was both properly and validly enacted under Morton Grove's police power. Therefore, the court concludes that ordinance #81-11 does not violate any of the plaintiff's rights under the Illinois Constitution.

In addition to their claims under the Illinois State Constitution, the plaintiffs also argue that the Morton Grove ordinance violates the United States Constitution, specifically the Second, Fifth, Ninth, and Fourteenth Amendments.

The Second Amendment provides as follows:

"A well regulated Militia, being necessary to the security of a free State, the right of the people to keep and bear Arms, shall not be infringed."

The plaintiffs rely substantially on historical arguments to buttress their contention that the Morton Grove ordinance infringes upon that Amendment. They review (1) the common law background of the right of individuals to possess weapons; (2) the impetus for the Second Amendment, which was the constitutional framers' fear that a national standing army would be inimical to personal rights and liberties; and (3) pre-Civil War judicial decisions in which the individual's right to bear arms was considered. Based on those materials, plaintiffs conclude that the Second Amendment conferred an individual right to keep and bear arms, including handguns, as opposed to a collective right in the states to maintain a militia separate from the federal standing army. After reaching that conclusion, plaintiffs then review the history of the Fourteenth Amendment and suggest that its framers intended that the Second Amendment should apply to the actions of the states.

Defendant Morton Grove's main response to plaintiffs' arguments is extremely simple. The Village points to the Supreme Court's decision in *Presser v. Illinois*, . . . in which the Court held that the prohibitions of the Second Amendment limited only the power of the United States Congress, and not the power of the individual states. Since this court is bound by the pronouncement of the Supreme Court, the village argues that plaintiff's contentions are largely irrelevant. In the alternative, Morton Grove also controverts the specific arguments made by the plaintiffs. The defendant claims that the Second Amendment does not create an individual right, but merely prohibits legislation that would impair the states' right to have a militia. . . . Also, the Village specifically refutes each of the plaintiffs' arguments, contending that they are not supported by common law traditions, the history of the Second Amendment, early state court decisions, or the statements of the framers of the Fourteenth Amendment. While some of those arguments are persuasive, there is no purpose in considering them further in view of the controlling *Presser* decision. . . .

Plaintiffs make two principal arguments in urging that this court not follow the holding in *Presser*. They argue first that *Presser*, when read properly, actually supports, rather than contradicts, their contention that the ordinance is unconstitutional. Second, they claim that irrespective of how *Presser* is read, it is no longer good law; in effect saying that the later cases incorporating several of the first ten amendments into the Fourteenth Amendment overrule *Presser sub silentio*. Neither of those arguments is persuasive.

Plaintiffs seize upon the phrase in *Presser* that "the States cannot, even laying the constitutional provision in question out of view, prohibit the people from keeping and bearing arms . . ." . . . to support their argument that defendant has misread that decision. When the phrase is read in context, however, it actually supports Morton Grove's position in this case, not the plaintiffs'.

The entire phrase referred to above, from which the plaintiffs have relied on but a portion, reads as follows:

> "[T]he States cannot, even laying the constitutional provision in question out of view, prohibit the people from keeping and bearing arms, so as to deprive the United States of their rightful resource for maintaining the public security, and disable the people from performing their duty to the general government."

Plaintiffs here have not suggested that the Morton Grove ordinance in any way interferes with the ability of the United States to maintain public security, nor could they make an argument to that effect. Irrespective of the Constitutional framers' fear of a national standing army, the United States currently has one and relies upon it, not upon armed private citizens, to maintain public security. . . .

Plaintiffs' second argument, that *Presser* has been overruled *sub silentio* by later decisions of the Supreme Court is equally unavailing. In their memorandum on this position, plaintiffs rely substantially on Justice Black's dissenting opinion in *Adamson v. California*. . . . Although three other Justices concurred with Justice Black that the Bill of Rights, in its entirety, should be incorporated into the protections offered by the Fourteenth Amendment, that position has never been accepted by a majority of the Supreme Court. . . . That situation is underscored by the fact that some provisions of the Bill of Rights, in addition to the Second Amendment, have never been held to apply to the states. . . .

*Presser* directly bears on the issue of whether the states or their political subdivisions are limited by the Second Amendment, and it is still good law, notwithstanding plaintiffs' arguments to the contrary. *Presser* controls this court and, therefore, requires it to hold that the Second Amendment does not apply to the states and localities and so is not infringed by the Morton Grove ordinance. Numerous state and lower federal courts who have considered the issue agree with this conclusion. . . .

The Ninth Amendment to the United States Constitution provides: The enumeration in the Constitution of certain rights, shall not be construed to deny or disparage others retained by the people. . . .

Although plaintiffs' arguments have an understandable facial appeal, the court is uanble to accept the argument that this claimed right is protected by the Ninth Amendment.

Neither plaintiffs, the defendant, nor this court has discovered a single instance in which the Supreme Court has explicitly held that a particular right was protected by the Ninth Amendment. In the situations where the Court has given protection to individual rights not explicitly listed in the first ten amendments, it has relied on "penumbras, formed by emanations from those guarantees that help give them life and substance."

Plaintiffs Quilici and Stengl both alleged in their complaints that the Morton Grove ordinance infringed the Fifth Amendment, which prohibits the taking of private property for public use, "without just compensation." Plaintiffs appear to have abandoned that argument, by failing to discuss it in their memoranda of law filed with this court. Nonetheless, for the sake of completeness, the court will address it briefly.

It is well established that a Fifth Amendment taking can occur through the exercise of the police power regulating property rights. In order for a regulatory taking to require compensation, however, the exercise of the police power must result in the destruction of the use and enjoyment of a legitimate private property right. . . . The Morton Grove ordinance does not go that far. The geographic reach of the ordinance is limited; gun owners who wish to may sell or otherwise dispose of their handguns outside of Morton Grove. . . . If handgun owners do not wish to sell their weapons they may simply register and store them at a licensed gun club. Finally, the ordinance has an exception for licensed collectors, for whom neither of those two alternatives may be acceptable.

In his memorandum, plaintiff Quilici implies that the ordinance is unconstitutionally vague. He suggests specifically that the ordinance's definition of "handgun" as a firearm of a size which may be concealed upon the person" might apply to shotguns and rifles in an unpredictable manner.

The conditions under which vagueness challenges to a statute may be considered have been clearly set out by the Supreme Court. "It is well-established that vagueness challenges to statutes which do not involve First Amendment freedoms must be examined in the light of the facts of the case at hand." . . . Plaintiff has failed to present an issue of the meaning of the statute as it applies to any weapon possessed by him. Rather, plaintiff, in his complaint, alleges that he owns handguns which are subject to the strictures of the ordinance. It is obvious that the ordinance gives Mr. Quilici "adequate warning" that his conduct would be illegal. . . .

Perhaps the clearest fact that emerges from this litigation is that the issue of gun control, in whatever form, is controversial. Reasonable people can, in good conscience, oppose what Morton Grove has done, while equally reasonable people can fully support this ordinance. Perhaps nowhere else is that situation more clearly demonstrated than in the lengthy and well thought out briefs filed by the opposing parties in this case.

After full consideration, the court has concluded that the Morton Grove ordinance was properly enacted pursant to the police power, and that it does not infringe upon the rights guaranteed by the United States Constitution. Although those legal questions decided by this court will reach finality at some point in time, the debate over the wisdom of this legislation will continue. Article 1, section 22 of the Illinois Constitution was drafted and presented to the voters of Illinois as a reflection of the conflicting views of the delegates. The voters of Illinois then approved the new Constitution with the express provision that the right to bear arms would be subject to the police power. The Trustees of Morton Grove, also acting in an atmosphere of pubic debate and conflict, have made a legislative decision that the danger posed by the easy availability of handguns is serious enough to warrant the banning of all handguns within this particular community. Before taking this action, the Morton Grove Trustees must have been aware of the deepseated conviction of a number of its citizens that they should be permitted to retain handguns for the protection of person and property. The Trustees concluded, however, that the public interest outweighed the claimed personal interests of the opponents of this legislation. The ultimate settlement of this troublesome political question must be returned to the citizens of Morton Grove where it properly belongs rather than in the courts.

For all the reasons stated above, the court finds that the Morton Grove ordinance is valid. It does not infringe any of the provisions of either the Illinois State Constitution or the United States Constitution. . . .

**Michael Kalodimos et al., Appellants,**
**v. The Village of Morton Grove, Appellee**
**Filed**
**October 19, 1984**
**Clerk Supreme Court**
**Illinois**

An ordinance of the village of Morton Grove banning the possession of all operable handguns, . . . withstood a challenge under the second and ninth amendments to the United States Constitution. (*Quilici v. Village of Morton Grove* (7th Cir. 1982), 695 F.2d 261, *cert. denied* (1983), ____ U.S. ____, 78 L. Ed. 2d 170, 104 S. Ct. 194). In that decision the Federal court also concluded that the ordinance was permissible under the Illinois Constitution. . . . This appeal calls upon this court to determine the meaning of our state constitution by defining the scope of the relevant state constitutional provision, deciding whether the ordinance passes muster under it, and, if so, deciding whether it is permissible under the constitutional home rule power and the police power.

The ordinance . . . provides that "[n]o person shall possess, in the Village . . . [a]ny handgun, unless the same has been rendered permanently inoperative." It exempts from its operation peace officers, prison officials, members of the armed forces, reserve units and the Illinois National Guard, security guards duly employed by a commercial or industrial enterprise or a public utility, and members of licensed gun clubs who entrust their handguns to the club for safekeeping when not using them for target shooting or other recreational purposes. Antique firearms are also specifically exempted from the ordinance.

Morton Grove residents filed this action seeking an injunction and a declaratory judgment that the ordinance violates article I, section 22, of the Illinois Constitution and is an unreasonable exercise of the police power. . . .

Article I, section 22, added to the Illinois Constitution in 1970, provides:

> "Subject only to the police power, the right of the individual citizen to keep and bear arms shall not be infringed."

The section does not mirror the Second Amendment to the federal Constitution . . . rather it adds the words "[s]ubject only to the police power," omits prefatory language concerning the importance of a militia, and substitutes "the individual citizen" for "the people." The majority report of the Bill of Rights Committee of the constitutional convention, which framed the provision, makes clear that the latter two changes were intended to broaden the scope of the right to arms from a collective one applicable only to weapons traditionally used by a regulated militia . . . to an individual right covering a wider variety of arms. . . .

Equally distinctive, however, is the explicit recognition of "the police power" as a limitation on the liberty the provision affords. The Bill of Rights Committee explained in its report that "[b]ecause arms pose an extraordinary threat to the safety and good order of society, the possession and use of arms is subject to an extraordinary degree of control under the police power." . . .

Plaintiffs contend that section 22 is ambiguous and that the ambiguity can only be resolved to mean that while the state and its subdivisions have the power to regulate the possession and use of weapons which are commonly used for recreation or protection of person and property, such as by requiring that all purchasers of handguns be licensed . . . they may not enact a flat ban on such weapons or any discrete category of them. Plaintiffs also argue that the proper focus in interpreting a constitutional provision such as section 22 must be on the common understanding of the citizens of the state who voted to adopt the Constitution.

The meaning of a constitutional provision depends, of course, on the common understanding of the citizens who, by ratifying the Constitution, gave it life. . . . This understanding, however, is best determined by referring to the common meaning of the words used. . . . The plain language of the provision clearly leaves the right to bear any type of arms subject to the police power. This belies any assertion that a majority of the voters must have interpreted the plain words of the provision as ruling out any specific regulatory measure. . . .

When presented with the report of the Bill of Rights Committee, the delegates to the convention were faced with a choice of adopting the so-called "majority report," which set forth section 22 in substantially the form in which it was enacted; adopting the "minority report," which recommended that the constitution remain silent concerning a right to arms; or adopting the "Lawlor amendment," which read: "The right of the individual to firearms or other means necessary for defense of his person or safeguarding of his property shall not be denied or infringed. The use of deadly weapons for hunting or other sports shall be subject to regulations established by law." . . . The Lawlor proposal and the minority report were both rejected. The majority report, which was accepted by the convention, was introduced by Delegate Leonard Foster. . . .

. . . Shortly before the vote which rejected the minority report, Mr. Foster stated:

> "It is the position of the majority that *under the police power of the state, the legislature would have the authority, for example, to forbid all handguns.* . . . [I]t is still the position of the majority that, short of an absolute and complete ban on the possession of *all firearms*, this provision would leave the legislature free to regulate the use of firearms in Illinois." . . .

Conspicuously absent from the debates is any expression by any delegate who favored the majority report that handguns could not be banned under the majority proposal. . . .

Plaintiffs contend that the natural interpretation of the words "police power," and that which the voter must have had in mind when considering section 22 under which all classes of firearms rather than merely military ones are protected, includes regulation of such firearms but not a prohibition of any class of arms. We see no basis for this argument. This court has long recognized that the police power comprehends laws "restraining or prohibiting anything harmful to the welfare of the people" . . ., and no convincing evidence has been produced that the voters ascribed a different meaning to the term in the context of section 22.

The plaintiffs refer to newspaper articles and editorials which they argue led voters to believe that no class of weapons would be subject to complete prohibition. . . .

. . . We are not aware of how many voters read the publications cited, how many of those read the particular articles in question, or how and to what extent those who did read the articles were influenced by them. By contrast, the text of the right-to-arms provision and the official explanation were made available to everyone who voted. Their import was that regulation consistent with the public welfare would be permitted; they did not suggest that such regulation would not include bans on discrete categories of weapons. For these reasons, we conclude that in this case, because of their inconclusive character, the newspaper articles on which the plaintiffs rely should not change our decision.

Based on the floor debates and the official explanation, as well as on the language of the provision, it is apparent to us that section 22, as submitted to the voters, meant that a ban on all firearms that an individual citizen might use would not be permissible, but a ban on discrete categories of firearms, such as handguns, would be. . . .

Plaintiffs point out that handguns are a form of weapon commonly used for defense of person and property and, consequently, they fall within the general protection of section 22. They argue that there is no principle which permits the complete abridgment of one form of constitutionally protected behavior whenever other forms of behavior which enjoy the same form of protection and lead to a substantially similar end are permitted. However, the authorities which plaintiffs cite for this proposition . . . arose in the context of the first amendment. Unlike that amendment, which is designed to encourage the propagation and dissemination of views and ideas . . . the amendment with which we are dealing was designed neither to encourage nor to discourage the possession of firearms, but merely to guard against the confiscation of all such arms.

Nor do we find merit in plaintiffs' argument that section 22 is a nullity if construed to permit a ban on some of the very categories of weapons it was enacted to protect. We emphasize again that section 22 bestows upon individual citizens for the first time a right to possess some form of weapon suitable for self-defense or recreation, regardless of the adaptability of the weapon for use in an organized militia or of whether it is possessed for the purposes of forming a militia. The enactment of such a provision can scarcely be regarded as an idle gesture. . . .

Plaintiffs argue that the regulation of firearms is inherently a matter of exclusive statewide concern because of the mobility of guns and gun owners, and that it is thus beyond the power of local governments acting under color of their home rule power . . . to enact an ordinance banning handguns. . . .

Whether a particular problem is of statewide rather than local dimension must be decided not on the basis of a specific formula or listing set forth in the Constitution but with regard for the nature and extent of the problem, the units of goverment which have the most vital interest in its solution, and the role traditionally played by local and statewide authorities in dealing with it. . . .

The plaintiffs seek to apply a free-wheeling preemption rule to the exercise of home rule power. They argue in effect that a subject is preempted whenever it is of significant concern to the State or whenever a uniform statewide solution to the problems it entails might arguably be more manageable than individual control by local units of government. Home rule, however, is predicated on the assmption that problems in which local governments have a legitimate and substantial interest should be open to local solution and reasonable experimentation to meet local needs, free from veto by voters and elected representatives of other parts of the State who might disagree with the particular approach advanced by the representatives of the locality involved or fail to appreciate the local perception of the problem. . . .

Although plaintiffs contend that weapons control and crime prevention are matters of statewide rather than local concern, villages such as Morton Grove have an obvious interest not only in reducing premeditated crime within their boundaries but also in minimizing the effects of domestic violence or spontaneous quarrels. They also have an interest in reducing the possibility of serious accidents resulting from the accessibility to children of attractive but dangerous instrumentalities such as handguns. Moreover, the delegates to the constitutional convention acknowledged that weapons control was a field suitable for local regulation pursuant to home rule authority. . . .

This case does not involve local regulation of a State institution such as the court system . . . or a regional institution such as a sanitary district. . . . Nor does it involve regulation of conduct outside the village of Morton Grove . . . except insofar as it may incidentally cause people who wish to carry a handgun while traveling to route themselves through other communities rather than Morton Grove. We do not view this as a reason to hold that weapons control does not pertain to local government or affairs, any more than the possibility that a village speed regulation might cause people who wish to go faster to route themselves around the village invalidates local speed laws. Nor would the possibility that different home rule units might adopt contradictory handgun laws be of concern in this regard. The grant of home rule powers contemplates that different communities which perceive a problem differently may adopt different measures to address the problem, provided that the legislature has taken no affirmative steps to circumscribe the measures that may be taken and that the measures taken are reasonable.

Plaintiffs finally contend that the enactment by the State of statutes bearing on gun ownership, possession and sale evidence an intent to preempt the field of firearms regulation either expressly or by implication, and leave no room for local laws regulating or restricting possession of firearms. . . .

Neither of these statutes suggests that firearms control is a subject for exclusive State involvement. In fact, the only statement in either act concerning the permissibility of more stringent local control is to the opposite effect: "The provisions of any ordinance enacted by any municipality which requires registration or imposes greater restrictions or limitation on the acquisition, possession and transfer of firearms than are imposed by this Act, are not invalidated or affected by this Act. . . ."

We likewise find no basis for concluding that the two acts on which plaintiffs rely leave no room for more restrictive local laws or are contradicted in any way by Morton Grove's ordinance. . . .

Plaintiffs argue that applying for an identification card in compliance with the Firarms and Ammunition Act involves disclosing certain information to State officials which may incriminate the applicant for purposes of prosecution under Morton Grove's ordinance in violation of the fifth and fourteenth amendments. . . . The ordinance with which we are dealing outlaws only the possession of handguns; permits everyone to possess a handgun that has been rendered permanently inoperative, or which is used solely for recreational purposes within the village and is kept on the premises of licensed gun clubs or outside village boundaries; and permits certain people, including commercial or industrial security guards, to possess operable handguns anywhere within the village. Inasmuch as the application for an identification card under the Firearms and Ammunition Act need not mention the applicant's occupation, the kind of firearm he wishes to possess, the place where he intends to keep it, or the purposes for which he intends to use it, the only information Morton Grove authorities could glean from the application is that a resident of Morton Grove desires to possess a firearm. This information by itself would be of virtually no use in establishing a violation of the ordinance.

We therefore conclude that the ordinance is a permissible exercise of Morton Grove's home rule powers. . . .

Plaintiffs contend that, inasmuch as guns and gun owners are highly mobile, the ordinance in question is valueless in preventing crime within the village of Morton Grove and may in fact encourage it by disarming law-abiding citizens. They argue that the ordinance is perverse as a safety measure and violates Federal and State guarantees of due process (U.S. Const., amends. V, XIV; Ill. Const. 1970, art. I, sec. 2). In related contentions, they argue that the ordinance, through its exemptions, arbitrarily discriminates between residents of the village in violation of equal protection guarantees,and that because of the fundamental nature of the right to bear arms in self-defense the ordinance is overbroad for purposes of due process and equal protection in that its substantive goals can be accomplished through various less restrictive means. . . .

Initially we observe that the search for less onerous alternative means of securing a governental interest is a hallmark of strict scrutiny, which comes into play only when a fundamental right is invaded. Not every right secured by the state or federal constitutions is fundamental, however, but only those which "lie at the heart of the relationship between the individual and a republican form of nationally integrated government". . . . While the right to possess firearms for purposes of self-defense may be necessary to protect important personal liberties from encroachment by other individuals, it does not lie at the heart of the relationship between individuals and their government. The right to bear arms guaranteed by the federal Constitution has never been thought to be an individual right, as distinguished from a collective right . . .; moreover, the right to arms secured by the Illinois Constitution, which did not exist prior to 1970, is subject, as we have explained, to substantial infringement in the exercise of the police power even though it operates on the individual level. . . .

Under the rational-basis test, which is the appropriate level of scrutiny when no fundamental right is involved, the relevant inquiry for purposes of due process and equal protection is whether the Morton Grove ordinance bears a rational relationship to a legitimate governmental interest, not whether it is overly broad. . . . In this regard the ordinance in its preamble defines the village's interest as reducing "the potentiality of firearm-related deaths and injuries" caused by "the easy and convenient availability of certain types of firearms and weapons" and finds that "handguns play a major role in the commission of homicide, aggravated assault, and armed robbery, and accidental injury and death." . . . Because of the ease with which handguns can be concealed and handled, as compared with other types of weapons, a ban on handguns under the conditions set forth in the ordinance could rationally have been viewed by the village as a way of reducing the frequency of premeditated violent attacks as well as unplanned criminal shootings in the heat of passion or in overreaction to fears of assault, accidental shootings by children or by adults who are unaware that a handgun is loaded, or suicides. We find of no significance the possibility that the ordinance was passed for the sole purpose of publicizing a political viewpoint, as the plaintiffs contend is demonstrated by the transcribed statements of the village trustees who approved the ordinance: police regulations and statutory classifications will be upheld "if any state of facts reasonably may be conceived to justify" them. . . .

For similar reasons, we find no constitutional infirmity in the fact that the ordinance permits security guards or special agents employed by railroads or public utilities to carry handguns regardless of their actual qualifications to possess or handle firearms without endangering the public, whereas ordinary citizens are not permitted to do so regardless of their qualifications or the urgency of their need to carry a gun. The village trustees could validly have believed that security guards as a group were likely to exercise greater responsibility in using their weapons than citizens generally, or it may simply have concluded that the private interest in protecting commercial premises was greater than the public interest in banning handgun possession in those few cases covered by the exemption of which plaintiffs complain. Because we cannot say that the classification is unrelated to the goals of the ordinance, we hold that it is a proper exercise of the police power.

Plaintiffs, noting that the case was dismissed upon the entry of summary judgment by the circuit court, urge us to remand the case to that court for consideration of additional evidence that may have a bearing on the rationality of the ordinance. Our review, however, is not one of fact but purely one of law, and our conclusion is compelled by the judgment that the ordinance bears a rational relation to the goal of reducing weapons-related injuries and accidents within the village of Morton Grove. Minimal scrutiny requires nothing more, and we do not perceive how a remand might alter this judgment. For the reasons stated, therefore, we conclude that the ordinance is a proper exercise of the police power authority.

The judgments of the appellate and circuit courts are affirmed.

## B. OPINIONS ILLUSTRATING THE "INDIVIDUAL" VIEW

### Bliss v. Commonwealth
### 12 Ky. (2 Litt.) 90 (1822)

This was an indictment founded on the act of the legislature of this state, "to prevent persons in this commonwealth from wearing concealed arms."

The act provides, that any person in this commonwealth, who shall hereafter wear a pocket pistol, dirk, large knife, or sword in a case, concealed as a weapon, unless when traveling on a journey, shall be fined in any sum not less than $100; which may be recovered in any court having jurisdiction of like sums, by action of debt, or on presentment of a grand jury.

The indictment, in the words of the act, charges Bliss with having *worn concealed as a weapon, a sword in a cane.*

Bliss was found guilty of the charge, and a fine of $100 assessed by the jury, and judgment was thereon rendered by the court. To reverse that judgment, Bliss appealed to this court.

In argument the judgment was assailed by the counsel of Bliss, exclusively on the ground of the act, on which the indictment is founded, being in conflict with the twenty-third section of the tenth article of the constitution of this state.

That section provides, "that the right of the citizens to bear arms in defence of themselves and the state, shall not be questioned."

The provision contained in this section, perhaps, is as well calculated to secure to the citizens the right to bear arms in defence of themselves and the state, as any that could have been adopted by the makers of the constitution. If the right be assailed, immaterial through what medium, whether by an act of the legislature or in any other form, it is equally opposed to the comprehensive import of the section. The legislature is nowhere expressly mentioned in the section; but the language employed is general, without containing any expression restricting its import to any particular department of government; and in the twenty-eighth section of the same article of the constitution, it is expressly declared, "that every thing in that article is excepted out of the general powers of government, and shall forever remain inviolate; and that all laws contrary thereto, or contrary to the constitution, shall be *void*."

It was not, however, contended by the attorney for the commonwealth, that it would be competent for the legislature, by the enactment of any law, to prevent the citizens from bearing arms either in defence of themselves or the state; but a distinction was taken between a law prohibiting the exercise of the right, and a law merely regulating the manner of exercising that right; and whilst the former was admitted to be incompatible with the constitution, it was insisted, that the latter is not so, and under that distinction, and by assigning the act in question a place in the latter description of laws, its consistency with the constitution was attempted to be maintained.

That the provisions of the act in question do not import an entire destruction of the right of the citizens to bear arms in defence of themselves and the state, will not be controverted by the court; for though the citizens are forbid wearing weapons concealed in the manner described in the act, they may, nevertheless, bear arms in any other admissible form. But to be in conflict with the constitution, it is not essential that the act should contain a prohibition against bearing arms in every possible form; it is the *right* to bear arms in defence of the citizens and the state, that is secured by the constitution, and whatever restrains the full and complete exercise of that right, though not an entire destruction of it, is forbidden by the explicit language of the constitution.

If, therefore, the act in question imposes any restraint on the right, immaterial what appellation may be given to the act, whether it be an act regulating the manner of bearing arms or any other, the consequence, in reference to the constitution, is precisely the same, and its collision with that instrument equally obvious.

And can there be entertained a reasonable doubt but the provisions of the act import a restraint on the right of the citizens to bear arms? The court apprehends not. The right existed at the adoption of the constitution; it had then no limits short of the moral power of the citizens to exercise it, and it in fact consisted in nothing else but in the liberty of the citizens to bear arms. Diminish that liberty, therefore, and you necessarily restrain the right; and such is the diminution and restraint, which the act in question most indisputably imports, by prohibiting the citizens wearing weapons in a manner which was lawful to wear them when the constitution was adopted. In truth, the right of the citizens to bear arms, has been as directly assailed by the provisions of the act, as though they were forbid carrying guns on their shoulders, swords in scabbards, or when in conflict with an enemy, were not allowed the use of bayonets; and if the act be consistent with the constitution, it cannot be incompatible with that instrument for the legislature, by successive enactments, to entirely cut off the exercise of the right of the citizens to bear arms. For, in principle, there is no difference between a law prohibiting the wearing concealed arms, and a law forbidding the wearing such as are exposed; and if the former be unconstitutional, the latter must be so likewise.

We may possibly be told, that although a law of either description may be enacted consistently with the constitution, it would be incompatible with that instrument to enact laws of both descriptions. But if either, when alone, be consistent with the constitution, which, it may be asked, would be incompatible with that instrument, if both were enacted?

The law first enacted would not be; for, as the argument supposes either may be enacted consistent with the constitution, that which is first enacted must, at the time of enactment, be consistent with the constitution; and if then consistent, it cannot become otherwise, by any subsequent act of the legislature. It must, therefore, be the latter act which the argument infers would be incompatible with the constitution.

But suppose the order of enactment were reversed, and instead of being the first, that which was first, had been the last; the argument, to be consistent, should, nevertheless, insist on the last enactment being in conflict with the constitution. So that the absurd consequence would thence follow, of making the same act of the legislature, either consistent with the constitution, or not so, according as it may precede or follow some other enactment of a different import. Besides, by insisting on the previous act producing any effect on the latter, the argument implies that the previous one operates as a partial restraint on the right of the citizens to bear arms, and proceeds on the notion, that by prohibiting the exercise of the residue of right, not affected by the first act, the latter act comes in collision with the constitution. But it should not be forgotten, that it is not only a part of the right that is secured by the constitution; it is the right entire and complete, as it existed at the adoption of the constitution; and if any portion of that right be impaired, immaterial how small the part may be, and immaterial the order of time at which it be done, it is equally forbidden by the constitution.

Hence, we infer, that the act upon which the indictment against Bliss is founded, is in conflict with the constitution; and if so, the result is obvious; the result is what the constitution has declared it shall be, that the act is *void*.

And if to be incompatible with the constitution makes void the act, we must have been correct, throughout the examination of this case, in treating the question of compatibility as one proper to be decided by the court. For it is emphatically the duty of the court to decide what the law is; and how is the law to be decided, unless it be known? And how can it be known without ascertaining, from a comparison with the constitution, whether there exist such an incompatibility between the acts of the legislature and the constitution, as to make void the acts?

A blind enforcement of every act of the legislature might relieve the court from the trouble and responsibility of deciding on the consistency of the legislative acts with the constitution; but the court would not be thereby released from its obligations to obey the mandates of the constitution, and maintain the paramount authority of that instrument; and those obligations must cease to be acknowledged, or the court becomes insensible to the impressions of moral sentiment, before the provisions of any act of the legislature, which in the opinion of the court, conflict with the constitution, can be enforced.

Whether or not an act of the legislature conflicts with the constitution, is at all times, a question of great delicacy, and deserves the most mature and deliberate consideration of the court. But though a question of delicacy, yet as it is a judicial one, the court would be unworthy its station, were it to shrink from deciding it whenever, in the course of judicial examination, a decision becomes material to the right in contest. The court should never, on slight implication or vague conjecture, pronounce the legislature to have transcended its authority in the enactment of law but when a clear and strong conviction is entertained, that an act of the legislature is incompatible with the constitution, there is no alternative for the court to pursue, but to declare that conviction, and pronounce the act inoperative and *void*. And such is the conviction entertained by a majority of the court (Judge Mills dissenting) in relation to the act in question.

The judgment must, consequently, be reversed.

## State v. Buzzard
## 4 Ark. 18 (1842)

***Lacy, J., dissenting.***

The defendant in the court below stands indicted by virtue of the authority of the 13th section of an act of the Legislature, prohibiting any person wearing a pistol, dirk, large knife, or sword-cane, *concealed as a weapon*, unless upon a journey, under the penalties of fine and imprisonment. . . .

The question now to be determined is, does this provision of the statute violate the second article of the amendments to the Constitution of the United States, or the 21st section of our Bill of Rights? The language in both instruments is nearly similar: the two clauses are as follows: "That a well regulated militia being necessary for the security of a free State, the right of the people to keep and bear arms shall not be infringed." "That the free white men of this State shall have a right to keep and bear arms in their common defence." The inquiry is restricted to a single point; but it is not, on that account, wholly free from difficulty. Several of the highest courts of the Union have adjudged it differently, upon the construction of statutes every way like our own; and their opinions are entitled to due consideration. . . . I know of no opinion ever delivered of the Supreme Court of the United States, bearing directly upon the point. The question, then, so far as this State is concerned, may be regarded open for investigation, and now brought up for adjudication upon error, for the first time. Both of my brother Judges have just pronounced separate opinions, each maintaining the constitutionality of the act. . . . Now, I take the expressions "a well regulated militia being necessary for the security of a free State," and the terms "common defence," to be the reasons assigned for the granting of the right, and not a restriction or limitation upon the right itself, or the perfect freedom of its exercise. The security of the State is the constitutional reason for the guaranty. But when was it contended before, that the reason given for the establishment of a right, or its uninterrupted enjoyment, not only limited the right itself, but restrained it to a single specific object? According to this construction, the right itself is not only abridged, but literally destroyed; and the security of a free State is made to depend exclusively and alone upon the force of the militia. And, in the opinion of one of my brother Judges, it is the militia alone who possess this right, in contradistinction from the mass of the people; and even they cannot use them for private defence or personal aggression, but must use them for public liberty, according to the discretion of the legislature. According to the rule laid down in their interpretation of this clause, I deem the right to be valueless, and not worth preserving; for the State unquestionably possesses the power, without the grant, to arm the militia, and direct how they shall be employed in cases of invasion or domestic insurrection. If this be the meaning of the Constitution, why give that which is no right in itself, and guaranties a privilege that is useless? This construction, according to the views I entertain, takes the arms out of the hands of the people, and places them in the hands of the legislature, with no restraint or limitation whatever upon their power, except their own free will and sovereign pleasure. Are great affirmative grants of political powers to be determined by this technical rule of verbal criticism? If so, its rigid application to other portions of the Constitution would erase from its pages many of its most important and salutary provisions. Such a principle, I apprehend, should never be recognized or adopted by any judicial tribunal, in determining the inherent and original rights of the citizen. It goes to abridge, instead of enlarging the constitutional guaranties of personal liberty.

If the legislature have the custody of the people's arms and the treasury of the State, what becomes of the separation and division of the political powers of the government? Are not those powers united in the same body of magistracy? And if this be the case, the balance of the Constitution is overthrown, and the State then possesses no real security for personal liberty. It is no answer to this argument, to say that the people may abuse the privilege or right of keeping and bearing arms. The Constitution thought and ordained it otherwise; and therefore it was deemed far safer to entrust the right to their own judgment and discretion, rather than to the will or ambition of the legislature; and this right was excepted out of the general powers of the government, and declared inviolate. Now, if the legislature had the right to forbid the people from keeping arms secretly, may they not prohibit them from carrying them openly or exposed? and if they could do this, may they not appoint the times and places when and where they shall be borne? And as the construction relied on assumes the principle that they can only be used for a specific and single purpose, then of course the whole subject matter, in regard to keeping and bearing either private or public arms, falls within the power of the legislature, and they can control or regulate it in any manner that they think proper. This principle I utterly repudiate. I deny that any just or free government upon earth has the power to disarm its citizens, and to take from them the only security and ultimate hope that they have for the defence of their liberties and their rights. I deny this, not only upon constitutional grounds, but upon the immutable principles of natural and equal justice, that all men have a right to, and which to deprive them of amounts to tyranny and oppression. Can it be doubted, that if the legislature, in moments of high political excitement or of revolution, were to pass an act disarming the whole population of the State, that such an act would be utterly void, not only because it violated the spirit and tenor of the Constitution, but because it invaded the original rights of natural justice? Now, if they are private and not public arms, the Constitution guaranties the right of keeping and bearing them.

The people are secured in their persons, houses, papers, and effects, against unwarrantable searches and seizures; but on probable cause, supported by oath or affirmation. Now, if the legislature possesses the power claimed for it, it surely has the means of carrying it into effect. Can it, directly or indirectly, invade the sanctuaries of private life and of personal security, by authorizing a public inquisition to search for either open or concealed weapons? Besides, private property cannot be taken for public uses without due compensation being first made according to law. A man's arms are his private property; how, then, can he be legally deprived of them? If they can forbid him, under the penalty of fine and imprisonment, to keep them concealed or exposed about his person, or on his own premises, although their unrestrained use may be necessary for all the purposes of his ordinary business and of personal defence, then certainly the right of keeping and bearing arms according to his own discretion, is infringed and violated, and his own free will in the management of this property abridged and destroyed.

If it means the public arms, then full power is given by the Constitution to Congress to organize and arm the militia, and prescribe rules for their use and regulation, when mustered into the service of the United States. Now, as full power is given to Congress over the subject, and the same power belongs to the State, which power shall be paramount, and to which of the two governments is entrusted the common defence of the country? Is the grant of the State Constitution void, being repugnant to the Constitution of the United States, or does it abrogate and annul that power? . . . According to the construction I design to give, there can be no conflict between these jurisdictions, nor any discrepancy arising from their action. I hold the doctrine that the Constitution of the United States, and the laws passed in pursuance of its authority, are supreme; and that all State constitutions and laws repugnant to them, are utterly null and void; and that the Constitution and laws of the federal government operate directly upon the people and the States, and all are bound to respect and obey them. Again; who compose the militia? Has not the State a right to desigate what part or portion of her citizens shall constitute this military corps? Then she can, by indirection, arm only those who are in her interest, or who are swayed by her ambition; and, by denying arms to every other class of her citizens, may she not subjugate the liberties of all, by the very means the Constitution gives for their protection and defence?

. . . Suppose the Legislature pass an act, that a man should not keep private arms in his own house secretly, or about his person concealed, although they should be every way necessary, in defence of his life, liberty, or property. Can it be doubted that such an act would be a palpable infraction of the Constitution, as well as an invasion of the natural rights of society? Has not every man a natural and an unalienable right to defend his life, liberty, or property, when a known felony is attempted to be committed upon either by violence or surprise? Can any laws deprive him of this right? Upon what principle has he a right to use force to repel force, and even to slay the aggressor, if he cannot make a successful repulsion otherwise? The laws of the land being unable to protect him, the laws of nature step in, and authorize him to defend himself. . . . To put this case in its true light—suppose a citizen of the State were indicted upon a charge of murder, and he could make out a clear case of justifiable homicide, the laws of nature, upon which the laws of society are presumed to be based, instead of punishing, commends him for the act; of course, he stands acquitted of all blame but, on the trial, the evidence shows that he was compelled to take life with a concealed weapon, and the State thinks proper to indict him for this new offence, which is forbidden by an act of the legislature; and the proof being clear upon the point, of course he may be convicted and rendered infamous for life. What then becomes of the right of self-defence? Is it not swept away from him by legislative discretion, and the doctrine of self-preservation destroyed, which nature has implanted in the breast of every living creature, and which no laws, either human or divine, can abrogate or annul? In such a case, could there by any hesitation in pronouncing the act that punished him for protecting his own life, absolutely null and void? I think not. All the authorities, upon natural as well as constitutional law, support and prove this position. Would the act forbidding a person to carry concealed weapons be constitutional if he used them in self-defence, and unconstitutional if he did not use them at all, or kept them in a secret manner? If that be the case, then it is the intent, and not the fact of carrying concealed weapons, that makes the law either void or valid. Can so fluctuating a rule be the standard by which to test the constitutionality of the acts of the legislature? I maintain that the simple fact of a man's keeping and bearing private arms, whether concealed or exposed, is an act innocent of itself, and its freedom secured from all legislative interference. The act being innocent and allowed, cannot be made penal, or prohibited by law. The existence and freedom of a right is one thing, and the culpable and criminal use of it another and a wholly different thing. A right, in itself innocent and guarantied by law, cannot be made illegal or punished as a crime; and the error into which the Court has fallen in the present instance, seems to me to result from confounding these two things, which are wholly separate and independent of each other.

I admit that it is somewhat difficult to determine the exact point where the freedom of a constitutional right stops, and where legislative regulation begins. I take this distinction, however, to run through the whole class of cases; that if the right be innocent of itself, it cannot be interdicted; but its unlawful exercise, degenerating into licentiousness, is subject to regulation. The principle assumed in this case is, that the fact of private arms being worn concealed is a criminal offence, and capable of being controlled by the legislature, and that they alone have the right to judge of its criminality. The propositions I do not believe, nor can I subscribe to them. It is true that the Legislature must judge, in the first case, whether the unrestrained freedom or use of a constitutional right is criminal or not; but having passed upon the subject, it then belongs to the judiciary to examine the question, and to declare the rule of action in regard to it. The citizen, in this instance, complains that his liberty has been improperly restrained, and he has appealed to the judiciary to shield him from this act of legislative injustice. That department is the last arbiter of his rights; and the point to be settled is, has the legislature judged wrongfully, or is the mere fact of a person's keeping his private arms concealed, an offence against the State, and liable to be controlled by legislative discretion?

I maintain that the act is not only lawful, but expressly secured by the Constitution, and of course cannot be controlled by ordinary legislation. I admit that, if a man uses his arms improperly, or in an unlawful manner, then it is competent for the legislature to punish him for the improper and illegal use of them; and it is right to do so; for everyone is bound so to exercise his own rights, as not to prejudice those of others. The legislature, in doing this, does not punish an innocent act, but an unwarrantable one; it does not abridge a natural and constitutional right, or in any manner interfere with its freedom. It merely punishes an unlawful use of a right; and it can do that only when the party has committed, with his own arms, unauthorized aggression upon the person or property of another. And the rights of the Constitution are guaranted upon this principle—that while their perfect freedom and enjoyment are secured, the Constitution utterly forbids any licentious or criminal indulgence in their exercise; for when that is the case, they can no longer be said to be the perfect and inviolable rights of the Constitution, but the unlawful and unauthorized acts of individuals. . . . The liberty of speech and of the press, and the freedom of religious toleration, are utterly incompatible, in the true constitutional meaning of those terms, with their licentiousness or criminal indulgence; and these latter or improper acts are in no manner connected with the invaluable franchises out of which they flow. Now, the right of the people to keep and bear arms is as free and unfettered, and as inviolable and important, as the liberty of speech and of the press, or the freedom of religious toleration; and it stands upon precisely the same constitutional ground, and supported by like reasons. . . .

It is further contended that the right should be restricted, because it is given alone for the security of a free State, which means nothing more or less than the defence of public liberty. Now, what constitutes the security of a free State, or what is public liberty? Does the security of a free State consist alone in repelling foreign aggression, or quelling domestic insurrection? How is the public liberty of a State to be preserved, and what is it? . . . The security of a free State, as I imagine, depends not only in upholding all its political institutions, but in sacredly performing all its legal and constitutional obligations, both to the government and to the people. Public liberty can only be secured and perpetuated by preserving inviolable the personal franchises and immunities of the citizen, as well as guarding and protecting the sovereign attributes of the State. To suppose that public liberty cannot be in danger, except from a foreign foe or internal disorder, is virtually to deny the importance and necessity of written constitutions. If there was no fear of our own rulers, why impose restraints upon them, and why commit the guardianship and care of the great principles of civil and religious liberty to separate and independent departments of the government, and bind each, by the most solemn injunctions, to preserve and defend them? And why trust the Constitution, in the last resort, to the interpretation of the Courts, to expound its meaning and declare its will? For this plain and obvious reason: because the Judiciary has few temptations to err, and possesses neither patronage or power, to make it popular or dangerous. I cannot separate the political freedom of the State from the personal rights of its citizens. They are indissolubly bound up together in the same great bond of union, and, to my mind, they are incapable of division. . . . Among these rights, I hold, is the privilege of the people to keep and to bear their private arms, for the necessary defence of their person, habitation, and property, or for any useful or innocent purpose whatever. We derive this right from our Anglo-Saxon ancestors, and under the form of that government it has ever been regarded as sacred and inviolable. It is of great antiquity and of invaluable price. Its necessary operation, in times of convulsion and of revolution, has been the only means by which public liberty or the security of free States has been vindicated and maintained. Here, the principles of equal and natural justice, as well as the obvious meaning and spirit of the Constitution, have placed it above legislative interference. To forbid a citizen, under the penalty of fine and imprisonment, to carry his own private arms about his person, in any manner that he may think proper for his security or safety, is, in my opinion, an unauthorized attempt to abridge a constitutional privilege, and therefore I hold the law in question to be of no effect.

## In re Brickey
## 8 Idaho 597, 70 P. 609 (1902)

The petitioner applies to this court for a writ of habeas corpus, and in the petition sets forth and shows that he is unlawfully imprisoned, confined, and restrained of his liberty by A. W. Kroutinger, sheriff of Nez Perce county, at the county jail in the county of Nez Perce, in the state of Idaho; that he is so imprisoned under a commitment which issued out of the justice's court of West Lewiston precinct, in the county of Nez Perce, in a criminal action wherein petitioner was convicted upon the charge of carrying a deadly weapon, to wit, a loaded revolver, within the limits and confines of the city of Lewiston, contrary to the provisions of the act of the territory of Idaho approved February 4, 1889 . . . and, in accordance with the prayer of said petition, the writ was issued, and return thereto duly made by the said sheriff. From the petition and return it appears that the only offense charged against the petitioner, of which he has been convicted, and is now restrained of his liberty, is that he carried a deadly weapon within the limits of the city of Lewiston, in contravention of the said act of February 4, 1889. The Second Amendment to the federal constitution is in the following language: "A well regulated militia, being necessary to the security of a free state, the right of the people to keep and bear arms, shall not be infringed." The language of section 11, art. 1, Const. Idaho, is as follows: "The people have the right to bear arms for their security and defense, but the legislature shall regulate the exercise of this right by law." Under these constitutional provisions, the legislature has no power to prohibit a citizen from bearing arms in any portion of the state of Idaho, whether within or without the corporate limits of cities, towns, and villages. The legislature may, as expressly provided in our state constitution, regulate the exercise of the police power of the state. But the statute in question does not prohibit the carrying of weapons concealed, which is of itself a pernicious practice, but prohibits the carrying of them in any manner in cities, towns, and villages. We are compelled to hold this statute void. The statute being void, the said justice's court had no jurisdiction of the subject-matter of the action, and the said judgment of conviction, and the commitment which issued thereon, and the detention of the petitioner under said commitment and judgment of conviction are illegal and void.

## State v. Rosenthal
## 75 Vt. 295, 55 A. 610 (1903)

Section 10 of the ordinances of the city of Rutland provides that no person shall carry within the city any steel or brass knuckles, pistol, slung shot, stiletto, or weapon of similar character, nor carry any weapon concealed on his person, without permission of the mayor or chief of police, in writing, and for violation thereof a penalty is provided by a subsequent section. A complaint was filed against the respondent in the city court for carrying within the city, in violation of said ordinance, a pistol loaded with powder and bullets, concealed on his person, without such permission. On demurrer to the complaint, the respondent contends, among other things, that said ordinance is illegal, for that, so far as it forbids the carrying of a pistol, it is repugnant to and inconsistent with the Constitution and the laws of this state.

Section 24 of the city charter gives the city council power to make, establish, alter, amend, or repeal ordinances, regulations, and by-laws, not inconsistent with the charter or with the Constitution or laws of the United States or of this state, for the purposes enumerated, and to inflict as a penalty for a violation thereof a fine not exceeding $50. After the special designations is the general clause, "And said city council may make and establish, and the same alter, amend or repeal, any other by-laws, rules and ordinances which they deem necessary for the well being of said city and not repugnant to the Constitution or laws of this state." Power to make the ordinance in question was not expressly given the council, and they had no power to make it, beyond what is given under the general clause above quoted. The people of the state have a right to bear arms for the defense of themselves and the state. Const. c. 1, art. 16. But by V. S. 4922, a person is prohibited from carrying a dangerous or deadly weapon, openly or concealed, with the intent or avowed purpose of injuring a fellow man; and by section 4923, no person can carry or have in his possession any firearm, dirk knife, bowie knife, dagger, or other dangerous or deadly weapon, while a member of and in attendance upon a school. Section 4924 provides a penalty for intentionally, without malice, pointing a firearm toward another person, and for discharging such firearm so pointed, without injury to another person; and by section 4925 a punishment is inflicted where another person is maimed or injured by the discharge of such firearm. But section 4926 provides that the two preceding sections shall not apply where firearms are used in self-defense or in the discharge of official duty, or in the case of justifiable homicide. Under the general laws, therefore, a person not a member of a school may carry a dangerous or deadly weapon, openly or concealed, unless he does it with the intent or avowed purpose of injuring another; and a person who is a member of a school, but not in attendance upon it, is at liberty, in a similar way, to carry such weapons. In State v. Carlton, 48 Vt. 636, it was held that the owner of land, having the right to use reasonable force in expelling a trespasser therefrom, had a right to go prepared to defend himself against any assault that the trespasser might make upon him while in the exercise of that right, and that if he only intended to use a pistol in such an emergency in defending his own life, or against the infliction of great bodily harm, the carrying of the pistol for such purpose would be lawful. By the ordinance in question, no person can carry such weapon concealed on his person within the city of Rutland in any circumstances, nor for any purpose, without the permission of the mayor or chief of police in writing. Therein neither the intent nor purpose of carrying them enters into the essential elements of the offense. Simply to carry them concealed without such permission constitutes a violation of the ordinance. But if a permission is procured from either of those officials there is no violation of the ordinance, even though the carrying of the weapon be with the intent or avowed purpose of injuring another person; and that a person is a member of a school, and in attendance upon it, forms no exception. Consequently, unless a special permission is granted by the mayor or chief of police for that purpose, a person is prohibited from carrying such weapons in circumstances where the same is lawful by the Constitution and the general laws of the state; and there is nothing in the ordinance to prevent the granting of such permission, notwithstanding it be in circumstances to constitute a crime under the general laws. The result is that Ordinance No. 10, so far as it relates to the carrying of a pistol, is inconsistent with and repugnant to the Constitution and the laws of the state, and it is therefore to that extent, void. Whether this renders the whole ordinance illegal, or whether it contains any other invalid provisions, are questions not now before the court.

Judgment reversed and sentence set aside, demurrer sustained, complaint adjudged insufficient and quashed, and the respondent discharged and let go without delay.

## State v. Kerner
## 181 N.C. 574, 107 S.E. 222 (1921)

The defendant was indicted on a first count for carrying a concealed weapon, and on the second count for carrying a pistol off his premises unconcealed. There was a special verdict which found the defendant was walking along the streets of the town of Kernersville in

Forsyth county carrying some packages, when he was accosted, for the purpose of engaging him in a fight, by one Matthews; that in the course of this altercation he set down his packages and went to his place of business and there procured a pistol, which he brought back with him unconcealed to the scene of the altercation. Section 3, c. 317, Public Local Laws of 1919, prohibits the carrying of such weapons off his own premises by any one in Forsyth without a permit, even though it was not concealed. The court, being of the opinion that this statute was in conflict with the constitutional provision that "the right to bear arms shall not be infringed," directed a verdict of not guilty, and the state appealed. . . .

The Constitution of this state, section 24, art. 1, which is entitled, "Declaration of Rights," provides: "The right of the people to keep and bear arms shall not be infringed," adding, "nothing herein contained shall justify the practice of carrying concealed weapons or prevent the Legislature from enacting penal statutes against said practice." This exception indicates the extent to which the right of the people to bear arms can be restricted; that is, the Legislature can prohibit the carrying of concealed weapons but no further. This constitutional guaranty was construed in State v. Speller, 86 N.C. 697, in which it was held that the distinction was between the "right to keep and bear arms" and the "practice of carrying concealed weapons." The former is a sacred right based upon the experience of the ages in order that the people may be accustomed to bear arms and ready to use them for the protection of their liberties or their country when occasion serves. The provision against carrying them concealed was to prevent assassinations or advantages taken by the lawless; i.e., against the abuse of the privilege. . . .

Chapter 317, Public Local Laws 1919, applicable only to Forsyth county, provides: Section 1 prohibits the carrying of concealed weapons; section 2 requires a permit; and section 3 provides:

> "If ay person, except when on his own premises, shall carry any weapon [named in section 1] without a permit, as provided in section 2, . . . he shall be guilty of a misdemeanor, and punished as provided in section 1 . . . for carrying a concealed weapon."

The weapons named in section 1 include pistols, and the question as presented is whether this conflicts with the constitutional provisions above cited.

The other weapons recited in section 1 of this act, besides "pistol," are "bowie knife, dirk, dagger, slung-shot, loaded cane, brass, iron or metallic knuckles or razor or other deadly weapon of like kind." None of these except "pistol" can be construed as coming within the meaning of the word "arms" used in the constitutional guaranty of the right to bear arms. We are of the opinion, however, that "pistol" ex vi termini is properly included within the word "arms," and that the right to bear such arms cannot be infringed. The historical use of pistols as "arms" of offense and defense is beyond controversy.

It is true that the invention of guns with a carrying range of probably 100 miles, submarines, deadly gases, and of airplanes carrying bombs and other modern devices, have much reduced the importance of the pistol in warfare except at close range. But the ordinary private citizen, whose right to carry arms cannot be infringed upon, is not likely to purchase these expensive and most modern devices just named. To him the rifle, the musket, the shotgun, and the pistol are about the only arms which he could be expected to "bear," and his right to do this is that which is guaranteed by the Constitution. To deprive him of bearing any of these arms is to infringe upon the right guaranteed to him by the Constitution.

It would be mockery to say that the Constitution intended to guarantee him the right to practice dropping bombs from a flying machine, to operate a cannon throwing missiles perhaps for a hundred miles or more, or to practice in the use of deadly gases. In Cooley, Con. Lims, the history and the intention of this provision is thus set forth:

"Among the other safeguards to liberty should be mentioned the right of the people to keep and bear arms. A standing army is peculiarly obnoxious in any free government, and the jealousy of such an army has at times been so strongly manifested in England as to lead to the belief that even though recruited from among themselves, it was more dreaded by the people as an instrument of oppression than a tyrannical monarch or any foreign power. So impatient did the English people become of the very army that liberated them from the tyranny of James II that they demanded its reduction even before the liberation became complete; and to this day the British Parliament render a standing army practically impossible by only passing a mutiny act from session to session. The alternative to a standing army is 'a well-regulated militia'; but this cannot exist unless the people are trained to bearing arms. The federal and state Constitutions therefore provide that the right of the people to bear arms shall not be infringed."

We know that in the past this privilege was guaranteed for the sacred purpose of enabling the people to protect themselves against invasions of their liberties. Had not the people of the Colonies been accustomed to bear arms, and acquire effective skill in their use, the scene at Lexington in 1775 would have had a different result, and when "the embattled farmers fired the shot that was heard around the world" it would have been fired in vain. Had not the common people, the rank and file, those who "bore the burden of the battle" during our great Revolution, been accustomed to the use of arms, the victories for liberty would not have been won and American independence would have been an impossibility.

If our pioneers had not been accustomed to the use of arms, the Indians could not have been driven back, and the French, and later the British, would have obtained possession of the valley of the Ohio and the Mississippi. If the frontiersmen had not been good riflemen, particularly the riflemen from Tennessee and Kentucky, the battle of New Orleans would have been lost and the frontiers of this country would have stood still at the Mississippi.

In our own state, in 1870, when Kirk's militia was turned loose and the writ of habeas corpus was suspended, it would have been fatal if our people had been deprived of the right to bear arms and had been unable to oppose an effective front to the usurpation.

The maintenance of the right to bear arms is a most essential one to every free people and should not be whittled down by technical constructions. It should be construed to include all "arms" as were in common use, and borne by the people as such when this provision was adopted. It does not guarantee on the one hand that the people have the futile right to use submarines and cannon of 100 miles range nor airplanes dropping deadly bombs, nor the use of poisonous gases, nor on the other hand does it embrace dirks, daggers, slung-shots and brass knuckles, which may be weapons but are not strictly speaking "arms" borne by the people at large, and which are generally carried concealed. The practical and safe construction is that which must have been in the minds of those who framed our organic law. The intention was to embrace the "arms," an acquaintance with whose use was necessary for their protection against the usurpation of illegal power—such as rifles, muskets, shotguns, swords, and pistols. These are now but little used in war; still they are such weapons that they or their like can still be considered as "arms," which they have a right to "bear."

It is dangerous to minimize these guaranties based upon the wisdom of the ages which have been imbedded in our organic law. It has been well said that when the word "weapon" is used in a statute it denotes firearms, which includes pistols, but does not embrace brass knuckles, slung-shots, or weapons of like description. . . .

It would also be a reasonable regulation and not an infringement of the right to bear arms to prohibit the carrying of deadly weapons when under the influence of intoxicating drink, or to a church, polling place, or public assembly, or in a manner calculated to inspire terror, which was forbidden at common law. These from a practical standpoint are mere regulations and would not infringe upon the object of the constitutional guaranty which is to preserve to the people the right to acquire and retain a practical knowledge of the use of firearms.

It is also but a reasonable regulation, and one which has been adopted in some of the states, to require that a pistol shall not be under a certain length, which if reasonable will prevent the use of pistols of small size which are not borne as arms but which are easily and ordinarily carried concealed. To exclude all pistols, however, is not a regulation, but a prohibition, of arms which come under the designation of "arms" which the people are entitled to bear. This is not an idle or an obsolete guaranty, for there are still localities, not necessary to mention, where great corporations, under the guise of detective agents or private police, terrorize their employees by armed force. If the people are forbidden to carry the only arms within their means, among them pistols, they will be completely at the mercy of these great plutocratic organizations. Should there be a mob, is it possible that law-abiding ciizens could not assemble with their pistols carried openly and protect their persons and their property from unlawful violence without going before an official and obtaining license and giving bond?

The usual method when a country is overborne by force is to "disarm" the people. It is to prevent the above and similar exercises of arbitrary power that the people, in creating this government "of the people, by the people and for the people," reserved to themselves the right to "bear arms," that, accustomed to their use, they might be ready to meet illegal force with legal force by adequate and just defense of their persons, their property, and their liberties, whenever necessary. We should be slow indeed to construe such guaranty into a mere academic expression which has become obsolete.

We can have no knowledge of the future except by the past, or, as Patrick Henry said, "The only light by which our feet are guided is the lamp of experience." The constitutional provision which forbids any prohibition upon the people to bear arms and use them effectively by being accustomed to their use should be strictly and stoutly maintained, for we know not when the occasion may again require the assertion of that doctrine which was once familiar throughout this country that "resistance to tyranny is obedience to God," or for the defense of person and property against mobs and violence.

The statute in this case, Public Local Laws 1919, c. 317, is especially objectionable in that it requires (section 2) that in order to carry a pistol off his own premises, even openly, and for a lawful purpose, the citizen must make application to the municipal court, if a resident of a town; or to the superior court, if not residing in town, describing the weapon and giving the time and purpose for which it may be carried off his premises and must pay to the clerk of the court the sum of $5 for each permit and must file a bond in the penalty of $500 that he will not carry the weapon except as so authorized. In the case of a riot or mob violence, or other emergency requiring the defense of public order, this would place law-abiding citizens entirely at the mercy of the lawless element. As a regulation even this is void because an unreasonable regulation, and, besides, it would be void because for all practical purposes it is prohibition of the constitutional right to bear arms. There would be no time or opportunity to get such permit and to give such bonds on an emergency.

On this occasion, the defendant threatened with violence was forced to abandon his property. He went to his place of business where he had the right to keep his pistol, "being on his own premises," and returned with it unconcealed. He was acting in self-defense of his person and in defense of his property. The court below most properly adjudged upon the special verdict that he was not guilty.

No error.

## People v. Zerillo
## 219 Mich. 635, 189 N.W. 927 (1922)

Defendant, an unnaturalized foreign-born resident, was convicted under a complaint charging him with possessing a revolver without a permit. . . .

The complaint was laid under the game law, but did not charge the defendant with hunting for or capturing or killing any wild bird or animal, or intending to do so. Does the game law make it unlawful for an unnaturalized foreign-born resident of the state to possess a revolver? . . .

Defendant insists that the act, so far as it deprives him of the right to possess a revolver, for a legitimate purpose, is in conflict with the provisions of the Constitution of the state, and therefore void. The Constitution of this state . . . provides: "Every person has a right to bear arms for the defense of himself and the state." . . .

Firearms serve the people of this country a useful purpose wholly aside from hunting, and under a constitution like ours, granting to aliens who are bona fide residents of the state the same rights in respect to the possession, enjoyment, and inheritance of property as native-born citizens, and to *every person* the right to bear arms for the defense of himself and the state, while the Legislature has power in the most comprehensive manner to regulate the carrying and use of firearms, that body has no power to constitute it a crime for a person, alien or citizen, to possess a revolver for the legitimate defense of himself and his property. The provision in the Constitution granting the right to all persons to bear arms is a limitation upon the power of the Legislature to enact any law to the contrary.

The exercise of a right guaranteed by the Constitution cannot be made subject to the will of the sheriff. The part of the act under which the prosecution was planted is not one of regulation, but is one of prohibition and confiscation. . . .

Game being property of the state the Legislature may enact laws for its protection, but under the guise of protection of game may not disarm any class, falling within the constitutional guaranty, of the right to bear arms in defense of themselves. The guaranty of the right to every person to bear arms in defense of himself means the right to possess arms for legitimate use in defense of himself, and necessarily includes the right to defend therewith, by lawful means, his property. . . .

Must an alien owner of a farm sit with folded arms and watch henhawks steal his chickens? No, the act permits him to kill noxious birds and animals, when necessary, in defense of his person or property. But what is he going to use for that purpose? Until the occasion arises, if this statute is given the construction contended for by the people, it is a crime for him to possess a firearm, and he therefore cannot be prepared to exercise the leave granted without committing a crime. Woodchucks could burrow in his yard and meadows with impunity, owls rob his henroost, rats run about his feet at chore time, and in some sections of the state wolves could sit on his very doorstep and howl defiance. Even the predatory skunk, in the open season, would be more offensively armed than the unnaturalized farmer faring forth to drive it away. Must such a farmer whistle off the dog discovered in the act of killing his sheep? Another statute gives him the right to kill such a dog discovered in the act. Must he request the burglar to come unarmed because he has been unarmed by the law? This act, if construed as contended for by the people, is so sharp-shod as to calk itself. The right to kill noxious birds and animals in defense of person or property would be but a joke if the means of exercising the right are take away by the general prohibition against possessing any firearms. . . .

It will be noticed that our Constitution is inclusive of the right of *every person* to bear arms for the defense of himself and the state, and not merely citizens, as in the state of Pennsylvania.

The part of the act making it a crime for an unnaturalized foreign-born resident to possess a revolver, unless so permitted by the sheriff, contravenes the guaranty of such right in the Constitution of the state, and is void. The statute must be construed in accord with the provisions of our Constitution, and it may stand as an act prohibiting the use of firearms by unnaturalized foreign-born residents in hunting or capturing or killing any wild bird or animals, either game or otherwise, of any description, excepting in defense of person or property, but so far as it makes it a crime for unnaturalized residents to possess a revolver for the legitimate defense of their persons and property it is void.

Under the complaint and warrant and the evidence the defendant should have been adjudged not guilty. The conviction is set aside, and defendant is discharged.

## City of Las Vegas v. Moberg
## 82 N.M. 626 (1971)

The defendant, Moberg, was convicted by the municipal court of the City of Las Vegas of violating the city ordinance No. 3-3, which reads as follows: "DEADLY WEAPONS. It shall be unlawful for any person to carry deadly weaons, concealed or otherwise, on or about their persons, within the corporate limits of the City of East Las Vegas. Deadly weapons shall consist of all kind of guns, pistols, knives with blades longer than two and half inches, slingshots, sandbags, metallic knuckles, concealed rocks, and all other weapons, by whatever name known, with which dangerous wounds can be inflicted."

The complaint charged the defendant with the violation of the ordinance by number and specifically by "carrying a concealed and deadly weapon." . . .

The evidence presented at the trial in the district court established, without dispute, that defendant went to the booking room of the city police department of the city of Las Vegas to report the theft of certain items from his automobile. At the time, defendant was carrying a pistol in a holster. The pistol was in plain view at all times. It appears that both parties at the trial in the district court treated the complaint as charging simply the carrying of a deadly weapon. No contention is made that the evidence supported the carrying of a concealed weapon. . . .

Defendant has appealed and challenges the constitutionality of the ordinance as it is applied to carrying arms openly and in plain view. He asserts that in this respect the ordinance is repugnant to Article II, Section 6 of the Constitution of the State of New Mexico. This section provides:

> "The people have the right to bear arms for their security and defense, but nothing herein shall be held to permit the carrying of concealed weapons."

It is a generally accepted principle that a municipal ordinance which denies rights protected by constitutional guaranty is void to the extent, at least, that it purports to deny such rights. . . .

Ordinances prohibiting the carrying of concealed weapons have generally been held to be a proper exercise of police power. . . .

Such ordinances do not deprive citizens of the right to bear arms; their effect is only to regulate the right. As applied to arms, other than those concealed, the ordinance under consideration purports to completely prohibit the "right to bear arms."

It is our opinion that an ordinance may not deny the people the constitutionally guaranteed right to bear arms, and to that extent the ordinance under consideration is void. . . .

**State v. Kessler**
**Or., 614 P.2d 94 (1980)**

The defendant in this case was convicted of "possession of a slugging weapon." . . . We allowed review to consider his claim that the legislative prohibition of the possession of a "billy" . . . violates Article I, section 27, of the Oregon Constitution. That provision states: "The people shall have the right to bear arms for the defence [sic] of themselves, and the State, but the Military shall be kept in strict subordination to the civil power." . . .

The scope of Article I, section 27, has not previously been analyzed by Oregon courts. The decisions construing the second amendment to the United States Constitution are not particularly helpful because the wording of the second amendment differs substantially from our state provision. The second amendment has not yet been held to apply to state limitations on the bearing of arms. The wording of Oregon's right to bear arms provision also differs from many other state constitutional provisions.

Despite the many variations in wording, the states' constitutional provisions guaranteeing the right to bear arms share a common historical background. . . . Oregon's right to bear arms provision therefore can be traced to state provisions drafted in the revolutionary and post-revolutionary war era.

The constitutions adopted by the original colonies generally included a bill or declaration of rights. Many of the declarations of rights were patterned largely upon the English Bill of Rights of 1689. . . . The state constitutions drafted in the revolutionary war era therefore included provisions guaranteeing the right to bear arms and prohibiting standing armies in times of peace. The relevant provisions of the English Bill of Rights of 1689 provided a useful model for the colonial drafters.

. . . Oregon's constitutional right to bear arms provision, . . . was taken verbatim from the Indiana constitutional provision drafted in

1816. The phrase "for defense of themselves and the state" in Indiana's provision was most likely taken from the Kentucky provision in its 1799 constitution, or the Ohio provision in its 1802 constitution. The phrase "for defense of themselves and the state" appears in the present day constitutions of Oregon, Indiana, and six other states. The language is subject to varying interpretations. It has been suggested that the language includes three separate justifications for a state constitutional right to bear arms: (a) The preference for a militia over a standing army; (b) the deterrence of governmental oppression; and (c) the right of personal defense.

The language "the right to bear arms . . . for defense of . . . the state" more likely refers to the historical preference for a citizen militia rather than a standing army as outlined above. . . . Self-defense has been recognized as a privilege in both civil and criminal law since about 1400 in England and at all times in the United States. Although the right to bear arms for self protection does not appear to have been an important development in England, the justification for a right to bear arms in defense of person and home probably reflects the exigencies of the rural American experience. . . .

The term "arms" is also subject to several interpretations. In the colonial and revolutionary war era, weapons used by militiamen and weapons used in defense of person and home were one and the same. A colonist usually had only one gun which was used for hunting, protection, and militia duty, plus a hatchet, sword, and knife. When the revolutionary war began, the colonists came equipped with their hunting muskets or rifles, hatchets, swords, and knives. The colonists suffered a severe shortage of firearms in the early years of the war, so many soldiers had to rely primarily on swords, hatchets, knives, and pikes (long staffs with a spear head).

Therefore, the term "arms" as used by the drafters of the constitutions probably was intended to include those weapons used by settlers for both personal and military defense. The term "arms" was not limited to firearms, but included several hand-carried weapons commonly used for defense. The term "arms" would not have included cannon or other heavy ordnance not kept by militiamen or private citizens. . . .

These advanced weapons of modern warfare have never been intended for personal possession and protection. When the constitutional drafters referred to an individual's "right to bear arms," the arms used by the militia and for personal protection were basically the same weapons. Modern weapons used exclusively by the military are not "arms" which are commonly possessed by individuals for defense, therefore, the term "arms" in the constitution does not include such weapons.

If the text and purpose of the constitutional guarantee relied exclusively on the preference for a militia "for defense of the State," then the term "arms" most likely would include only the modern day equivalents of the weapons used by colonial militiamen. The Oregon provision, however, guarantees a right to bear arms "for defense of *themselves*, and the State." The term "arms" in our constitution therefore would include weapons commonly used for either purpose, even if a particular weapon is unlikely to be used as a militia weapon. . . .The defendant was involved in an off and on verbal argument with his apartment manager. . . . The dispute escalated into name calling, colorful words, and object throwing. At one point the defendant kicked the elevator door in the apartment building. The police were called and arrested the defendant. . . . The officers found two "billy clubs" in the defendant's apartment.

The defendant was charged with disorderly conduct, . . . and possession of a slugging weapon, . . . The matter went to trial without a jury. The defendant at trial demurred to and moved to dismiss the second charge on the grounds that it failed to state a crime. The motion was denied and the defendant was found guilty as charged on both counts. . . .

The defendant appealed to the Court of Appeals, contending first that his acts did not amount to the crime of disorderly conduct, and second that the statute prohibiting possession of billy clubs, . . . violates Article I, section 27, of the Oregon Constitution. . . .

The defendant contends that his conviction for possession of a billy club violates his right to possess arms in his home for personal defense. Pursuant to our previous discussion regarding the purpose and scope of the right to bear arms provision, we hold that Article I, section 27, of the Oregon Constitution includes a right to possess certain arms for defense of person and property. The remaining question is whether the defendant's possession of a billy club in this case is protected. . . .

The club is considered the first personal weapon fashioned by humans. . . . The club is still used today as a personal weapon, commonly carried by the police. ORS 166.510 prohibits possession of a "billy;" however, ORS 166.520 states that peace officers are not prohibited from carrying or possessing a weapon commonly known as a "blackjack" or "billy."

The statute in this case, . . . prohibits the mere possession of a club. The defendant concedes that the legislature could prohibit carrying a club in a public place in a concealed manner, but the defendant maintains that the legislature cannot prohibit all persons from possessing a club in the home. The defendant argued that a person may prefer to keep in his home a billy club rather than a firearm to defend against intruders.

Our historical analysis of Article I, section 27, indicates that the drafters intended "arms" to include the hand-carried weapons commonly used by individuals for personal defense. The club is an effective hand-carried weapon which cannot logically be excluded from this term. We hold that the defendant's possession of a billy club in his home is protected by Article I, section 27, of the Oregon Constitution.

## Schubert v. DeBard
## 398 N.E. 2d 1339 (1980)

Appellant, Joseph L. Schubert, applied . . . for a license to carry a handgun. . . . A hearing was held and . . . Schubert [was] . . . denied the permit. The trial court sustained . . . and this appeal follows.

The evidence disclosed that . . . appellant applied for a permit to carry a handgun for self-protection. He had previously held such permits. . . . He had carried a handgun when engaged in part-time employment in the nature of security work. He also had held a special police commission from the City of Fort Wayne and a St. Joseph's County Deputy Sheriff's commission. Both commissions had been revoked prior to his application for the license.

Schubert offered as evidence of the need to protect himself two items he had received in the mail in 1975. One was a copy of a picture of a pig with appellant's name written above it. The other was a letter, signed "The Assassinater's," demanding $1250 or "Pig, you are dead." No method or place of payment was specified. Appellant stated he suspected his brother might have sent the letters. However, he did not discuss the matter with his brother nor report it to the police. He also testified that while photographing the house where his mother lived, in connection with "secret" work for the U.S. Department of the Treasury, his brother ordered him out of the area and fired a rifle at the van in which he was riding. He did notify the prosecutor's office about the shooting incident, but no charges were brought. He claims that as a result of these incidents he fears for his life and needs to carry a gun to protect himself.

A report summarizing a background investigation made of appellant when he applied for a private detective's license in 1971 was admitted without objection. The report concluded that appellant was a "chronic liar" suffering from a "gigantic police complex." . . . Several of those interviewed during the course of the investigation, including former employers and the sheriff who both created and revoked his deputy sheriff's commission, felt appellant had "mental problems."

The licensing statute, . . . provides . . . "(a) A person desiring a license to carry a handgun shall apply to the chief of police or corresponding police officer of the municipality in which he resides. If that municipality has no such officer, or if the applicant does not reside in a municipality, he shall apply to the sheriff of the county in which he resides, . . . The officer to whom the application is made shall conduct an investigation into the applicant's official records and verify thereby the applicant's character and reputation, and shall in addition verify for accuracy the information contained in the application, and shall forward this information together with his recommendation for approval or disapproval . . . to the superintendent who may make whatever further investigation he deems necessary. In addition, whenever disapproval is recommended, the officer to whom the application is made shall provide the superintendent and the applicant with his complete and specific reasons, in writing, for the recommendation or disapproval. *If it appears to the superintendent that the applicant has a proper reason for carrying a handgun and is of good character and reputation and a proper person to be so licensed,* he shall issue to the applicant either a qualified or an unlimited license to carry any handgun or handguns lawfully possessed by the applicant. . . .

Establishing such a licensing procedure for handguns is not violative of the right to bear arms as guaranteed by the Second Amendment or Art. 1, Sec. 32 of the Indiana Constitution.

Schubert contends, however, that the Indiana Constitution affords him the right to bear arms for his own defense. Thus, he urges that where self-defense is properly asserted as the reason for desiring a firearms license, and the applicant is otherwise qualified, the license cannot be withheld upon an administrative official's subjective determination of whether the applicant needs defending.

Our Art. 1, Sec. 32, is worded differently than the Second Amendment. It states simply and plainly, "The people shall have a right to bear arms, for the defense of themselves and the State."

It is well settled that we are to presume that constitutional language was carefully chosen to express the framer's intention. . . . The words used are to be taken in their general and ordinary sense. . . . We think it clear that our constitution provides our citizenry the right to bear arms for their self-defense. Furthermore, . . . our Supreme Court held that if it is determined . . . that the applicant has met the conditions of the statute, the superintendent has no discretion to withhold the license. . . .

In Schubert's case it is clear from the record that the superintendent decided the application on the basis that the statutory reference to "a proper reason" vested in him the power and duty to subjectively evaluate an assignment of "self-defense" as a reason for desiring a license and the ability to grant or deny the license upon the basis of whether the applicant "needed" to defend himself.

Such an approach contravenes the essential nature of the constitutional guarantee. It would supplant a right with a mere administrative privilege which might be withheld simply on the basis that such matters as the use of firearms are better left to the organized military and police forces even where defense of the individual citizen is involved.

We therefore hold that Schubert's assigned reason which stood unrefuted was constitutionally a "proper reason."

## Shettle v. Shearer
## Ind. App., 425 N.E. 2d 739 (1981)

John T. Shettle, Superintendent of the Indiana State Police Department appeals the trial court's order directing him to issue an unlimited handgun license to James F. Shearer. . . .

The only question in issue at the hearing was whether Shearer had a proper reason for carrying a handgun. Shearer's asserted reason for carrying a handgun was a medical condition in which any assault upon his person could cause anything ranging from a brief period of incapacitation to death. In support of his testimony, Shearer presented a letter from his physician.

In *Schubert v. DeBard* (1980) . . . the question of what is a proper reason for carrying a handgun was decided by this Court. *Schubert* held that under Art. 1, § 32 of the Indiana Constitution self-defense ws a proper reason. . . . Furthermore, *Schubert* determined that absent some evidence to refute self-defense as a reason, the superintendent could not deny an applicant a license on the basis of the superintendent's subjective evaluation of the asserted reason.

Shettle argues that Shearer did not properly assert self-defense as his reason for requesting a handgun license. At the hearing Shearer stated that due to phlebitis in his left leg, any assault upon him could result in his death. Additionally, when asked if there were any reasons other than medical, Shearer answered, "It is my feeling that such licensing would allow me to protect myself." It is clear that self-defense was the motive for the application and that the normal need for self-defense was heightened by Shearer's medical problems.

Shearer testified that he had not been a victim of a violent crime, nor had he been threatened. Additionally, Shearer said that his employment does not require him to be in contact with "undesirable people." These factors, however, are not sufficient to justify the denial of Shearer's application. . . . Shearer's unrefuted testimony regarding his medical problems and his desire for self-defense are proper reasons for acquiring a handgun license. Absent other justifications for denial, the application should have been granted by Shettle.

**Michael Kalodimos et al., Appellants,**
**v. The Village of Morton Grove, Appellee**
**Filed**
**October 19, 1984**
**Clerk Supreme Court**
**Illinois**

***Chief Justice Ryan, dissenting:***

I join in the very convincing dissent of my colleague, Justice Moran. In addition, I wish to address the question of the use of police power by the village of Morton Grove to ban the ownership of handguns.

The majority opinion concedes that section 22 of article I of our Illinois Constitution broadened the scope of the right to arms from the limited collective right of the Federal Constitution to an individual right covering a wider variety of arms and that the Illinois Constitution bestows upon individual citizens the right to possess weapons suitable for self-defense and recreation. This constitutionally granted right is subject only to regulation through the use of the police power.

This court, in *Nahser v. City of Chicago* . . . addressed what constitutes a legitimate use of the police power by stating:

> "Under what circumstances or conditions the police power of the State may be exercised was defined . . . as follows: 'In order to sustain legislative interference with the business of the citizen by virtue of the police power it is necessary that the act should have some reasonable relation to the subjects included in such power. If it is claimed that the statute or ordinance is referable to the police power, the court must be able to see that it tends in some degree towards the prevention of offenses or the preservation of the public health, morals, safety or welfare. It must be apparent that some such end is the one actually intended and that there is some connection between the provisions of the law and such purpose. If it is manifest that the statute or ordinance has no such object, but, under the guise of a police regulation, is an invasion of the property rights of the individual, it is the duty of the court to declare it void.'"

The majority uses equal protection standards relating to statutory classification to support its statement that police regulations will be upheld if any state of facts may be reasonably conceived to justify them, . .

I am not concerned with an equal protection question. We are here dealing with a due process question: the taking away of a constitutionally given right—the right to arms—through the exercise of the police power. The language of this court . . . quoted above specifies under what circumstances the police power may be exercised. . . .

This court's inquiry in reviewing the legislative exercise of the police power should be whether the legislation represents a rational means to accomplish a proper purpose. . . . Thus, the inquiry must be: First, what purpose does the legislative body seek to accomplish by depriving the residents of Morton Grove of the constitutionally given right to arms? Second, is it a *proper* purpose; that is, one that may be constitutionally achieved by the use of the police power? Lastly, does the ordinance use a rational means of accomplishing the purpose? As noted . . . in order for such a regulation to be lawfully imposed on a constitutional right of an individual, the act passed under the guise of a measure to protect the public health, safety and welfare must have a definite relation to the ends sought to be attained.

As the majority opinion notes, the ordinance, in its preamble, cites certain interests of the village, such as reducing "the potentiality of firearm related deaths and injuries" caused by "the easy and convenient availability of certain types of firearms and weapons," and finds that "handguns play a major role in the commission of homicide, aggravated assault, and armed robbery, and accidental injury and death."

Although the recited purposes of the ordinance would appear to be laudable and supportive of the exercise of the police power to achieve these ends, the minutes of the meeting of the board of trustees of the village at which the ordinance was adopted do not reflect any discussion of these purposes, or that the ordinance was adopted to achieve them. There was no discussion as to how many, if any, deaths, injuries or crimes involving handguns had been committed in Morton Grove. In this litigation, at the trial level, an affidavit of the chief of police was presented that showed that over a 24-year period there had been a total of 155 incidents of handgun misuse in the village, or an average of about six incidents a year. The statistics presented reveal that the incidents had declined since the late 1970s. The statistics compiled by the chief of police did not disclose the nature of the handgun misuse, or whether the misuse involved a crime, death or injury. Also, the statistics did not disclose if the misuses were committed by residents of Morton Grove. Meager as these statistics are, they reveal that the misuse of handguns is a very minimal problem in Morton Grove. . . .

The purposes of the ordinance cited in its preamble were therefore pure and simple litany, inserted in the ordinance for window dressing and to help withstand constitutional challenge. Since no discussion was had at the meeting of the village board concerning handgun misuse in the village, and since these statistics concerning such misuse were not compiled until after the ordinance was adopted and were not presented to the village board, it is apparent that some other purpose motivated the adoption of the ordinance. This purpose is disclosed by the minutes of the meeting at which the ordinance was adopted. . . .

The majority opinion acknowledges that these statements reflect the possibility that the ordinance was passed for the sole purpose of publicizing a political viewpoint. I am in accord with that conclusion. I am shocked, however, that the majority opinion finds no significance in this possibility. If the police power can be exercised for the sole purpose of publicizing a political viewpoint, then I feel that our constitutionally guaranteed rights are in serious jeopardy.

As stated in the language quoted above from *Nahser*, it must be apparent that the legislation tends in some degree toward the prevention of offenses, or the preservation of public health, morals, safety or welfare; that such an end is the one *actually intended*; and that there is some connection between the ordinance and such purpose. If it is manifest that the legislation *has no such object*, but under the guise of a police regulation is an invasion ofthe property rights of the individual, it is the duty of the court to declare it void. . . .

. . . If we permit the constitutionally given right to arms to be nullified by simply inserting a few "magic words" in an ordinance which gives the ordinance an appearance of being a valid exercise of the police power, when it is in fact only the assertion of a political philosophy and a publicizing of that viewpoint, then we have in effect eliminated this right that has been granted by the Constitution. . . .

Thus, it is not sufficient when considering constitutional rights that there be a bare assertion or recital of a proper purpose for the exercise of the police power. As held in *City of Chicago v. Wilson*, there must be some valid existing reason for the intrusion. In summary, it is my position that although the ordinance recites an accepted purpose for the exercise of the police power, we must not accept such a recitation without question. In looking behind the ordinance under consideration, the village has not shown a need or justification for the infringement on the constitutional right to arms. The sole purpose behind the ordinance was to assert and publicize a particular political belief, "to send a message to other legislative bodies across the country." Such a purpose is not a sufficient reason for infringing on a constitutional right by the exercise of the police power. I therefore dissent.

**Michael Kalodimos et al., Appellants,**
**v. The Village of Morton Grove, Appellee**
**Filed**
**October 19, 1984**
**Clerk Supreme Court**
**Illinois**

***Justice Moran, also dissenting:***

For more than a decade, the bill of rights to the Illinois Constitution has included a provision on the right to keep and bear arms. . . . I agree with the majority opinion that the language of section 22 of article I indicates that the right to keep and bear arms is a qualified, not an absolute, right. Nevertheless, I disagree with the conclusion that . . . municipalities may enact flat bans on the possession of ordinary handguns. Under the opinion announced today, so long as municipalities allow residents to possess "some form of weapon suitable for self-defense or recreation" municipalities may ban all other weapons. . . . The majority's strained reading of section 22 defies logic and runs counter to the history surrounding the enactment of the right-to-bear-arms guarantee.

To the contrary, section 22 prohibits a flat ban on those types of firearms that "law-abiding citizens commonly employ for purposes of recreation or the protection of person and property," including ordinary handguns and long guns. . . .

Today's opinion places considerable reliance on the comments of certain delegates to the constitutional convention to justify the conclusion that section 22 does not prohibit municipalities from enacting a flat ban on the possession of ordinary handguns. Although this court on occasion has consulted such debates when the meaning of the constitutional provision was in doubt, it has done so only when it appeared that the delegates reached a consensus as to the meaning of the provision. . . .

After considering the debates on section 22, I am of the opinion that, at most, the debates reflect a lack of consensus as to the meaning of section 22. The debates illustrate that the issue of whether Illinois' citizens should have the right to bear arms was a highly controversial and emotional issue. . . .

The lack of consensus as to the meaning of section 22 was not lost on a number of delegates. Delegate William Fay, during the course of the debates, noted that "the fact that we have just seen the last two or three speakers here unite in support of this measure for different reasons indicates how this proposal will mean different things to different people." . . . Delegate Jeffrey Ladd commented that it "seems we got people together on this bill for different reasons, and maybe we ought to know which side is really going to prevail." Delegate Jeanette Mullen stated, "Seldom have I heard such contradictory argument as has been presented today by the supporters of the majority [committee] report." . . . I feel the court's reliance, in this instance, on the constitutional debates is misplaced.

On the other hand, the report of the convention's Committee on the Bill of Rights left the understanding that municipalities would be prohibited from enacting total bans on the possession of ordinary handguns. . . . The committee report at the time that the 1970 Constitution was ratified stated:

> "By referring to 'the individual citizen' and to the right to 'keep' as well as to 'bear' arms, the proposed new provision guarantees an individual right rather than a collective right and seeks to assure that the 'arms' involved are not limited by the armaments or needs of the state militia or other military body. The substance of the right is that a citizen has the right to possess and make reasonable use of arms that law-abiding persons commonly employ for purposes of recreation or the protection of person and property." . . .

The committee report also stated:

> "Laws that attempted to ban all possession or use of such arms [handguns], or laws that subjected possession or use of such arms to regulation or taxes so onerous that all possession or use was effectively banned, would be invalid." . . .

The above-quoted language, I submit, gave the understanding that section 22 prohibits municipalities from enacting total bans on the possession of handguns. This conclusion is further bolstered by the cases refered to in the committee report in support of the proposition that a ban on "all possession or use of such arms" would be unconstitutional under section 22. All of these cases involved attempts to ban, directly or indirectly, the possession of handguns. In each of these cases cited by the committee report, the courts held that the governmental body involved exceeded the police powers, and, thus, that the law violated their respective State constitutional provisions on the right to keep and bear arms. . . . Nowhere did the committee report indicate that a total ban on handguns would be permissible. The list of permissible regulations contained in the committee reports, along with appropriate case citations, included the prohibition of "certain deadly weapons *not* commonly and peacefully used by individuals." . . . The committee report also stated that certain individuals, such as minors, incompetents and convicted felons, could be prohibited from possessing firearms. . . . Finally, the report indicated that gun licensing and permit laws, as well as taxes on firearms, would continue to be valid under section 22. . . .

Moreover, the Committee on the Bill of Rights and convention delegates specifically declined to adopt proposals which would have allowed the prohibition of ordinary handguns. . . . If committee members or convention delegates had desired to give municipalities such wide-ranging power, they would not have rejected every proposal authorizing the right to prohibit handguns.

In my opinion, municipalities cannot, consistent with section 22, enact flat bans on the possession of handguns or any other firearm which is commonly used by law-abiding citizens for recreation or protection of person or property. I would therefore hold that Morton Grove's ordinance banning the possession of handguns is unconstitutional.

In addition, I strongly disagree with the majority's conclusion that Morton Grove has not exceeded its home rule powers in enacting the handgun ban. . . .

The problems associated with the use of handguns and other firearms are similarly a subject for State, not local, regulation. Like municipal noise ordinances, municipal handgun ordinances will be conflicting and counterproductive. Municipalities may, consistent with today's opinion, ban the possession of any weapon so long as residents are allowed to possess one type of weapon. Thus, Morton Grove may ban handguns and a neighboring municipality may ban rifles, shotguns or both. Another neighboring community may decide to require persons to own and possess guns. Indeed, two Illinois municipalities have enacted ordinances purporting to require handgun ownership. . . . As plaintiffs correctly point out, today's opinion will create a "crazy quilt of conflicting and unenforceable home rule ordinances." . . .

Although the ordinance does not purport to regulate conduct outside Morton Grove, the ordinance will affect nonresidents as well as influence conduct outside the village boundaries. Nonresidents are required by the ordinance to make their handguns "permanently inoperable" before transporting their guns through Morton Grove (Morton Grove, Ill., Ordinance 81 – 11 (June 8, 1981). The ordinance has the practical effect of forcing nonresidents to avoid Morton Grove if they wish to carry their firearms to a neighboring community where handguns are permitted. Secondly, by banning the possession of handguns within its boundaries, Morton Grove has presumably increased the number of handguns that are present in adjacent communities, since the ordinance does not prohibit its residents from storing, selling, or using their handguns outside the village.

Moreover, today's decisions fails to adequately consider the potential problems that could result from inconsistent local gun laws. Inconsistent local gun laws could make it difficult for gun owners to lawfully use their firearms, since gun owners must often travel from one community to another in order to use their firearms lawfully. Those gun owners wishing to use their firearms for hunting, target shooting or other lawful recreational activity could be subject to a wide range of criminal penalities merely because they unknowingly violated one or more local gun-control laws. Furthermore, under the majority's reasoning, there is nothing to prohibit municipalities from enacting gun-control laws that are more permissive than State gun-control laws. If so, these gun-control ordinances would undoubtedly have an effect on nearby communities' law-enforcement efforts.

The issue of whether an Illinois citizen may or may not possess a handgun has never, until today, been thought to be a matter for local governments. The Morton Grove ordinance is the first of its kind. Instead, handguns and other firearms have been subject to extensive regulation by our State government. . . . The deadly-weapons statute was adopted with the purpose of creating "one comprehensive, integrated statute, dealing in an orderly manner with deadly weapons," so that State gun-control laws are "consistent with one another." . . .

In the present case, the State regulation of firearm possession has been long standing, comprehensive and, for the most part, exclusive. Until now, home rule municipalities have not attempted to enact ordinances of the type adopted by Morton Grove. Until now, the issue of whether or not a person may possess a firearm has been resolved by looking to a State regulatory scheme intended by the General Assembly to deal with firearms in an orderly and consistent manner. The Morton Grove ordinance directly conflicts with the express policy of the deadly-weapons statute. Under the Morton Grove ordinance, persons are prohibited from possessing handguns in their home, on their land, or in their "fixed place of business" despite the express authorization for such uses by the General Assembly. The Morton Grove ordinance, in effect, is an attempt by a municipality to preempt clearly defined State policy in an area where the State, not municipalities, has authority to act. . . .

Thus, because the possession of firearms has traditionally been regulated by State law, and because local firearms laws like the one adopted by Morton Grove would necessarily affect persons beyond municipal boundaries, confuse law-abiding citizens and are counterproductive, I am of the opinion that this subject is of State and not local concern. I would therefore hold that Morton Grove has exceeded its home rule authority under article VII, section 6(a), of our constitution in enacting this ordinance.

For the above-stated reason, I must respectfully dissent.

## C. OPINIONS OF THE UNITED STATES SUPREME COURT

### United States v. Cruikshank
### 92 U.S. 542 (1876)

This was an indictment for conspiracy under the sixth section of the act of May 30, 1870, known as the Enforcement Act (16 Stat. 140), and consisted of thirty-two counts.

The *first* count was for banding together, with intent "unlawfully and feloniously to injure, oppress, threaten, and intimidate" two citizens of the United States, "of African descent and persons of color," "with the unlawful and felonious intent thereby" them "to hinder and prevent in their respective free exercise and enjoyment of their lawful right and privilege to peaceably assemble together with each other and with other citizens of the said United States for a peaceable and lawful purpose."

The *second* avers an intent to hinder and prevent the exercise by the same persons of the "right to keep and bear arms for a lawful purpose."

The *third* avers an intent to deprive the same persons "of their respective several lives and liberty of person, without due process of law."

The *fourth* avers an intent to deprive the same persons of the "free" exercise and enjoyment of the right and privilege to the full and equal benefit of all laws and proceedings for the security of persons and property" enjoyed by white citizens.

The *fifth* avers an intent to hinder and prevent the same persons "in the exercise and enjoyment of the rights, privileges, immunities, and protection granted and secured to them respectively as citizens of the said United States, and as citizens of the said State of Louisiana, by reason of and for and on account of the race and color" of the said persons.

The *sixth* avers an intent to hinder and prevent the same persons in "the free exercise and enjoyment of the several and respective right and privilege to vote at any election to be thereafter by law had and held by the people in and of the said State of Louisiana."

The *seventh* avers an intent "to put in great fear of bodily harm, injure, and oppress" the same persons, "because and for the reason" that, having the right to vote, they had voted.

The *eighth* avers an intent "to prevent and hinder" the same persons "in their several and respective free exercise and enjoyment of every, each, all, and singular the several rights and privileges granted and secured" to them "by the constitution and laws of the United States."

The next eight counts are a repetition of the first eight, except that, instead of the words "band together," the words "combine, conspire, and confederate together" are used. . . .

The Circuit Court for the District of Louisiana . . . presents for our consideration an indictment . . . based upon sect. 6 of the Enforcement Act of May 31, 1870. That section is as follows:

> "That if two or more persons shall band or conspire together, or go in disguise upon the public highway, or upon the premises of another, with intent to violate any provision of this act, or to injure, oppress, threaten, or intimidate any citizen, with intent to prevent or hinder his free exercise and enjoyment of any right or privilege granted or secured to him by the constitution or laws of the United States, or because of his having exercised the same, such persons shall be held guilty of felony, and, on conviction thereof, shall be fined or imprisoned, or both, at the discretion of the court, — the fine not to exceed $5,000, and the imprisonment not to exceed ten years; and shall, moreover, be thereafter ineligible to, and disabled from holding, any office or place of honor, profit, or trust created by the constitution or laws of the United States."

The question certified arose upon a motion in arrest of judgment after a verdict of guilty generally upon the whole sixteen counts, and is stated to be, whether "the said sixteen counts of said indictment are severally good and sufficient in law, and contain charges of criminal matter indictable under the laws of the United States."

The general charge in the first eight counts is that of "banding," and in the second eight, that of "conspiring" together to injure, oppress, threaten, and intimidate Levi Nelson and Alexander Tillman, citizens of the United States, of African descent and persons of color, with the intent thereby to hinder and prevent them in their free exercise and enjoyment of rights and privileges "granted and secured" to them "in common with all other good citizens of the United States by the constitution and laws of the United States."

The offenses provided for by the statute in question do not consist in the mere "banding" or "conspiring" of two or more persons together, but in their banding or conspiring with the intent, or for any of the purposes, specified. To bring this case under the operation of the statute, therefore, it must appear that the right, the enjoyment of which the conspirators intended to hinder or prevent, was one granted or secured by the constitution or laws of the United States. If it does not so appear, the criminal matter charged has not been made indictable by any act of Congress.

We have in our political system a government of the United States and a government of each of the several states. Each one of these governments is distinct from the others, and each has citizens of its own who owe it allegiance, and whose rights, within its jurisdiction, it must protect. The same person may be at the same time a citizen of the United States and a citizen of a State, but his rights of citizenship under one of these governments will be different from those he has under the others. . . .

Experience made the fact known to the people of the United States that they required a national government for national purposes. The separate governments of the separate States, bound together by the articles of confederation alone, were not sufficient for the promotion of the general welfare of the people in respect to foreign nations, or for their complete protection as citizens of the confederated States. For this reason, the people of the United States, "in order to form a more perfect union, establish justice, insure domestic tranquillity, provide for the common defence, promote the general welfare, and secure the blessings of liberty" to themselves and their posterity (Const. Preamble), ordained and established the government of the United States, and defined its powers by a constitution, which they adopted as its fundamental law, and made its rule of action.

The government thus established and defined is to some extent a government of the States in their political capacity. It is also, for certain purposes, a government of the people. Its powers are limited in number, but not in degree. Within the scope of its powers, as enumerated and defined, it is supreme and above the States; but beyond, it has no existence. It was erected for special purposes, and endowed with all the powers necessary for its own preservation and the accomplishment of the ends its people had in view. It can neither grant nor secure to its citizens any right or privilege not expressly or by implication placed under its jurisdiction.

The people of the United States resident within any State are subject to two governments: one State, and the other National; but there need be no conflict between the two. The powers which one possesses, the other does not. They are established for different purposes, and have separate jurisdictions. . . .

The government of the United States is one of delegated powers alone. Its authority is defined and limited by the Constitution. All powers not granted to it by that instrument are reserved to the States or the people. No rights can be acquired under the constitution or laws of the United States, except such as the government of the United States has the authority to grant or secure. All that cannot be so granted or secured are left under the protection of the States.

We now proceed to an examination of the indictment, to ascertain whether the several rights, which it is alleged the defendants intended to interfere with, are such as had been in law and in fact granted or secured by the constitution or laws of the United States.

The first and ninth counts state the intent of the defendants to have been to hinder and prevent the citizens named in the free exercise and enjoyment of their "lawful right and privilege to peaceably assemble together with each other and with other citizens of the United States for a peaceful and lawful purpose." The right of the people peaceably to assemble for lawful purposes existed long before the adoption of the Constitution of the United States. In fact, it is, and always has been, one of the attributes of citizenship under a free government. It "derives its source," to use the language of Chief Justice Marshall, in *Gibbons v. Ogden*, . . . "from those laws whose authority is acknowledged by civilized man throughout the world." It is found wherever civilization exists. It was not, therefore, a right granted to the people by the Constitution. The government of the United States when established found it in existence, with the obligation on the part of the States to afford it protection. As no direct power over it was granted to Congress, it remains . . . subject to State jurisdiction. Only such existing rights were committed by the people to the protection of

Congress as came within the general scope of the authority granted to the national government.

The first amendment to the Constitution prohibits Congress from abridging "the right of the people to assemble and to petition the government for a redress of grievances." This, like the other amendments proposed and adopted at the same time, was not intended to limit the powers of the State governments in respect to their own citizens, but to operate upon the National government alone. . . .

The particular amendment now under consideration assumes the existence of the right of the people to assemble for lawful purposes, and protects it against encroachment by Congress. The right was not created by the amendment; neither was its continuance guaranteed, except as against congressional interference. For their protection in its enjoyment, therefore, the people must look to the States. The power for that purpose was originally placed there, and it has never been surrendered to the United States.

The right of the people peaceably to assemble for the purpose of petitioning Congress for a redress of grievances, or for anything else connected with the powers or the duties of the national government, is an attribute of national citizenship, and, as such, under the protection of, and guaranteed by, the United States. The very idea of a government, republican in form, implies a right on the part of its citizens to meet peaceably for consultation in respect to public affairs and to petition for a redress of grievances. If it had been alleged in these counts that the object of the defendants was to prevent a meeting for such a purpose, the case would have been within the statute, and within the scope of the sovereignty of the United States. Such, however, is not the case. The offence, as stated in the indictment, will be made out, if it be shown that the object of the conspiracy was to prevent a meeting for any lawful purpose whatever.

The second and tenth counts are equally defective. The right there specified is that of "bearing arms for a lawful purpose." This is not a right granted by the Constitution. Neither is it in any manner dependent upon that instrument for its existence. The second amendment declares that it shall not be infringed; but this, as has been seen, means no more than that it shall not be infringed by Congress. This is one of the amendments that has no other effect than to restrict the powers of the national government, leaving the people to look for their protection against any violation by their fellow-citizens of the rights it recognizes, to what is called, in *The City of New York v. Miln*, 11 Pet. 139, the "powers which relate to merely municipal legislation, or what was, perhaps, more properly called internal police," "not surrendered or restrained" by the Constitution of the United States.

The third and eleventh counts are even more objectionable. They charge the intent to have been to deprive the citizens named, they being in Louisiana, "of their respective several lives and liberty of person without due process of law." This is nothing else than alleging a conspiracy to falsely imprison or murder citizens of the United States, being within the territorial jurisdiction of the State of Louisiana. The rights of life and personal liberty are natural rights of man. "To secure these rights," says the Declaration of Independence, "governments are instituted among men, deriving their just powers from the consent of the governed."The very highest duty of the States, when they entered into the Union under the Constitution, was to protect all persons within their boundaries in the enjoyment of these "unalienable rights with which they were endowed by their Creator." Sovereignty, for this purpose, rests alone with the States. It is no more the duty or within the power of the United States to punish for a conspiracy to falsely imprison or murder within a State, than it would be to punish for false imprisonment or murder itself.

The fourteenth amendment prohibits a State from depriving any person of life, liberty, or property, without due process of law; but this adds nothing to the rights of one citizen as against another. It simply furnishes an additional guaranty against any encroachment by the States upon the fundamental rights which belong to every citizen as a member of society. As was said by Mr. Justice Johnson, in *Bank of Columbia v. Okely*, 4 Wheat. 244, it secures "the individual from the arbitrary exercise of the powers of government, unrestrained by the established principles of private rights and distributive justice." These counts in the indictment do not call for the exercise of any of the powers conferred by this provision in the amendment.

. . . When stripped of its verbiage, the case as presented amounts to nothing more than that the defendants conspired to prevent certain citizens of the United States, being within the State of Louisiana, from enjoying the equal protection of the laws of the State and of the United States.

The fourteenth amendment prohibits a State from denying to any person within its jurisdiction the equal protection of the laws; but this provision does not, any more than the one which precedes it, and which we have just considered, add anything to the rights which one citizen has under the Constitution against another. The equality of the rights of citizens is a principle of republicanism. Every republican government is in duty bound to protect all its citizens in the enjoyment of this principle, if within its power. That duty was originally assumed by the States; and it still remains there. The only obligation resting upon the United States is to see that the States do not deny the right. This the amendment guarantees, but no more. The power of the national government is limited to the enforcement of this guaranty.

No question arises under the Civil Rights Act of April 9, 1866 (14 Stat. 27), which intended for the protection of citizens of the United States in the enjoyment of certain rights, without discrimination on account of race, color, or previous condition of servitude, because, as has already been stated, it is nowhere alleged in these counts that the wrong contemplated against the rights of these citizens was on account of their race or color. . . .

We are, therefore, of the opinion that the first, second, third, fourth, sixth, seventh, ninth, tenth, eleventh, twelfth, fourteenth, and fifteenth counts do not contain charges of a criminal nature made indictable under the laws of the United States, and that consequently they are not good and sufficient in law. They do not show that it was the intent of the defendants, by their conspiracy, to hinder or prevent the enjoyment of any right granted or secured by the Constitution.

. . .it is needless to pursue the argument further. The conclusion is irresistible, that these counts are too vague and general. They lack the certainty and precision required by the established rules of criminal pleading. It follows that they are not good and sufficient in law. They are so defective that no judgment of conviction should be pronounced upon them.

The order of the Circuit Court arresting the judgment upon the verdict is, therefore, affirmed; and the cause remanded, with instructions to discharge the defendants.

## Presser v. Illinois
## 116 U.S. 252 (1886)

Herman Presser, the plaintiff in error, was indicted on September

24, 1879, in the Criminal Court of Cook County, Illinois, for a violation of the following sections of Art. XI. of the Military Code of that State, . . .

"§ 5. It shall not be lawful for any body of men whatever, other than the regular organized volunteer militia of this State, and the troops of the United States, to associate themselves together as a military company or organization, or to drill or parade with arms in any city, or town, of this State, without the license of the Governor thereof, which license may at any time be revoked: *And provided, further*, that students in educational institutions, where military science is a part of the course of instruction, may, with the consent of the Governor, drill and parade with arms in public, under the superintendence of their instructors, and may take part in any regimental or brigade encampment, under command of their military instructor; and while so encamped shall be governed by the provisions of this act. They shall be entitled only to transportation and subsistence, and shall report and be subject to the commandant of such encampment: *Provided*, that nothing herein contained shall be construed so as to prevent benevolent or social organizations from wearing swords.

"§ 6. Whoever offends against the provisions of the preceding section, or belongs to, or parades with, any such unauthorized body of men with arms shall be punished by a fine not exceeding the sum of ten dollars ($10), or by imprisonment in the common jail for a term not exceeding six months, or both."

The indictment charged in substance that Presser, on September 24, 1879, in the county of Cook, in the State of Illinois, "did unlawfully belong to, and did parade and drill in the city of Chicago with an unauthorized body of men with arms, who had associated themselves together as a military company and organization, without having a license from the Governor, and not being a part of, or belonging to, 'the regular organized volunteer militia' of the State of Illinois, or the troops of the United States."

A motion to quash the indictment was overruled. Presser then pleaded not guilty, and both parties having waived a jury the case was tried by the court, which found Presser guilty and sentenced him to pay a fine of $10.

The bill of exceptions taken upon the trial set out all the evidence, from which it appeared that Presser was thirty-one years old, a citizen of the United States and of the State of Illinois, and a voter; that he belonged to a society called the Lehr and Wehr Verein, a corporation organized April 16, 1875, in due form, under chapter 32, Revised Statutes of Illinois, called the General Incorporation Laws of Illinois, "for the purpose," as expressed by its certificate of association, "of improving the mental and bodily condition of its members, so as to qualify them for the duties of citizens of a republic. Its members shall therefore obtain, in the meetings of the association, a knowledge of our laws and political economy, and shall also be instructed in military and gymnastic exercises;" that Presser, in December, 1879, marched at the head of said company, about four hundred in number, in the streets of the city of Chicago, he riding on horseback and in command; that the company was armed with rifles and Presser with a cavalry sword; that the company had no license from the governor of Illinois to drill or parade as a part of the militia of the State, and was not a part of the regular organized militia of the State, nor a part of troops of the United States, and had no organization under the militia law of the United States. The evidence showed no other facts. Exceptions were reserved to the ruling of the court upon the motion to quash the indictment, to the finding of guilty, and to the judgment thereon. The case was taken to the Supreme Court of Illinois, where the judgment was affirmed. Thereupon Presser brought the present writ of error for a review of the judgment of affirmance. . . .

Mr. Justice Woods delivered the opinion of the court. After stating the facts in the language above reported, he continued:

The position of the plaintiff in error in this court was, that the entire statute under which he was convicted was invalid and void, because its enactment was the exercise of a power by the legislature of Illinois forbidden to the States by the Constitution of the United States.

The clauses of the Constitution of the United States referred to in the assignments of error, were as follows:

Art. I., sec. 8. "The Congress shall have power . . . To raise and support armies . . . . To provide for calling forth the militia to execute the laws of the Union, suppress insurrections, and repel invasions. To provide for organizing, arming, and disciplining the militia, and for governing such part of them as may be employed in the service of the United States, reserving to the States, respectively, the appointment of the officers, and the authority of training the militia, according to the discipline prescribed by Congress. . . . To make all laws which shall be necesary and proper, for carrying into execution the foregoing powers, &c.

Art. I., sec. 10. "No State shall, without the consent of Congress, keep troops . . . in time of peace."

Art. II. of Amendments. "A well regulated militia being necessary to the security of a free State, the right of the people to keep and bear arms shall not be infringed."

The plaintiff in error also contended that the enactment of the 5th and 6th sections of Article XI. of the Military Code was forbidden by subdivision 3 of section 9, Art. I., which declares "No bill of attainder or *ex post facto* law shall be passed,' and by Art. XIV of Amendments, which provides that "No State shall make or enforce any law which shall abridge the privileges or immunities of citizens of the United States, nor shall any State deprive any person of life, liberty, or property without due process of law."

The first contention of counsel for plaintiff in error is that . . . the legislature of Illinois had no power to pass the act approved May 28, 1879, "to provide for the organization of the State militia, entitled the Military Code of Illinois," under the provisions of which . . . the plaintiff in error was indicted.

The argument in support of this contention is, that the power of organizing, arming, and disciplining the militia being confided by the Constitution to Congress, when it acts upon the subject, and passes a law to carry into effect the constitutional provision, such action excludes the power of legislation by the State on the same subject.

It is further argued that the whole scope and object of the Military Code of Illinois is in conflict with that of the law of Congress. It is said that the object of the act of Congress is to provide for organizing, arming, and disciplining all the able-bodied male citizens of the States, respectively, between certain ages, that they may be ready at all times to respond to the call of the nation to enforce its laws, suppress insurrection, and repel invasion, and thereby avoid the necessity for maintaining a large standing army, with which liberty can never be safe, and that on the other hand, the effect if not object of the Illinois statute is to prevent such organizing, arming, and disciplining of the militia.

The plaintiff in error insists that the act of Congress requires absolutely all able-bodied ciizens of the State between certain ages, to be enrolled in the militia; that the act of Illinois makes the enrollment dependent on the necessity for the use of troops to execute the laws and suppress insurrections, and then leaves it discretionary with the governor by proclamation to require such enrollment; that the act of Congress requires the entire enrolled militia of the State, with a few exemptions made by it and which may be made by State laws, to be formed into companies, batallions, regiments, brigades, and divisions, that every man shall be armed and supplied with ammunition, provides a system of discipline and field exercises for companies, regiments, &c., and subjects the entire militia of the State to the call of the President to enforce the laws, suppress insurrection, or repel invasion, and provides for the punishment of the militia officers and men who refuse obedience to his orders. On the other hand, it is said that the State law makes it unlawful for any of its able-bodied citizens, except eight thousand, called the Illinois National Guard, to associate themselves together as a military company, or to drill or parade with arms without the license of the governor, and declares that no military company shall leave the State with arms and equipments without his consent; that even the eight thousand men styled the Illinois National Guard, are not enrolled or organized as required by the act of Congress, nor are they subject to the call of the President, but they constitute a military force sworn to serve in the military service of the State, to obey the orders of the governor, and not to leave the State without his consent; and that, if the State act is valid, the national act providing for organizing, arming, and disciplining the militia is of no force in the State of Illinois, for the Illinois act, so far from being in harmony with the act of Congress, is an insurmountable obstacle to its execution.

We have not found it necessary to consider or decide the question thus raised, as to the validity of the entire Military Code of Illinois, for, in our opinion, the sections under which the plaintiff in error was convicted may be valid, even if the other sections of the act were invalid. For it is a settled rule "that statutes that are constitutional in part only will be upheld so far as they are not in conflict with the Constitution, provided the allowed and prohibited parts are separable." . . . We are of opinion that this rule is applicable in this case. . . .

We are next to inquire whether the 5th and 6th sections of article XI. of the Military Code are in violation of the other provisions of the Constitution of the United States relied on by the plaintiff in error.

The first of these is the Second Amendment, which declares: "A well regulated militia being necessary to the security of a free State, the right of the people to keep and bear arms shall not be infringed."

We think it clear that the sections under consideration, which only forbid bodies of men to associate together as military organizations, or to drill or parade with arms in cities and towns unless authorized by law, do not infringe the right of the people to keep and bear arms. But a conclusive answer to the contention that this amendment prohibits the legislation in question lies in the fact that the amendment is a limitation only upon the power of Congress and the National government, and not upon that of the States. It was so held by this court in the case of *United States v. Cruikshank*, . . .

It is undoubtedly true that all citizens capable of bearing arms constitute the reserved military force or reserve militia of the United States as well as of the States, and, in view of this prerogative of the general government, as well as of its general powers, the States cannot, even laying the constitutional provision in question out of view, prohibit the people from keeping and bearing arms, so as to deprive the United States of their rightful resource for maintaining the public security, and disable the people from performing their duty to the general government. But, as already stated, we think it clear that the sections under consideration do not have this effect.

The plaintiff in error next insists that the sections of the Military Code of Illinois, under which he was indicted, are an invasion of that clause of the first section of the Fourteenth Amendment to the Constitution of the United States which declares: "No State shall make or enforce any law which shall abridge the privileges or immunities of citizens of the United States."

It is only the privileges and immunities of citizens of the United States that the clause relied on was intended to protect. A State may pass laws to regulate the privileges and immunities of its own citizens, provided that in so doing it does not abridge their privileges and immunities as citizens of the United States. . . .

The plaintiff in error was not a member of the organized volunteer militia of the State of Illinois, nor did he belong to the troops of the United States or to any organization under the militia law of the United States. On the contrary, the fact that he did not belong to the organized militia or the troops ofthe United States was an ingredient in the offence for which he was convicted and sentenced. The question is, therefore, had he a right as a citizen of the United States, in disobedience of the State law, to associate with others as a military company, and to drill and parade with arms in the towns and cities of the State? If the plaintiff in error has any such privilege he must be able to point to the provision of the Constitution or statutes of the United States by which it is conferred. . . .

The right voluntarily to associate together as a military company or organization, or to drill or parade with arms, without, and independent of, an act of Congress or law of the State authorizing the same, is not an attribute of national citizenship. Military organization and military drill and parade under arms are subjects especially under the control of the government of every country. They cannot be claimed as a right independent of law. Under our political system they are subject to the regulation and control of the State and Federal governments, acting in due regard to their respective prerogatives and powers. The Constitution and laws of the United States will be searched in vain for any support to the view that these rights are privileges and immunities of citizens of the United States independent of some specific legislation on the subject.

It cannot be successfully questioned that the State governments, unless restrained by their own Constitutions, have the power to regulate or prohibit associations and meetings of the people, except in the case of peaceable assemblies to perform the duties or exercise the privileges of citizens of the United States; and have also the power to control and regulate the organization, drilling, and parading of military bodies and associations, except when such bodies or associations are authorized by the militia laws of the United States. The exercise of this power by the States is necessary to the public peace, safety and good order. To deny the power would be to deny the right of the State to disperse assemblages organized for sedition and treason, and the right to suppress armed mobs bent on riot and rapine. . . .

The argument of the plaintiff in error that the legislation mentioned deprives him of either life, liberty or property without due process of law, or that it is a bill of attainder or *ex post facto* law, is so clearly untenable as to require no discussion.

It is next contended by the plaintiff in error that sections 5 and 6 of Art. XI. of the Military Code, under which he was indicted, are in conflict with the acts of Congress for the organization of the militia. But this position is based on what seems to us to be an unwarranted construction of the sections referred to. It is clear that their object was to forbid voluntary military associations, unauthorized by law, from organizing or drilling and parading with arms in the cities or towns of the State, and not to interfere with the organization, arming and drilling of the militia under the authority of the acts of Congress. If the object and effect of the sections were in irreconcilable conflict with the acts of Congress they would of course be invalid. But it is a rule of construction that a statute must be interpreted so as, if possible, to make it consistent with the Constitution and the paramount law. . . . If we yielded to this contention of the plaintiff in error we should render the sections invalid by giving them a strained construction, which would make them antagonistic to the law of Congress. We cannot attribute to the legislature, unless compelled to do so by its plain words, a purpose to pass an act in conflict with an act of Congress on a subject over which Congress is given authority by the Constitution of the United States. We are therefore of opinion that fairly construed the sections of the Military Code referred to do not conflict with the laws of Congress on the subject of the militia.

The plaintiff in error further insists that the organization of the Lehr and Wehr Verein as a corporate body, under the general corporation law of the State of Illinois, was in effect a license from the governor, within the meaning of section 5 of Article XI. of the Military Code, and that such corporate body fell within the exception of the same section "of students in educational institutions where military science is a part of the course of instruction."

In respect to these points we have to say that they present no Federal question. It is not, therefore, our province to consider or decide them.

All the Federal questions presented by the record were rightly decided by the Supreme Court of Illinois.

Judgment affirmed.

## Miller v. Texas
## 153 U.S. 535 (1894)

Motion to dismiss. The plaintiff in error was indicted by the grand jury of Dallas County, Texas, for the murder of one Riddle on June 18, 1892. He was convicted July 23, 1892, and sentenced to death. From the judgment of the District Court of Dallas County, before which he was tried, he appealed to the Court of Criminal Appeals of Texas, the court of last resort in criminal cases, where the judgment of the court below was affirmed. A motion for a rehearing was then made and overruled. Defendant thereupon sued out this writ, assigning as error that the statute of the State of Texas prohibiting the carrying of dangerous weapons on the person, by authority of which statute the court charged the jury that, if defendant was on a public street carrying a pistol, he was violating the law, infringed the right of the defendant as a citizen of the United States, and was in conflict with the Second Amendment to the Constitution of the United States, providing that the right of the people to keep and bear arms shall not be infringed; *second*, that the same statute, which provided that any person carrying arms in violation of the previous section, might be arrested without warrant, under which the court charged the jury that defendant, if he were carrying arms in violation of the statute, was subject to arrest without warrant, was in contravention of the Fourth Amendment of the Constitution, which provides that the right of the people to be secure in their persons against unreasonable searches and seizures shall not be violated; and of the Fifth and Fourteenth Amendments, which provide that no person shall be deprived of life, liberty, or property without due process of law, and that no State shall pass or enforce any law which shall abridge the privileges or immunities of citizens of the United States. . . .

Mr. Justice Brown, after stating the case, delivered the opinion of the court.

Motion is made to dismiss the writ of error in this case upon the ground that it was issued and signed by the clerk of the Court of Criminal Appeals of Texas, and was, therefore, insufficient to give this court jurisdiction, . . .

In this case the writ runs in the name of the President of the United States, to the judges of the Court of Criminal Appeals, is tested in the name of the Chief Justice of the Supreme Court of the United States, signed by the clerk of the Court of Criminal Appeals, and allowed by its presiding judge. If there was any error, it was in the signature of the writ by the clerk of the Court of Appeals, instead of by the clerk of this court, or of the Circuit Court of the United States for the proper district, . . . and such error would be amendable. . . .

Without, however, expressing a decided opinion upon the invalidity of the writ as it now stands, we think there is no Federal question properly presented by the record in this case, and that the writ of error must be dismissed upon that ground. The record exhibits nothing of what took place in the court of original jurisdiction, and begins with the assignment of errors in the Court of Criminal Appeals. In this assignment no claim was made of any ruling of the court below adverse to any constitutional right claimed by the defendant, nor does any such appear in the opinion of the court, which deals only with certain alleged errors relating to the impanelling of the jury, the denial of a continuance, the admission of certain testimony, and certain exceptions taken to the charge of the court. In his motion for a rehearing, however, defendant claimed that the law of the State of Texas forbidding the carrying of weapons, and authorizing the arrest without warrant of any person violating such law, under which certain questions arose upon the trial of the case, was in conflict with the Second and Fourth Amendments to the Constitution of the United States, one of which provides that the right of the people to keep and bear arms shall not be infringed, and the other of which protects the people against unreasonable searches and seizures. We have examined the record in vain, however, to find where the defendant was denied the benefit of any of these provisions, and even if he were, it is well settled that the restrictions of these amendments operate only upon the Federal power, and have no reference to proceedings in state courts. . . .

And if the Fourteenth Amendment limited the power of the States as to such rights as pertaining to citizens of the United States, we think it was fatal to this claim that it was not set up in the trial court. . . .

There was no other question under the Fourteenth Amendment to the Constitution. As the proceedings were conducted under the ordinary forms of criminal prosecutions there certainly was no denial of due process of law, or did the law of the State, to which reference was made, abridge the privileges or immunities of *citizens of the United States*. . . .

The writ of error is, therefore, Dismissed.

## United States v. Miller
## 307 U.S. 174 (1939)

An indictment in the District Court Western District Arkansas, charged that Jack Miller and Frank Layton "did unlawfully, knowingly, wilfully, and feloniously transport in interstate commerce from the town of Claremore in the State of Oklahoma to the town of Siloam Springs in the State of Arkansas a certain firearm, to-wit, a double barrel 12-gauge Stevens shotgun having a barrel less than 18 inches in length, . . . said defendants, at the time of so transporting said firearm in interstate commerce . . . not having registered said firearm as required by Title 26, United States Code, . . . and not having in their possession a stamp-affixed written order for said firearm . . . under authority of the . . . Act of Congress known as the 'National Firearms Act' approved June 26, 1934, contrary to the form of the statute in such case made and provided, and against the peace and dignity of the United States."

A duly interposed demurrer alleged: The National Firearms Act is not a revenue measure but an attempt to usurp police power reserved to the States, and is therefore unconstitutional. Also, it offends the inhibition of the Second Amendment to the Constitution. . . .

The District Court held that section eleven of the Act violates the Second Amendment. It accordingly sustained the demurrer and quashed the indictment.

The cause is here by direct appeal. . . .

In the absence of any evidence tending to show that possession or use of a "shotgun having a barrel of less than eighteen inches in length" at this time has some reasonable relationship to the preservation or efficiency of a well regulated militia, we cannot say that the Second Amendment guarantees the right to keep and bear such an instrument. Certainly it is not within judicial notice that this weapon is any part of the ordinary military equipment or that its use could contribute to the common defense. . . .

The Constitution as originally adopted granted to the Congress power—"To provide for calling forth the Militia to execute the Laws of the Union, suppress Insurrections and repel Invasions; To provide for organizing, arming, and disciplining, the Militia, and for governing such Part of them as may be employed in the Service of the United States, reserving to the States respectively, the Appointment of the Officers, and the Authority of training the Militia according to the discipline prescribed by Congress." With obvious purpose to assure the continuation and render possible the effectiveness of such forces the declaration and guarantee of the Second Amendment were made. It must be interpreted and applied with that end in view.

The Militia which the States were expected to maintain and train is set in contrast with Troops which they were forbidden to keep without the consent of Congress. The sentiment of the time strongly disfavored standing armies; the common view was that adequate defense of country and laws could be secured through the Militia—civilians primarily, soldiers on occasion.

The signification attributed to the term Militia appears from the debates in the Convention, the history and legislation of Colonies and States, and the writings of approved commentators. These show plainly enough that the Militia comprised all males physically capable of acting in concert for the common defense. "A body of citizens enrolled for military discipline." And further, that ordinarily when called for service these men were expected to appear bearing arms supplied by themselves and of the kind in common use at the time. . . .

. . . Osgood, Vol. 1, ch. XIII, affirms in reference to the early system of defense in New England—"In all the colonies, as in England, the militia system was based on the principle of the assize of arms. This implied the general obligation of all adult male inhabitants to possess arms, and, with certain exceptions, to cooperate in the work of defence." "The possession of arms also implied the possession of ammunition, and the authorities paid quite as much attention to the latter as to the former." "A year later . . . it was ordered that any single man who had not furnished himself with arms might be put out to service, and this became a permanent part of the legislation of the colony [Massachusetts]."

Also "Clauses intended to insure the possession of arms and ammunition by all who were subject to military service appear in all the important enactments concerning military affairs. Fines were the penalty for delinquency, whether of towns or individuals. . . .

The General Court of Massachusetts, . . . provided for the organization and government of the Militia. It directed that the Train Band should "contain all able bodied men, from sixteen to forty years of age, and the Alarm List, all other men under sixty years of age, . . ." Also, "That every non-commissioned officer and private soldier of the said militia not under the controul of parents, masters or guardians, and being of sufficient ability therefor in the judgment of the Selectmen of the town in which he shall dwell, shall equip himself, and be constantly provided with a good fire arm," &c.

By an Act passed April 4, 1786 the New York Legislature directed:

'That every able-bodied Male Person, being a Citizen of this State, or of any of the United States, and residing in this State, (except such Persons as are hereinafter excepted) and who are of the Age of Sixteen, and under the Age of Forty-five Years, shall, by the Captain or commanding Officer of the Beat in which such Citizens shall reside, within four Months after the passing of this Act, be enrolled in the Company of such Beat. . . . That every Citizen so enrolled and notified, shall, within three Months thereafter, provide himself, at his own Expense, with a good Musket, or Firelock, a sufficient Bayonet and Belt, a Pouch with a Box therein to contain not less than Twenty-four Cartridges suited to the Bore of his Musket or Firelock, each Cartridge containing a proper Quantity of Powder and Ball, two spare Flints, a Blanket and Knapsack; . . ."

The General Assembly of Virginia, October, 1785, . . . declared, "The defense and safety of the commonwealth depend upon having its citizens properly armed and taught the knowledge of military duty." . . . And every of the said officers, non-commissioned officers, and privates, shall constatly keep the aforesaid arms, accoutrements, and ammunition, ready to be produced whenever called for by his commanding officer. If any private shall make it appear to the satisfaction of the court hereafter to be appointed for trying delinquencies under this act that he is so poor that he cannot purchase the arms herein required, such court shall cause them to be purchased out of the money arising from delinquents."

Most if not all of the States have adopted provisions touching the right to keep and bear arms. Differences in the language employed in these have naturally led to somewhat variant conclusions concerning the scope of the right guaranteed. But none of them seem to afford any material support for the challenged ruling of the court below. . . .

We are unable to accept the conclusion of the court below and the challenged judgment must be reversed. The cause will be remanded for further proceedings.

## Chapter IV

# "TO KEEP AND BEAR ARMS": A CONTINUING AMERICAN DILEMMA

IT HAS BECOME virtually a cliché to observe that the incidence of violence in American culture is of staggering proportions,[1] ". . . higher . . . than almost anywhere else in the industrialized West."[2] Aside from the fact that statistics on crime and violence may be considerably inaccurate,[3] there are enough historic and contemporary examples to suggest that violence has been something of a tradition in the United States.

The United States was, of course, born in violent revolution. From the beginning, therefore, violence—and perhaps especially that in which guns have played a role—has had both positive *and* negative connotations for Americans. Indeed,

> . . . violence has formed a seamless web with some of the most positive events of U.S. history: independence (revolutionary violence),

[1]The literature dealing with American violence is itself of staggering proportions. See, for example, James D. Wright, Peter H. Rossi, Kathleen Daly, and Eleanor Weber-Burden, *Weapons, Crime and Violence in America: A Literature Review and Research Agenda* (Washington, D.C.: U.S. Department of Justice, National Institute of Justice, 1981); Hugh Davis Graham and Ted Robert Gurr, eds., *Violence in America: Historical and Contemporary Perspectives* (Beverly Hills: Sage Publications, rev. ed., 1979); *Violent Crime in the United States* (Washington, D.C.: U.S. Department of Justice, 1981); Carl Bakal, *The Right to Bear Arms* (New York: McGraw-Hill, 1966), among hundreds of others.

[2]James D. Wright, Peter H. Rossi, Kathleen Daly, and Eleanor Weber-Burden, *Weapons, Crime and Violence in America: A Literature Review and Research Agenda* (Washington, D.C.: U.S. Department of Justice, national Institute of Justice, 1981), p. 2.

[3]Ibid.

> the freeing of the slaves and the preservation of the Union (Civil War violence), the occupation of the land (Indian wars), the stabilization of frontier society (vigilante violence), the elevation of the farmer and the laborer (agrarian and labor violence), and the preservation of law and order (police violence). The patriot, the humanitarian, the nationalist, the pioneer, the landholder, the farmer, . . . the laborer (and the capitalist), have used violence as a means to a higher end.[4]

In much of this violence, the gun has been constructively associated with just causes. As one student of the subject has observed, ". . . the [American] revolution [itself] was a people's war the victory of which would have been uncertain without the American tradition of the individual right to keep and bear arms."[5] Widespread private ownership of firearms has thus been the historical reality in the United States. Likewise, firearms continue to play a significant role in contemporary American culture.

The number of firearms currently owned by Americans is, like the extent of violence in this country, of staggering proportions. Estimates of gun ownership have varied from a low of about 50,000,000 to well over 200,000,000.[6] As one researcher has stated, "There is an estimated 50,000,000 handguns in the United States today; double the number from 1968. . . . A handgun is sold new in this country every 13 seconds. . . ."[7] In short, "About half the people in America own a gun of some kind. . . ."[8]

Ultimately, of course, no one knows for certain how many guns there are in the United States, and figures which are presented in the literature as estimates may in fact err on the conservative side. Whatever the actual number of firearms—and especially handguns—owned

---

[4]Richard Maxwell Brown, "Historical Patterns of American Violence," in Hugh Davis Graham and Ted Robert Gurr, eds., *Violence in America: Historical and Contemporary Perspectives* (Beverly Hills: Sage Publications, rev. ed., 1979), pp. 40-41.

[5]Stephen P. Halbrook, "The Jurisprudence of the Second and Fourteenth Amendments," *George Mason University Law Review*, Volume 4, 1981, p. 8.

[6]See, for example, George D. Newton, Jr., and Franklin E. Zimring, *Firearms and Violence in the United States: A Staff Report to the National Commission on the Causes and Prevention of Violence* (Washington, D.C.: U.S. Government Printing Office, 1969); and Sam Fields, "Handgun Prohibition and Social Necessity," *Saint Louis University Law Journal*, Volume 23, 1979).

[7]Windle Turley, "Manufacturers' and Suppliers' Liability to Handgun Victims," *Northern Kentucky Law Review*, Volume 10, No. 1, 1982, p. 41.

[8]David Lester, *Gun Control: Issues and Answers* (Springfield: Charles C Thomas, Publisher, 1984), p. 45.

by Americans, it should be noted that

> . . . it is generally in the best interests of *both* sides [of the gun controversy] to overstate the private ownership of guns: The pro-gun-control forces, that is, are interested in the highest possible numbers because they illustrate in the most dramatic way the extent and 'urgency' of the 'gun problem,' and the anti-gun-control forces are interested in the highest possible numbers because they illustrate most dramatically the number of citizens whose rights and prerogatives would be infringed by additional weapons regulations.[9]

As to whether the reduction or the elimination of guns, especially handguns, would necessarily reduce the amount of violence in the United States, the evidence remains inconclusive. Yet, the *directionality* of the findings of the major studies appears to suggest that the mere possession or widespread distribution of firearms are not in themselves a cause of violence; indeed their widespread possession may in some cases actually discourage violence from occurring.[10] Perhaps one example of this occurred in Kennesaw, Georgia where in reaction to *Quilici* an ordinance was passed *requiring* ownership of guns in every noncriminal household, and where crime reportedly dropped nearly 90 percent in the ten months following enactment of the law. Likewise, in some cultures where weapons density equals or even exceeds that of the United States—Switzerland is a notable example—the frequency of violence is among the lowest in the world. Thus, according to Tonso, ". . . the whole notion of a gun culture has been called into question."[11] In short, "The proportion of gun offenders among private gun owners is extremely low . . ." and it is very difficult to assert that private weapons are a cause of violence when there ". . . is no direct evidence of the connection."[12]

---

[9]James D. Wright, Peter H. Rossi, Kathleen Daly, and Eleanor Weber-Burden, *Weapons, Crime and Violence in America: A Literature Review and Research Agenda* (Washington D.C.: U.S. Department of Justice, National Institute of Justice, 1981), p. 70.

[10]Space limitations do not permit an article-by-article discussion of these findings. Two of the best recent summaries are James D. Wright, Peter H. Rossi, Kathleen Daly, and Eleanor Weber-Burden, *Ibid.*, and David Lester, *Gun Control: Issues and Answers* (Springfield: Charles C Thomas, Publisher, 1984).

[11]See William R. Tonso, *Gun and Society: The Social and Existential Roots of the American Attachment to Firearms* (Washington, D.C.: University Press of America, 1982), p. 9. The term "gun culture" was used pejoratively by Richard Hofstadter in "America As A Gun Culture," *American Heritage*, Volume XXI, October, 1970).

[12]James D. Wright, Peter H. Rossi, Kathleen Daly, and Eleanor Weber-Burden, *Weapons, Crime and Violence in America: A Literature Review and Research Agenda* (Washington D.C.: U.S. Department of Justice, National Institute of Justice, 1981), pp. 218-219.

The lack of a supportable correlation between widespread ownership of firearms and widespread violence in the United States may be a consequence of the simple fact that most people who own guns are law-abiding citizens and that they own their weapons—rifles, shotguns, and handguns, in that order of frequency—for legitimate purposes: hunting, sports, recreation, and self-protection. Wright and Marston for example, point out that ". . . the vast, overwhelming majority of . . . privately-owned weapons are *not* involved in accidental shooting or intentional death. Most of the gun-owners . . . are probably responsible persons who use their weapons for legitimate recreational activities."[13] Moreover, persons who own guns are not much different from the rest of us. They tend to be, among other things, male, relatively affluent, middle class, and Protestant, most of whom, incidentally, have apparently had some prior experience with weapons. In short, ". . . there is no evidence suggesting . . . [gun-owners] to be an especially unstable or violent or maladapted lot; their 'personality profiles' are largely indistinct from those of the rest of the population."[14] On the other hand, it is probably also true that the typical gun owner and the typical felon are economically, sociologically, psychologically and otherwise "different" from each other. Cultural, historical, psychological, and other socialization patterns are very likely more directly related to the misuse of firearms than is the ownership of a weapon. In brief, "The idea that common, ordinary citizens are somehow transformed into potential perpetrators of criminally violent acts once they have acquired a firearm seems far-fetched. . . ."[15]

This fact nothwithstanding, most students of the subject would probably agree that the indiscriminate use of firearms must somehow be regulated. And that attempts have been made to do this is obvious from the fact that there are already well over 20,000 laws in the United States which attempt to regulate the use of firearms. These

---

[13]James D. Wright and Linda L. Marston, "The Ownership of the Means of Destruction: Weapons in the United States," *Social Problems*, Volume 23, No. 1, October, 1975, p. 106.

[14]James D. Wright, Peter H. Rossi, Kathleen Daly, and Eleanor Weber-Burden, *Weapons, Crime and Violence in America: A Literature Review and Research Agenda* (Washington D.C.: U.S. Department of Justice, National Institute of Justice, 1981), p. 203. See also David Lester, *Gun Control: Issues and Answers* (Springfield: Charles C Thomas, Publisher, 1984), p. 45; and Alan J. Lizotte and David J. Bordua, "Firearms Ownership for Sport and Protection: Two Divergent Models," *American Sociological Review*, Volume 45, April, 1980.

[15]James D. Wright, Peter H. Rossi, Kathleen Daly, and Eleanor Weber-Burden, *Weapons, Crime and Violence in America: A Literature Review and Research Agenda* (Washington D.C.: U.S. Department of Justice, National Institute of Justice, 1981), p. 237.

laws vary widely, ranging from federal acts such as the National Firearms Act of 1934, the Federal Firearms Act of 1938, the Gun Control Act and Omnibus Crime Control and Safe Streets Act of 1968, to a maze of state and local ordinances which are relatively stringent or relatively loose in their intent. They run the gamut from requiring licensing, banning the assembling of handguns with imported parts, requiring registration, prohibiting the carrying of handguns on the person or in other places, requiring permits to purchase, to requiring waiting periods, requiring minimum age to purchase, reporting sales to the police, and dozens of other specific conditions which must be satisfied before guns can be owned and used. Gun laws in the United States thus constitute something of a virtually incomprehensible maze. The handgun ban in Morton Grove, Illinois, may add only further to the confusion which already exists in attempts to regulate the use of firearms in the United States.[16]

It is legitimate to raise the question as to the actual effectiveness of all of these firearms regulations. It has been found, for example, that even relatively severe gun control laws have not had an impact on lowering the rate of violence nor, indeed, on the access to firearms. This has been true in the United States and in England as well—a country which is usually cited as an example of a particularly law-abiding nation, presumably because of its ostensibly restrictive gun laws. One author notes, however, that ". . . even with England's strict handgun laws, no reduction has been noted in violent crime. . . . The conclusion . . . must be reached from these facts . . . that handgun control laws do not effectively control the illegal possession of handguns, nor do such laws affect their use in violent crimes."[17]

The point is well summarized by David T. Hardy:

---

[16]The literature dealing with firearms regulation is extensive. Only a few examples include Fred E. Inbau, "Firearms and Legal Doctrine," *Tulane Law Review*, Volume VII, No. 4, June 1983; Alan Gottlieb, *The Rights of Gun Owners* (Aurora, Ill.: Caroline House Publishers, Inc., 1981); United States Department of the Treasury, Bureau of Alcohol, Tobacco and Firearms, *Your Guide to Firearms Regulation* (Washington, D.C.: U.S. Government Printing Office, 1978); Barnes Company, *Handgun Laws of the United States* (Fairfield: Barnes Company, 1974); Franklin E. Zimring, "Firearms and Federal Law: The Gun Control Act of 1968," *The Journal of Social Issues*, Volume IV, No. 1, January, 1975; and Edward H. Sheppard, "Control of Firearms," *Missouri Law Review*, Volume 34, 1969, among dozens of others.

[17]Robert G. Newman, "A Farewell to Arms—An Analysis of Texas Handgun Control Laws," *St. Mary's Law Journal*, Volume 13, 1982, p. 613.

> After more than a century of experience with firearm laws at the state and federal level, and after more than a decade of advanced statistical analysis of such statutes, the conclusion remains that firearm regulatory statutes are as much a failure in controlling violent crime as were the alcohol prohibition statutes of a half century ago.[18]

Thus, decisions like those reached in *Quilici* and *Kalodimos* leave unanswered a host of philosophical, legal, and practical questions. Leaving aside, for the moment, the Second Amendment itself as a potential bar to the banning of private ownership of firearms, it seems evident that future courts will have to address in further detail at least the following issues.

How could the banning, confiscation, or even a national registration requirement be enforced? The Fourth Amendment to the Constitution—which protects "the right of the people to be secure in their person, houses, papers and effects, against unreasonable searches and seizures . . ."—would appear to stand as a significant impediment to the enforcement of such laws. It can be assumed that most private firearms are kept in one's home or place of residence. Would any attempt to enforce laws involving firearms thus involve the widespread searching of private homes and other places in order to ferret out the guns of those who choose not to comply with the law—or even of those who do? And how would information about the private possession of firearms be gathered? Those who respond by saying that official efforts to prod the public toward voluntary surrender of their

[18]David T. Hardy, "Legal Restriction of Firearm Ownership As An Answer to Violent Crime: What Was the Question?" *Hamline Law Review*, Volume 6, No. 2, July, 1983, p. 408. Other examples of literature dealing with the effectiveness of firearms legislation include Don B. Kates, Jr., "Why Gun Control Won't Work," *Commonweal*, Volume CVIII, No. 5, 1976; Matthew G. Yaeger, "Do Mandatory Prison Sentences for Handgun Offenders Curb Violent Crime?" United States Conference of Mayors, 2d. ed., 1976; Douglas R. Murray, "Handguns, Gun Control Laws, and Firearms Violence," *Social Problems*, Volume 23, No. 1, October, 1975; Carol Skalnik Leff and Mark H. Leff, "The Politics of Ineffectiveness: Federal Firearms Legislation, 1919-38," *The Annals of the American Academy of Political and Social Science*, May, 1981; Martin S. Geisel, Richard Roll, and R. Stanton Wettick, Jr., "The Effectiveness of State and Local Regulation of Handguns: A Statistical Analysis," *Duke Law Journal*, Volume 1969, No. 4; Colin Greenwood, *Firearms Control: A Study of Armed Crime in England and Wales* (London: Routledge and Kegan Paul, 1972); Krug, Alan S., "The Relationship Between Firearms Licensing Laws and Crime Rates," *Congressional Record*, Vol. 113, Part 15, July 25, 1967, and Krug, "The Relationship Between Firearms Ownership and Crime Rates: A Statistical Analysis," *Congressional Record*, Vol. 114, Part 2, January 30, 1968.

weapons would largely solve this problem may seriously misinterpret the attitudes of the people on this issue. It might be just as reasonable to assume that Americans would not willingly give up their firearms if they felt that their rights would be violated in the process. Selective enforcement may thus stand as an alternative. But, as has been the experience of both police and courts, selective enforcement is often essentially ineffective in bringing a problem under control.

The Fifth Amendment to the Constitution may likewise pose an impediment to the enforcement of firearms regulation. The Fifth Amendment states, in part, that "No person . . . shall be compelled in any criminal case to be a witness against himself . . . nor shall private property be taken for public use, without just compensation." To illustrate this point, let us refer to a 1968 case decided by the United States Supreme Court.[19] The case involved the conviction in lower courts of one Haynes on the grounds that he knowingly possessed a sawed-off shotgun which he had failed to register with the Secretary of the Treasury as required by the National Firearms Act. This Act, since amended, contained provisions dealing with the acquisition, transportation, and importation of firearms, which, if not complied with, constituted grounds for criminal prosecution. The Act also required an individual who possessed a firearm acquired in violation of its provisions to register. Thus, the issue of the Fifth Amendment's guarantee against self-incrimination was nicely presented.

The Supreme Court reversed Haynes' conviction, stating ". . . a proper [Fifth Amendment] claim . . . provides a full defense to prosecutions either for failure to" register ". . . or for possession of an unregistered firearm under . . ." the National Firearms Act, since such provision requires admission of unlawful possession.[20] An interesting anomoly presents itself here: such a registration provision would require those who legally possess a firearm to register, but would not require those who have illegally gained possession to do so. In any event, future gun control laws may have to be couched in language which does not violate a person's Fifth Amendment privilege against self-incrimination.

The second clause from the excerpt of the Fifth Amendment quoted above—that dealing with the guarantee against government's

[19] *Haynes v. U.S.*, 390 U.S. 85 (1968).
[20] *Ibid.*, p. 100.

taking of private property without just compensation—was dealt with in *Quilici*. Plaintiffs argued that Morton Grove's statute prohibiting handguns violated this provision of the Fifth Amendment. The Court rejected this assertion, stating, in part, that if a taking of property is to require a compensation, then ". . . the exercise of the police power must result in the destruction of the use and enjoyment of a legitimate private property right. . . . The . . . ordinance does not go that far."[21] The Court pointed out that handguns could in fact be used at licensed gun clubs (provided that the club maintained possession and control over them) and that the weapons could be stored at those clubs. The Court thus felt that the plaintiff's reasonable use of the guns had not been significantly infringed and hence that the Morton Grove statute resulted in a noncompensable taking. Yet, Justice Rehnquist, in a strong dissent in another Fifth Amendment case, once asserted that taking someone's property ". . . does not become a noncompensable exercise of police power simply because the government in its grace allows the owner to make some 'reasonable' use of his property."[22] The decision in *Quilici* does not seem to sufficiently rebut Rehnquist's opinion. It would appear that this issue deserves more extended examination in future cases of this type.

The *Quilici* court also dismissed Ninth Amendment considerations as essentially irrelevant to the right to keep and bear arms. The Ninth Amendment reads: "The enumeration in the Constitution, of certain rights, shall not be construed to deny or disparage others retained by the people." Inasmuch as the Ninth Amendment has rarely been the basis of litigation, its language remains largely undefined.

Bennett Patterson has written that the Ninth Amendment acknowledges ". . . that everyone of the people of the United States owns a residue of individual rights and liberties which have never been, and which are never to be surrendered to the State, but which are still to be recognized, protected, and secured . . . and that such rights are not derived from the Constitution, but belong to the individual by natural

[21]*Quilici v. Village of Morton Grove*, 532 F. Supp. 1169 (N.D. Ill. 1981), p. 1184. For a more extended discussion of the relevance and implication of this clause to the issue of gun control, see Mark Benedict, "Second Amendment Right to Bear Arms," *Akron Law Review*, Volume 16, Fall, 1982.

[22]Rehnquist, J., dissenting, in *Penn Central Transportation Co., v. New York City*, 438 U.S. 104, 149 (1978).

endowment."[23] Edwards, indeed, puts the matter even more boldly. He suggests,

> The federal government is a government of limited power which has only the power expressly given by the Constitution. All other power remains in the states and in the people. . . . Therefore, it makes no difference whether the Second Amendment refers to the militia or not. The right to bear arms is not dependent upon militia service but is one of the broad, general rights reserved to the states and to the people.[24]

The Court in *Quilici* took an opposite view. It asserted that rights growing out of the Ninth Amendment are related essentially to procreational matters,[25] as recognized by the United States Supreme Court. In other words, the *Quilici* court denied the argument that the Ninth Amendment might be used as a rationale to protect the right to keep and bear arms on the basis of the rather bizarre logic that such a right does not exist under the Ninth Amendment because it has not been recognized by the Supreme Court. Yet, the *Quilici* court might have looked more closely at Justice Goldberg's comments in his concurring opinion in *Griswold*. He suggested, for example, that ". . . the Ninth Amendment shows a belief of the Constitution's authors that fundamental rights exist that are not expressly enumerated in the first eight . . . and an intent that the list of rights included there not be deemed exhaustive."[26] Indeed, he went on to say that "The Ninth Amendment simply shows the intent of the Constitution's authors that other fundamental personal rights should not be denied such protection or disparaged in any other way simply because they are not specifically listed in the first eight constitutional amendments."[27] And, even beyond this, there may be principles founded on the "'. . . traditions and [collective] conscience of our people . . .'" which may in short "'. . . be ranked as fundamental.'"[28] The right to keep and bear arms is deemed by some interpreters of the Constitution to be one of

[23]Bennett P. Patterson, *The Forgotten Ninth Amendment* (Indianapolis: The Bobbs-Merrill Company, Inc., 1955), pp. 1-2.

[24]James E. Edwards, *Myths About Guns*. (Coral Springs, Florida: Peninsula Press, 1978), pp. 86-87.

[25]*Griswold v. Connecticut*, 381 U.S. 479 (1965).

[26]*Ibid.*, p. 492.

[27]*Ibid.*

[28]*Ibid.*, p. 493.

the rights so rooted. Whatever the ultimate outcome of the interpretation of the Ninth Amendment as it relates to the Second, it would seem an issue requiring further examination.

The Fourteenth Amendment likewise requires further examination in terms of its relevance to the right to keep and bear arms. The Amendment reads, in part, ". . . No State shall make or enforce any law which shall abridge the privileges or immunities of citizens of the United States; nor shall any State deprive any person of life, liberty, or property, without due process of law. . . ."

It was for many years accepted judicial doctrine that the Bill of Rights of the United States Constitution was inoperative upon the States. This position has long since been overturned, however, and many provisions of the Bill of Rights have now been incorporated into the due process clause. Interestingly, the Second Amendment has been absent from such incorporation. Interpretations of the materials available on the development of the Fourteenth Amendment are, as can be expected, inconsistent and conflicting. Only a few examples of these conflicting interpretations will be given here.[29]

Morrison and Fairman, for example, in two early articles on the subject, vehemently asserted that the Fourteenth Amendment does not incorporate the Bill of Rights.[30] Hugo Black, on the other hand, once observed, "I believe that by virtue of the Fourteenth Amendment, the first ten amendments are now applicable to the states. . . .[31] Moreover, he argued, "It is my belief that there *are* 'absolutes' in our Bill of Rights, and that they were put there on purpose by men who

[29]See, for example Stephen P. Halbrook, "The Fourteenth Amendment and the Right to Keep and Bear Arms: The Intent of the Framers," in *The Right to Keep and Bear Arms*, Report of the Subcommittee on the Constitution of the Committee on the Judiciary, United States Senate, 97th Congress, 2d Session, February, 1982; Halbrook, "The Jurisprudence of the Second and Fourteenth Amendments," *George Mason University Law Review*, Volume 4, 1981; Alan M. Gottlieb, "Gun Ownership: A Constitutional Right," *Northern Kentucky Law Review*, Volume 10, No. 1, 1982; Howard Jay Graham, "The Early Antislavery Backgrounds of the Fourteenth Amendment," *Wisconsin Law Review*, May and July, 1950; Stanley Morrison, "Does the Fourteenth Amendment Incorporate the Bill of Rights? The Judicial Interpretation," *Stanford Law Review*, Volume 2, December, 1949; Charles Fairman, "Does the Fourteenth Amendment Incorporate the Bill of Rights? The Original Understanding," *Stanford Law Review*, Volume 2, December, 1949; and Thomas A. Wallitsch, "Right to Bear Arms in Pennsylvania: The Regulation of Possession," *Duquesne Law Review*, Volume 11, Summer, 1973.

[30]See Morrison and Fairman as cited in note 29.

[31]Hugo Black, "The Bill of Rights," *New York University Law Review*, Volume 35, No. 4, April, 1960, p. 866.

knew what the words meant, and meant their prohibitions to be 'absolutes.'" Then, in a direct reference to the Second Amendment, Black stated "Although the Supreme Court has held this amendment to include only arms necessary to a well-regulated militia, as so construed, its prohibition is absolute."[32]

Given the general tendency of the Supreme Court in recent decades to incorporate more of the Bill of Rights by way of the Fourteenth Amendment, one might conclude, as Risely does, that "If the Supreme Court is in the future to avoid holding the second amendment to be included in the fourteenth, it would have to reverse its present trend and return to its former interpretation of the Bill of Rights."[33] The Supreme Court could accomplish an incorporation of the Second Amendment through either the due process clause or the privileges and immunities clause, or it might avail itself of ". . . a broader 'penumbra' theory perhaps involving the first, second, fourth, fifth, ninth, tenth, and fourteenth amendments. . . ."[34]

Thus there are a number of unresolved constitutional issues which are related both directly and indirectly to the interpretation and the application of the Second Amendment. Each of these requires pondering to a degree well beyond that yet given them by the courts. Surely the decisions in both *Quilici* and *Kalodimos* have left them unclear and undecided.[35]

---

[32]*Ibid.*, pp. 867, 873.

[33]Richard F. Riseley, Jr., "The Right to Keep and Bear Arms: A Necessary Constitutional Guarantee or an Outmoded Provision of the Bill of Rights?" *Albany Law Review*, Volume 31, March/April, 1966, p. 80.

[34]Stephen P. Halbrook, "The Jurisprudence of the Second and Fourteenth Amendments," *George Mason University Law Review*, Volume 4, 1981, p. 66.

[35]Aside from the related constitutional issues, there are a number of other questions which must be addressed with respect to a "final solution" to the Second Amendment question. Again, space does not permit an elaborate discussion of all of them here. However, at least the following require judicial and scholarly deliberation, as suggested in the literature.

What is meant by the term "militia" in modern times? Is it to be construed as an "organized" military body? In historical context, this would seem incorrect, inasmuch as there *was* no organized militia until passage of the Militia Act of 1792— long after the concept of the militia had becme widely recognized. If, on the other hand, the term refers to the so-called National Guard, then why do the members thereof not keep their weapons at home? Are handguns militia weapons? Catalogs of weaponry suggest that they are. What is the *wisdom* of firearms legislation? Are we as a nation confronting a kind of second "Prohibition" which cannot in the long run be enforced? The likelihood of massive noncompliance with highly restrictive gun laws seems high—and one is forced to at least raise the question about

→

Although the debate regarding the correct interpretation of the Second Amendment continues, it would appear—as was pointed out in Chapter I—that the best and most recent scholarship supports the view that the Framers intended the right to keep and bear arms as an individual right. Joyce Lee Malcolm, for example, reminding us that "Every generation suffers to some extent from historic amnesia,"[36] concludes that the right is firmly imbedded in the English common law and that, the language of the amendment ". . . should properly be read to extend to every citizen the right to have arms for personal defense. . . . Thus, in guaranteeing the individual right to keep and bear arms, and the collective right to maintain a general militia, the Second Amendment amplified the tradition of the English Bill of Rights for the purpose of preserving and protecting government by and for the people."[37]

Although this individual rights view is not supported by a majority of legal scholars, law professors, practicing attorneys and the American Bar Association, it is the position taken by a majority of non-legal

---

whether making criminals out of otherwise law-abiding citizens is a rational approach to an admittedly complex problem. Even if it were possible to enforce a massive gun ban, the courts and penal systems would probably suffer from such a staggering workload that coping with the problem would be virtually impossible. In other words, the costs involved may not reap nearly the amount of benefits which some expect.

Would gun prohibitions prevent criminals from acquiring firearms? Would political assassinations and other crimes of violence be prevented? These are questions to which the answer is probably in the negative. Those intent upon perpetrating a crime or an assassination will undoubtedly always find the way to do so.

How shall provisions of state constitutions—in their diverse forms—dealing with the right to keep and bear arms be construed? Should state legislatures have authority to pass pre-emptive legislation in order to prevent local governments from passing inconsistent and diverse local laws which might lead to chaotic conditions?

What will happen to the right of self-defense?

Is the issue ultimately political? That is, does the citizen ultimately not have the right to defend himself from despotic government? The fear of tyranny and oppression has not just "gone away." In short, the question may be asked whether the citizen of the United States will ever have to exercise his right to cast off an oppressive government again. It is a question which at least needs to be addressed.

[36]Joyce Lee Malcolm, "The Right of the People to Keep and Bear Arms: The Common Law Tradition," *Hastings Constitutional Law Quarterly*, Volume 10, 1983, p. 285. See also Stephen P. Halbrook. *That Every Man Be Armed: The Evolution of a Constitutional Right* (Albuquerque: University of New Mexico Press, 1984).

[37]Joyce Lee Malcolm, "The Right of the People to Keep and Bear Arms: The Common Law Tradition," *Hastings Constitutional Law Quarterly*, Volume 10, 1983, p. 314.

scholars.[38] Likewise, most courts have taken a position different from that to which the empirical evidence would lead: they have endosed a collective interpretation of the language of the Second Amendment.

As was observed in Chapter III, the Supreme Court has ruled in only four instances on Second Amendment issues. In Cruikshank,[39] for example, a case which involved the allegation that a number of Southern whites had, among other things, intended to obstruct and prevent plaintiff's "right to keep and bear arms for a lawful purpose,"[40] the Court did not analyze the Second Amendment in detail, but did argue that such a right was not absolute and that it was not guaranteed by the Constitution. The Court merely stated that the amendment only prevented *Congress* from interfering with the right to bear arms—it limited only the powers of the federal government.

In *Presser v. Illinois*,[41] the Supreme Court, again without any significant exploration of the meaning of the language of the Second Amendment, suggested that Presser's action as a member of the Lehr and Wehr Verein society in marching through the streets of Chicago without a license from the governor violated the Military Code of Illinois. The Court asserted that the Second Amendment limited the powers of the Congress, not the power of the states. It chose to ignore whether states may forbid citizens from bearing arms for purposes other than military.

In *Miller v. Texas*,[42] in which Miller had been convicted of murder and on appeal claimed that his Second Amendment rights had been violated, the Court once again held that the amendment limited only federal, not state, powers. Thus it merely reiterated its holding in *Cruikshank*.

In *United States v. Miller*,[43] in which Jack Miller and Frank Layton were accused of violating the National Firearms Act, the Supreme Court reversed the district court's decision that the Act violated the Second Amendment. This time the Supreme Court stated

> In the absence of any evidence tending to show that possession or

---

[38]See Don B. Kates, Jr., "Handgun Prohibition and the Original Meaning of the Second Amendment," *Michigan Law Review*, Volume 82, November, 1983, pp. 206-207.
[39]United States v. Cruikshank, 92 U.S. 542 (1875).
[40]*Ibid.*, p. 545.
[41]116 U.S. 252 (1886).
[42]153 U.S. 535 (1894).
[43]307 U.S. 174 (1939).

> use of a 'shotgun having a barrel of less than eighteen inches in length' at this time has some reasonable relationship to the preservation or efficiency of a well-regulated militia, we cannot say that the Second Amendment guarantees the right to keep and bear such an instrument. Certainly it is not within judicial notice that this weapon is any part of the ordinary military equipment or that its use could contribute to the common defense.[44]

Thus, the question of the *individual's* right to keep and bear arms has never been directly settled by the United States Supreme Court.

Moreover, most state court decisions have followed the leadership of the Supreme Court in holding that the amendment is applicable to the federal government only, that the right to keep and bear arms is not an absolute right, and that the intention of the Second Amendment was to assure a collective, not an individual, right to keep and bear arms.

Is, then, the right to keep and bear arms a fundamental right? If it is to be so construed, laws aimed at its regulation must be examined far more searchingly than would normally be required to satisfy due process. For a fundamental right is considered ingrained in the historical experience of a people and is regarded as independent of specific constitutional provisions. The framers undoubtedly considered the right fundamental, in the sense that without arms for self defense and defense of the state the perpetuation of a free democracy would be in jeopardy.

But, as has been observed, both federal and state courts have moved away from this point of view. Indeed,

> Even if one takes it for granted that the Framers would have considered arms 'fundamental' without hesitation, the inquiry is not complete. Social and technological change, along with a reluctance on the part of the modern Supreme Court to further expand the boundaries of substantive due process, will probably conspire to prevent judicial recognition of the 'fundamental' nature of the right to possess arms.[45]

Having made these observations, Barrett then attempts a reconciliation between the two points of view by positing an analogy with the

---

[44]*Ibid.*, p. 178.

[45]Sidney R. Barrett, Jr., "The Right to Bear Arms and Handgun Prohibition: A Fundamental Rights Analysis," *North Carolina Central Law Journal*, Volume 14, 1983, pp. 307-308.

First Amendment. Just as the First Amendment does not absolutely protect all types of speech—libel and obscenity, for example—likewise the Second Amendment may not protect ownership and use of all types of weapons. In other words, both amendments "may be said to contain a 'core content' of a political nature which justifies a lesser degree of protection to the exercise of that right outside of that scope."[46] The "core" of the Second Amendment may reside in the ownership of arms by private citizens for protection against tyrannical government. If gun ownership does not "contribute significantly to this goal,"[47] then, presumably, under this analogy, it may be regulated. In the words of Barrett, "the 'core content' approach does offer a principled basis on which to resolve the libertarian traditions of the framers and the need of an evolving society to protect itself from the criminal's hidden arsenal."[48]

As eminently reasonable as this approach appears to be, it is, in conclusion, nevertheless necessary to present two other views on the subject.

One author has observed that the Second Amendment may very well have become the "lost amendment."[49] Robert Sprecher, in 1965, suggested that the Second Amendment may have become "lost" because the concept of a citizens' militia has long passed out of everyday usage, and that individuals today rely essentially upon police and legal institutions to ensure their rights. He pointed out that ". . . the rights of the other first eight amendments have been given so much judicial and popular attention that the Second Amendment has been all but overlooked."[50] Yet, he emphasized also that even if the Second Amendment had not been included in the Constitution, the rights of citizens would hardly be any different now. As he stated so eloquently,

> Perhaps the people have lost a valuable right and privilege which should be cherished rather than forgotten. Perhaps the Founding Fathers, as they so often seem to have done, gave the people an enduring right which changing history does not outmode but merely

[46] *Ibid.*, p. 309.
[47] *Ibid.*, p. 310.
[48] *Ibid.*, p. 311.
[49] Robert A. Sprecher, "The Lost Amendment," *American Bar Association Journal*, Volume 51, June and July, 1965.
[50] *Ibid.*, July, 1965, p. 667.

places in a new context—often more compelling than the old.[51]

Ultimately, however, regardless of recent scholarship which concludes that the framers intended the right to keep and bear arms as an individual right, it may one day be determined that the intentions of the framers are no longer relevant to twentieth and twenty-first century America. After all, it may be argued that the era when all men were part of the militia and were expected to maintain their own private arms to defend their state or community has long since passed. Or has it? One might speculate at length on this, of course. In a frequently-cited case it was stated that

> . . . what was once deemed a stable and essential bulwark of freedom, 'a well-regulated militia,' though the clause still remains in our Constitutions, both State and Federal, has, as an organization, passed away in almost every State of the Union, and only remains to us as a memory of the past, probably never to be revived.[52]

Yet, the potential of external invasion and internal oppression has not disappeared. While some may argue that the weapons of any modern militia have become far too sophisticated for private possession (notwithstanding the fact that small arms remain among militia weapons), the fact remains that much of the world's warfare is fought by individuals attempting to free themselves from both internal and external oppression—and by the use of relatively primitive weapons.

Perhaps, however, future jurists, lawyers, and philosophers will simply deny that a right to bear arms ever existed. The entire notion that the possession of arms, even for self defense, and, indeed, as a natural right, might one day be viewed as nothing more than the figment of the imagination of those who lived in the distant past. Writing over 50 years ago, Daniel J. McKenna asked, ". . . will the courts ever say that the Constitution would protect the right to keep and bear arms, if there were such a right, but that it does not exist and never did exist except in the minds of discredited theorists? Who knows?"[53]

Who knows indeed. *Do* the American people continue to have the right to keep and bear arms? If the answer proves to be "No," then it

---

[51] *Ibid.*

[52] See *Andrews v. State*, 3 Heisk. (Tenn.) 165, (1871).

[53] Daniel J. McKenna, "The Right to Keep and Bear Arms," *Marquette Law Review*, Volume 12, 1928, p. 149.

will be up to jurists, lawyers, and scholars to reconcile this position with the findings of historical research. If the answer is "Yes," then the question becomes one of how to regulate the indiscriminate use of firearms in a society which is demonstrably less than peaceful.

In short, the issue of whether the people have the right to keep and bear arms is nothing less than a continuing American dilemma.

# APPENDICES

## APPENDIX 1

# Provisions of State Constitutions Dealing with the Right to Keep and Bear Arms*

| *State* | *Constitutional Reference* | *Text Language* |
|---|---|---|
| Alabama | Article I, Section 26 | "That every citizen has a right to bear arms in defense of himself and the state." |
| Alaska | Article I, Section 19 | "A well regulated militia being necessary to the security of a free state, the right of the people to keep and bear arms shall not be infringed." |
| Arizona | Article II, Section 26 | "The right of the individual citizen to bear arms in defense |

*Source: Legislative Drafting Research Fund of Columbia University, *Constitutions of the United States, National and State*, 2nd Edition (Dobbs Ferry: Oceana Publications, Inc., 1984).

For other listings of state constitutional provisions dealing with the right to keep and bear arms during earlier periods, see Daniel J. McKenna, "The Right to Keep and Bear Arms," *Marquette Law Review*, Volume 12, 1928; Ralph J. Rohner, "The Right to Bear Arms: A Phenomenon of Constitutional History," *Catholic University Law Review*, Volume 16, September, 1966; Robert Dowlut and Janet A. Knoop, "State Constitutions and The Right to Keep and Bear Arms," *Oklahoma City University Law Review*, Volume 7, No. 2, Summer, 1982; and David I. Caplan, "The Right of the Individual to Bear Arms; A Recent Judicial Trend," *Detroit College of Law Review*, Volume 1982, Winter, Issue 4.

See also the 1962 edition of *Constitutions of the United States, National and State*, cited above.

| *State* | *Constitutional Reference* | *Text Language* |
|---|---|---|
| | | of himself or the State shall not be impaired but nothing in this section shall be construed as authorizing individuals or corporations to organize, maintain, or employ an armed body of men." |
| Arkansas | Article II, Section 5 | "The citizens of this state shall have the right to keep and bear arms for their common defense." |
| California | The Constitution is silent on the issue.<br>Article I, Section 5, refers to the subordination of military to civil power and to limits on standing armies and the quartering of soldiers. | |
| Colorado | Article II, Section 13 | "The right of no person to keep and bear arms in defense of his home, person and property, or in aid of the civil power when there legally summoned, shall be called in question; but nothing herein contained shall be construed to justify the practice of carrying concealed weapons. |
| Connecticut | Article I, Section 15 | "Every citizen has a right to bear arms in defense of himself and the State." |
| Delaware | The Constitution is silent on the issue.<br>Article I, Sections 17 and 18, refer to limitations on standing | |

| *State* | *Constitutional Reference* | *Text Language* |
|---|---|---|
| | armies, the subordination of military to civil power, and prohibitions against the quartering of soldiers. | |
| Florida | Declaration of Rights, Section 8 | "The right of the people to bear arms in defense of themselves and the lawful authority of the State shall not be infringed, except that the manner of bearing arms may be regulated by law." |
| Georgia | Article I, Section 1, Paragraph V | "The right of the people to keep and bear arms shall not be infringed, but the General Assembly shall have the power to prescribe the manner in which arms may be borne." |
| Hawaii | Article I, Section 17 | "A well regulated militia being necessary to the security of a free state, the right of the people to keep and bear arms shall not be infringed." |
| Idaho | Article I, Section 11 | "The people have the right to keep and bear arms, which right shall not be abridged; but this provision shall not prevent the passage of laws to govern the carrying of weapons concealed on the person nor prevent passage of legislation providing minimum sentences for crimes committed while in possession of a firearm, nor prevent the passage of legislation providing penalties for the possession of firearms |

| *State* | *Constitutional Reference* | *Text Language* |
|---|---|---|
| | | by a convicted felon, nor prevent the passage of any legislation punishing the use of a firearm. No law shall impose licensure, registration or special taxation on the ownership or possession of firearms or ammunition. Nor shall any law permit the confiscation of firearms, except those actually used in the commission of a felony." |
| Illinois | Article I, section 22 | "Subject only to the police power, the right of the individual citizen to keep and bear arms shall not be infringed." |
| Indiana | Article I, Section 32 | "The people shall have a right to bear arms, for the defense of themselves and the State." |
| Iowa | The Constitution is silent on the issue. Article I, Sections 14 and 15, refer to subordination of military to civil power, limitations on standing armies, limitations on appropriations for standing armies, and limitations on the quartering of soldiers. | |
| Kansas | Bill of Rights, Section 4 | "The people have the right to bear arms for their defense and security; but standing armies, in time of peace, are dangerous to liberty, and shall not be |

| *State* | *Constitutional Reference* | *Text Language* |
|---|---|---|
| | | tolerated, and the military shall be in strict subordination to the civil power." |
| Kentucky | Section 1, Seventh | "All men are, by nature, free and equal, and have certain inherent and inalienable rights, among which may be reckoned: . . . The right to bear arms in defense of themselves and of the State, subject to the power of the General Assembly to enact laws to prevent persons from carrying concealed weapons." |
| Louisiana | Article I, Section 11 | "The right of each citizen to keep and bear arms shall not be abridged, but this provision shall not prevent the passage of laws to prohibit the carrying of weapons concealed on the person." |
| Maine | Article I, Section 16 | "Every citizen has a right to keep and bear arms for the common defence; and this right shall never be questioned." |
| Maryland | The Consitution is silent on the issue. Declaration of Rights, Articles 28, 29, 30, 31, and 32, refer, respectively, to a well regulated militia; to limitations on standing armies; to subordination of military to civil power; | |

| *State* | *Constitutional Reference* | *Text Language* |
|---|---|---|
| | to limitations on quartering troops; and to limitations on the application of martial law. | |
| Massachusetts | Part the First, Article XVII | "The people have a right to keep and bear arms for the common defence. And as, in time of peace, armies are dangerous to liberty, they ought not to be maintained without the consent of the Legislature and the military power shall always be held in an exact subordination to the Civil authority, and be governed by it." |
| Michigan | Article I, Section 6 | "Every person has a right to keep and bear arms for the defense of himself and the state." |
| Minnesota | The Constitution is silent on the issue. Article I, Section 14, refers to the subordination of the military to the civil power and to limitations on standing armies. | |
| Mississippi | Article 3, Section 12 | "The right of every citizen to keep and bear arms in defense of his home, person or property, or in aid of the civil power when thereto legally summoned, shall not be called in question, but the legislature |

| *State* | *Constitutional Reference* | *Text Language* |
|---|---|---|
| | | may regulate or forbid carrying concealed weapons." |
| Missouri | Article I, Section 23 | "That the right of every citizen to keep and bear arms in defense of his home, person, and property or when lawfully summoned in aid of the civil power shall not be questioned; but this shall not justify the wearing of concealed weapons." |
| Montana | Article II, Section 12 | "The right of any person to keep or bear arms in defense of his own home, person, or property, or in aid of the civil power when thereto legally summoned, shall not be called in question, but nothing herein contained shall be held to perrmit the carrying of concealed weapons." |
| Nebraska | The Constitution is silent on the issue. Article I, Sections 17 and 18, refer to the subordination of the military to the civil power and to limitations on the quartering of soldiers. | |
| Nevada | The Constitution is silent on the issue. Article I, Section 1, refers to "certain inalienable rights among which are those of enjoying and defending life and | |

| State | Constitutional Reference | Text Language |
|---|---|---|
| | liberty;" Section 12 places limitations on the quartering of soldiers; and Section 20 emphasizes that "this enumeration of rights shall not be construed to impair or deny others retained by the people." | |
| New Hampshire | The Constitution is silent on the issue. | |
| | Part First, Article 2d, states "all men have certain natural, essential, and inherent rights—among which are, the enjoying and defending life and liberty; acquiring, possessing, and protecting, property;" Article 10th refers to a "right of revolution" against an oppressive government; Article 24th refers to a "well regulated militia" as "the proper, natural, and sure defense, of a state;" and Articles 25th, 26th, and 27th place limitations on standing armies, subordinate military to civil power, and place limitations on quartering of soldiers, respec- | |

| *State* | *Constitutional Reference* | *Text Language* |
|---|---|---|
| | tively. Article 32d limits martial law. | |
| New Jersey | The Constitution is silent on the issue. Article I, Paragraphs 15 and 16, refer to the subordination of the military to the civil power, and to limitations on the quartering of soldiers. | |
| New Mexico | Article II, Section 6 | "No law shall abridge the right of the citizen to keep and bear arms for security and defense, for lawful hunting and recreational use and for other lawful purposes, but nothing herein shall be held to permit the carrying of concealed weapons." |
| New York | The Constitution is silent on the issue. | |
| North Carolina | Article I, Section 30 | "A well regulated militia being necessary to be the security of a free State, the right of the people to keep and bear arms shall not be infringed; and, as standing armies in time of peace are dangerous to liberty, they shall not be maintained, and the military shall be kept under strict subordination to, and governed by, the civil power. Nothing herein shall justify the practice of carrying concealed weapons, or prevent the General Assembly from |

| *State* | *Constitutional Reference* | *Text Language* |
|---|---|---|
| | | enacting penal statutes against that practice." |
| North Dakota | The Constitution is silent on the issue. Article I, Section 19, refers to the subordination of military to civil power, and to limitations on standing armies and the quartering of soldiers. | |
| Ohio | Article I, Section 4 | "The people have the right to bear arms for their defense and security; but standing armies, in time of peace, are dangerous to liberty; and shall not be kept up; and the military shall be in strict subordination to the civil power." |
| Oklahoma | Article II, Section 26 | "The right of a citizen to keep and bear arms in defense of his home, person, or property, or in aid of the civil power, when thereunto legally summoned, shall never be prohibited; but nothing herein contained shall prevent the Legislature from regulating the carrying of weapons." |
| Oregon | Article I, Section 27 | "The people shall have the right to bear arms for the defence of themselves, and the State, but the Military shall be kept in strict subordination to the civil power." |
| Pennsylvania | Article I, Section 21 | "The right of the citizens to bear arms for the defence of |

| *State* | *Constitutional Reference* | *Text Language* |
|---|---|---|
| | | themselves and the State shall not be questioned." |
| Rhode Island | Article I, Section 22 | "The right of the people to keep and bear arms shall not be infringed." |
| South Carolina | Article I, Section 20 | "A well regulated militia being necessary to the security of a free State, the right of the people to keep and bear arms shall not be infringed. As, in times of peace, armies are dangerous to liberty, they shall not be maintained without the consent of the General Assembly. The military power of the State shall always be held in subordination to the civil authority and be governed by it. No soldier shall in time of peace be quartered in any house without the consent of the owner nor in time of war but in the manner prescribed by law." |
| South Dakota | Article VI, Section 24 | "The right of the citizens to bear arms in defense of themselves and the state shall not be denied." |
| Tennessee | Article I, Section 26 | "That the citizens of this State shall have a right to keep and bear arms for their common defense; but the Legislature shall have power, by law, to regulate the wearing of arms with a view to prevent crime." |
| Texas | Article I, Section 23 | "Every citizen shall have the right to keep and bear arms in |

| *State* | *Constitutional Reference* | *Text Language* |
|---|---|---|
| | | the lawful defense of himself or the State; but the Legislature shall have power, by law, to regulate the wearing of arms, with a view to prevent crime." |
| Utah | Article I, Section 6 | "The people have the right to bear arms for their security and defense, but the Legislature may regulate the exercise of this right by law." |
| Vermont | Chapter I, Article 16th | "That the people have a right to bear arms for the defence of themselves and the State—and as standing armies in time of peace are dangerous to liberty, they ought not to be kept up; and the military should be kept under strict subordination to and governed by the civil power." |
| Virginia | Article I, Section 13 | "That a well regulated militia composed of the body of the people, trained to arms, is the proper, natural, and safe defense of a free state, therefore, the right of the people to keep and bear arms shall not be infringed; that standing armies, in time of peace, should be avoided as dangerous to liberty; and that in all cases the military should be under strict subordination to, and governed by, the civil power." |
| Washington | Article I, Section 24 | "The right of the individual citizen to bear arms in defense |

| *State* | *Constitutional Reference* | *Text Language* |
|---|---|---|
| | | of himself, or the state, shall not be impaired, but nothing in this section shall be construed as authorizing individuals or corporations to organize, maintain, or employ an armed body of men." |
| West Virginia | The Constitution is silent on the issue. Article III, 12, refers to limitations on standing armies and their subordination to civil power, limitations on military courts, and to the quartering of soldiers. | |
| Wisconsin | The Constitution is silent on the issue. Article I, Section 20, refers to the subordination of the military to the civil power. | |
| Wyoming | Article I, Section 24 | "The right of citizens to bear arms in defense of themselves and of the state shall not be denied." |

# APPENDIX 2

## Selected Cases Dealing with the Right to Keep and Bear Arms and the Power to Regulate*

Akron v. Dixon, 303 N.E.2d 923, 36 Ohio Misc. 133

Akron v. Williams, 113 Ohio App. 293, 17 Ohio Ops 2d 317, 177 N.E.2d 802, app. dismd. 172 Ohio St. 287, 16 Ohio Ops 2d 6, 175 N.E.2d 174

Andrews v. State, 3 Heisk. 165

Application of Atkinson, 291 N.W.2d 396

Application of Cassidy, 51 N.Y. S.2d 202, 268 App. Div. 282, rearg. den. 63 N.Y.S.2d 840, 270 App. Div. 1046, affd. 73 N.E.2d 41, 299 N.Y. 926

Application of Grauling, 183 N.Y.S.2d 654, 17 Misc. 2d 1021

Aymette v. State, 2 Humphr. 154

Biffer v. Chicago, 278 Ill. 562, 116 N.E. 182

Bliss v. Commonwealth, 2 Litt. 90

Brown v. City of Chicago, 250 N.E.2d 129, 42 Ill.2d 501

Burton v. Sills, 240 A.2d 462, 99 N.J. Super. 516, affd. 240 A.2d 432, 99 N.J. Super. 459, affd. 248 A.2d 521, 53 N.J. 86, 28 A.L.R. 3d 829, app. dism. 89 S.Ct. 1486, 394 U.S. 812, 22 L.Ed.2d 748

---

*Sources: *Corpus Juris Secundum* (Brooklyn: The American Law Book Company, 1956), Volume 94 and Pocket Supplement; *American Jurisprudence* (Rochester: The Lawyers Co-Operative Publishing Company, and San Francisco: Bancroft-Whitney Company, 1975), Second Edition, Volume 79 and Pocket Supplement; *West's Federal Practice Digest 2d* (St. Paul: West Publishing Company, 1978), Volume 80 and Pocket Supplement; and *United States Code Annotated, Amendments 1 to 3, Cumulative Supplement* (St. Paul: West Publishing Company, 1983).

Carson v. State, 247 S.E.2d 68, 241 Ga. 622

Cases v. U.S., C.C.A., Puerto Rico, 131 F.2d 916, cert. den. Cases Valazquez v. U.S., 63 S.Ct. 1431, 319 U.S. 770 87 L.Ed. 1718, reh. den. 65 S.Ct. 1010, 324 U.S. 889, 89 L.Ed. 1437

Cody v. U.S., C.A. Mo., 460 F.2d 34, cert. den. 93 S.Ct. 454, 409 U.S. 1010, 34 L.Ed.2d 303

Commonwealth v. McHarris, 246 Pa. Super. 488, 371 A.2d 941

Commonwealth v. Ray, 218 Pa. Super. 72, 272 A.2d. 275, vac. on other grounds 448 Pa. 307, 292 A.2d 410

Davis v. State, 146 So.2d 892

Detroit v. Judge, Recorder's Court, Traffic & Ordinance Div., 56 Mich. App. 224, 223 N.W.2d 722

Dunne v. People, 94 Ill. 120, 34 Am. R. 213

Eckert v. City of Philadelphia, D.C.Pa., 329 Supp. 845, affd., C.A., 477 F.2d 610, cert. den. 94 S.Ct. 89, 414 U.S. 839, 38 L.Ed.2d 74, and 94 S.Ct.104, 414 U.S. 843, 38 L.Ed.2d 81

Eckert v. State of Pa., D.C.Pa., 331 F.Supp, 1361, affd. C.A., 474 F.2d 1339, cert. den. 93 S.Ct. 1522, 410 U.S. 989, 36 L.Ed.2d 187, and 93 S.Ct. 1560, 411 U.S. 920, 36 L.Ed.2d 313

Engblom v. Carey, D.C.N.Y., 522 F. Supp. 57, affd. in part, revd. in part on oth. grds., C.A., 677 F.2d 957, on remand, D.C., 572 F. Supp. 44, affd. C.A., 724 F.2d 28

English v. State, 35 Tex. 473, 14 Am.R. 374

Ex parte Ramirez, 226 P. 914, 193 Cal. 633

Ex parte Thomas, 97 P. 260, 21 Okl. 770, 20 L.R.A., N.S. 1007, 17 Ann. Cas. 566

Fall v. Esso Standard Oil Co. (CA5 Fla) 297 F.2d 411, cert.den. 371 U.S. 814, 9 L.Ed.2d 55, 83 S.Ct. 24

Fife v. State, 31 Ark. 455, 25 Am.R. 556

Galloway v. State, 69 S.W.2d 89, 125 Tex. Cr. 524

Galvan v. Superior Court of San Francisco, 70 Cal. 2d 851, 76 Cal. Rptr. 642, 452 P.2d 930

Glasscock v. City of Chattanooga, 11 S.W.2d 678, 157 Tenn. 518

Grimm v. City of New York, 289 N.Y.S.2d 358, 56 Misc. 2d 525

Guida v. Dier, 375 N.Y.S.2d 826, 84 Misc.2d 110, revd. on oth. grds. 387 N.Y.S.2d 720, 54 A.D.2d 86

Haile v. State, 38 Ark. 564

Hardison v. State, 437 P.2d 868, 84 Nev. 125

Harris v. State, 432 P.2d 929, 83 Nev. 404, 30 A.L.R.3d 1412
Hetherton v. Sears, Roebuck & Co., C.A.Del., 62 F.2d 1152
Holland v. State, 33 Ark. 560
In re Brickey, 70 P. 609, 8 Idaho 597, 101 Am.S.R. 215, 1 ann.Cas. 55
In re Opinion of Justices, 14 Gray 614
In re Reilly, 31 Ohio Dec. 364 (C.P. 1919)
Jackson v. State, 68 So.2d 850, 37 Ala. App. 335, cert. den. 58 So.2d 853, 260 Ala. 698
Jennings v. State, 5 Tex. Crim. App. 298
Jones v. U.S., 97 S.Ct. 384, 429 U.S. 960, 50 L.Ed.2d 327
Junction City v. Lee, 532 P.2d 1929, 316 Kan. 495
Klinger v. Erickson, 328 F.Supp. 674
Lakewood v. Pillow, 180 Colo. 20, 501 P.2d 744 (en banc)
Lally v. Department of Police, App., 306 So.2d 65
Las Vegas v. Moberg (App) 82 N.M. 626, 485 P.d 737
Maryland & District of Columbia Rifle and Pistol Ass'n. Inc., v. Washington, C.A., 442 F.2d 123, 142 U.S. App.D.C. 375
Matthews v. State, 148 N.E.2d 334, 237 Ind. 677
Miller v. Texas, 153 U.S. 535, 38 L.Ed. 812, 14 S.Ct. 874
Moore v. Gallup, 45 N.Y.S.2d 63, 267 App. Div. 64, affd. 59 N.E.2d 439, 293 N.Y. 846, motion grntd. 60 N.E.2d 847, 294 N.Y. 699
Morrison v. State, 170 Tex. Crim. 218, 339 S.W.2d, 529
Mosher v. City of Dayton, 358 N.E.2d 540, 48 Ohio St.2d 243, 2 0.0.3d 412
Mowels v. State, 211 S.W.2d 213, 152 Tex. Cr. 135
Nunn v. State, 1 Ga. (1 Kelly) 243
Onderdonk v. Handgun Permit Review Bd. of Dept. of Public Safety and Correctional Services of Maryland, 407 A.2d 763, 44 Md. App. 132
People v. Blue, 544 P.2d 385, 190 Colo. 95
People v. Brown, 235 N.W. 245, 253 Mich. 537, 82 A.L.R. 341
People ex rel. Darling v. Warden of City Prison, 154 App. Div. 413, 139 NYS 277
People v. Dubose, 117 Cal. Rptr. 235, 42 C.A.3d
People ex rel. Ferris v. Horton, 264 N.Y.S. 84, 147 Misc. 506, affd. 269 N.Y.S. 579, 239 Div. 610
People v. Garcia, 595 P.2d 228, 197 Colo. 550
People v. Nakamura, 99 Colo. 262, 62 P.2d 246 (en banc)

People v. Seale, 78 Cal. Rptr. 811, 274 C.A.2d 107
People v. Warden of City Prison, 139 N.Y.S. 277, 154 App. Div. 413, 29 N.Y.Cr. 74
People v. Zerillo, 189 N.W. 927, 219 Mich. 635, 24 A.L.R. 1115
Photos v. City of Toledo, 250 N.E.2d 916, 19 Ohio Misc. 147
Prater v. Burns, App., 525 S.W.2d 846
Presser v. Illinois, 6 S.Ct. 580, 116 U.S. 252, 29 L.Ed. 615
Quilici v. Village of Morton Grove, 532 F. Supp. 1169 (N.D. Ill.), affd. 695 F.2d 261, cert. den. 104 S.Ct. 194
R. G. Industries, Inc., v. Askew, 276 S. 2d 1
Rawlings v. Illinois Dept. of Law Enforcement, 391 N.E.2d 758, 29 Ill. Dec. 333, 73 Ill. App. 3d 267
Rinzler v. Carson, 262 So.2d 661
Robertson v. Baldwin, 165 U.S. 275, 41 L.Ed. 715, 17 S.Ct. 326
Salina v. Blaksley, 72 Kan. 230, 83 P. 619
Schubert v. DeBard, 398 N.E.2d 1339
Sklar v. Byrne, 556 F. Supp. 736·
Sonzinsky v. United States, 300 U.S. 506, 81 L.Ed. 772, 57 S.Ct 554
State v. Amos, 343 So.2d 166
State v. Beorchia, 530 P.2d 813
State v. Bias, 37 La.Ann. 259
State v. Blocker, 291 Or. 255, 630 P.2d 824
State v. Bolin, 200 Kan. 369, 436 P.2d 978
State v. Buzzard, 4 Ark. 18
State v. Dawson, 159 S.E.2d 1, 272 N.C. 535
State v. Duke, 42 Tex. 455
State v. Fant, 371 N.E.2d 588, 53 Ohio App.2d 87, 7 0.0.3d 58
State v. Hart, 157 P.2d 72, 66 Idaho 217
State v. Hogan, 63 Ohio St. 202, 58 N.E. 572
State v. Keet, 269 Mo. 206, 190 S.W. 573
State v. Kerner, 107 S.E. 222, 181 N.C. 574
State v. Kessler, 614 P.2d 94, 289 Or. 359
State v. Krantz, 164 P.2d 453, 24 Wash.2d 350
State v. Montoya, App., 572 P.2d 1270, 91 N.M. 262
State v. Nickerson, 247 P.2d 188, 126 Mont. 157
State v. Reid, 1 Ala. 612
State v. Robinson, 343 P.2d 886, 217 Or. 612
State v. Rosenthal, 75 Vt. 295, 55 A. 610

State v. Rupp, 282 N.W.2d 125
State v. Sanne, 364 A.2d 630, 116 N.H. 583
State v. Schutzler, 249 N.E.2d 549, 20 Ohio Misc. 79
State v. Swanton, App., 629 P.2d 98, 129 Ariz. 131
State v. Wilburn, 66 Tenn. 57
State v. Winkelman, 442 N.E.2d 811, 2 Ohio App. 3d 465, 2 O.B.R. 561
State v. Workman, 14 S.E. 9, 35 W. Va. 367, 14 L.R.A. 600
Stevens v. U.S., C.A. Ky., 440 F.2d 144
Strickland v. State, 137 Ga. 1, 72 S.E. 260
Taylor v. McNeal, 523 S.W.2d 148
Thompson v. Dereta, 549 F.Supp. 297
United States v. Adams, 11 F. Supp. 216
United States v. Birmley, 529 F.2d 103
United States v. Bowdach, 414 F. Supp. 1346
United States v. Brooks, 330 A.2d 245
United States v. Casson, 288 F. Supp. 86
United States v. Cruikshank, 92 U.S. 542, 23 L.Ed. 588
United States v. Day, 476 F.2d 562
United States v. Decker, 292 F.2d 89, cert. den. 368 U.S. 834, 7 L.Ed.2d 36, 82 S.Ct. 58
United States v. Friday, 404 F.Supp. 1343
United States v. Gross, 313 F.Supp, 1330, affd. 451 F.2d 1355
United States v. Gurrola-Garcia, 547 F.2d 1075
United States v. Houston, 547 F.2d 104
United States v. Johnson, 441 F.2d 1134
United States v. Kilburn, 596 F.2d 928
United States v. Kozerski, 518 F.Supp. 1082
United States v. Kraase, 340 F. Supp. 147, rev. 484 F.2d 549
United States v. Melville, 309 F.Supp. 774
United States v. Miller, 59 S.Ct. 816, 307 U.S. 174, 83 L.Ed. 1206
United States v. Oakes, 564 F.2d 384, cert. den. 98 S.Ct. 1493, 435 U.S. 926, 55 L.Ed.2d 521
United States v. Romero, 484 F.2d 1324
United States v. Rose, 695 F.2d 1356
United States v. Rubino, 320 F.Supp. 613
United States v. Swinton, 521 F.2d 1255
United States v. Synnes, 438 F.2d 764, disapproved on other

grounds, United States v. Bass, 404 U.S. 336, 30 L.Ed.2d 488, 92 S.Ct 515, and vac. on other grds., 404 U.S. 1009, 30 L.Ed.2d 657, 92 S.Ct 687

United States v. Three Winchester 30-30 Caliber Lever Action Carbines, 504 F.2d 1288

United States v. Tomlin, 454 F.2d 176, cert. den. 92 S.Ct 1792, 406 U.S. 924, 32 L.Ed.2d 125

United States v. Tot, 131 F.2d 261, rev. on other grnds 63 S.Ct. 1241, 319 U.S. 463, 87 L.Ed. 1519

United States v. Warin, 530 F.2d 103, cert. den. 96 S.Ct. 3168, 426 U.S. 948, 49 L.Ed.2d 1185

United States v. Wiley, 309 F.Supp, 141, affd. 438 F.2d 773, following opinion 438 F.2d 764

United States v. Wilson, 440 F.2d 1068

Vietnamese Fishermen's Ass'n v. Knights of the Ku Klux Klan, 453, F.Supp. 198

Watson v. Steon, 4 So.2d. 700, 148 Fla. 516

Williams v. Commonwealth, 261 S.W.2d 807

Wilson v. State, 33 Ark. 557

# SELECTED BIBLIOGRAPHY


*A Collection of State Tracts Published During the Reign of King William III*. London. 3 Volumes. 1705, 1706, 1707.

Abbey, Edward. *Abbey's Road*. New York: E. P. Dutton, 1979.

Adair, Douglass, and Schultz, John A., eds. *Peter Oliver's Origin & Progress of The American Rebellion*. San Marino: The Huntington Library, 1961.

Adams, John. *A Defence of the Constitutions of Government of the United States of America*. 3 Volumes. London: 1787, 1788. Da Capo Press Reprint Edition. New York: Da Capo Press, 1971.

Allen, William Sheridan. *The Nazi Seizure of Power: The Experience of a Single German Town, 1930-1935*. Chicago: Quadrangle Press, 1965.

Alviani, Joseph D., and Drake, William R. *Handgun Control: Issues and Alternatives*. United States Conference of Mayors, 1975.

American Enterprise Institute for Public Policy Research. *Gun Control*. Washington, D.C.: American Enterprise Institute for Public Policy Research, 1976.

Andreski, Stanislav. *Military Organization and Society*. Berkeley and Los Angeles: University of California Press, Second Edition, 1968.

Ansell, S. T.: "Legal and Historical Aspects of the Militia." *Yale Law Journal*, Volume XXVI, No. 5, March, 1917.

Aristotle. *Politics*. Translated by Benjamin Jowett. New York: The Modern Library, 1943.

Asbury, Charles J. "The Right to Keep and Bear Arms: The Origins and Application of the Second Amendment to the Constitution." Ph.D. Dissertation, University of Michigan, 1974.

Ascione, Alfred M. "The Federal Firearms Act." *St. John's Law Review*, Volume 13, April, 1939.

Ashbrook, John M. "Against Comprehensive Gun Control." *Current History*, Volume 71, No. 418, July/August, 1976.

Ashman, Martin C. "Handgun Control by Local Government." *Northern*

*Kentucky Law Review*, Volume 10, No. 1, 1982.

Bagley, J. J., and Rowley, P. D. *A Documentary History of England, Volume I, 1066-1540*. Baltimore: Penguin Books, 1966.

Bailyn, Bernard. *The Ideological Origins of the American Revolution*. Cambridge: The Belknap Press of Harvard University Press, 1967.

———, *Pamphlets of the American Revolution, 1750-1776*. Cambridge: The Belknap Press of Harvard University Press, 1965.

Bakal, Carl. *The Right to Bear Arms*. New York: McGraw-Hill Book Company, 1966.

Barlow, Joel. *Advice to the Privileged Orders in the Several States of Europe, Resulting from the Necessity and Propriety of a General Revolution in the Principle of Government*. London, 1792, 1795. Ithaca: Great Seal Books, 1956.

Barnes Company. *Handgun Laws of the U.S.* Fairfield, CT.: Barnes Company, 1974.

Barrett, Sidney R., Jr. "The Right to Bear Arms and Hangdun Prohibition: A Fundamental Rights Analysis." *North Carolina Central Law Journal*, Volume 14, 1983.

Bass, Howard I. "Quilici v. Village of Morton Grove: Ammunition for a National Handgun Ban." *DePaul Law Review*, Volume 32, Winter, 1983.

Becarria, Cesare. *On Crimes and Punishments*. Translated, and with an Introduction by Henry Paolucci. Indianapolis: The Bobbs-Merrill Company, Inc., 1963. Originally published 1764.

Beha, James A., II. "'An *Nobody* Can Get You Out:' The Impact of a Mandatory Prison Sentence for the Illegal Carrying of a Firearm on the Use of Firearms and on the Administration of Criminal Justice in Boston—Part I." *Boston University Law Review*, Volume 57, No. 1, Jauary, 1977.

———, "'And Nobody Can Get You Out:'" Part II, *Ibid.*, No. 2, March, 1977.

Benedict, Mark. "Second Amendment Right to Bear Arms: Quilici v. Village of Morton Grove, 532 F. Supp. 1169 (N. D. Ill. 1981)." *Akron Law Review*, Volume 16, No. 2, Fall, 1982.

Bennenson, Mark K. "A Controlled Look at Gun Controls." *New York Law Forum*, Volume 14, 1968.

Black, Hugo. "The Bill of Rights." *New York University Law Review*, Volume 35, No. 4, April, 1960.

Blackmore, Howard L. *Guns and Rifles of the World*. London: B. T. Batsford, Ltd., 1965.

*Blackstone's Commentaries*. Many Editions.

Bodin, Jean. *The Six Books of a Commonweale*. Edited, and with an Introduction by Kenneth Douglas McRae. Cambridge: Harvard University Press, 1962.

Boorstin, Daniel J. *The Americans: The Colonial Experience*. New York: Random House, 1958.

_______, *The Americans: The National Experience*. New York: Random House, 1965.

Borden, Morton, ed. *The Antifederalist Papers*. East Lansing: Michigan State University Press, 1965.

Bork, Robert H. "Neutral Principles and Some First Amendment Problems." *Indiana Law Journal*, Volume 47, No. 1, Fall, 1971.

Boskin, Joseph. "The Essential American Soul: Violent." In Joseph Boskin, ed., *Issues in American Society*. Encino: Glencoe, 1978.

Boston, Noel. *Old Guns and Pistols*. London: Ernest Been Limited, 1958.

Boynton, Lindsay. *The Elizabethan Militia 1558-1638*. London: Routledge & Kegan Paul, 1967.

Brabner-Smith, John. "Firearm Regulation." *Law and Contemporary Problems*, Volume I, No. 4, October, 1934.

Bracton, Henrici de. *De Legibus et Consuetudinibus Angliae*. Ed. George E. Woodbine. Translated, and with revisions and notes, by Samuel E. Thorne. 2 Volumes. Cambridge: Belknap Press of Harvard University Press, 1968.

*Brassey's Infantry Weapons of the World, 1950-1975*. Ed. Major General J. I. H. Owen. London: Brassey's, 1975.

Breen, Victor; Garrett, Virgil; Kandt, William; and Shinkle, Frank. "Federal Revenue as a Limitation on State Police Power and the Right to Bear Arms—Purpose of Legislation as Affecting Its Validity." *Journal of the Kansas Bar Association*, Volume 9, November, 1940.

Brest, Paul. "The Misconceived Quest for the Original Understanding." *Boston University Law Review*, Volume 60, No. 2, March, 1980.

Brill, Steven. *Firearm Abuse: A Research and Policy Report*. Washington, D.C.: Police Foundation, 1977.

Brown, Joe B. "Firearms Legislation." *Vanderbilt Law Review*, Volume 18, 1965.

Bruce-Briggs, B. "The Great American Gun War." *The Public Interest*, Fall, 1976.

Bureau of Alcohol, Tobacco, and Firearms. *Project Identification: A Study of Crime Handguns*. Washington, D.C., 1976.

Bureau of Alcohol, Tobacco, and Firearms. *Your Guide to Firearms Regulation*. Washington, D.C., 1978.

Bureau of Alcohol, Tobacco, and Firearms. *Federal Regulation of Firearms and Ammunition*. Washington, D.C., 1980.

Burgh, James. *Political Disquisitions*. London: 1774.

Caplan, David I. "Decisions Sound Death Knell for 'Collective Right' Theory." *Gun Week*, Friday, October 24, 1980.

_______. "Handgun Control: Constitutional or Unconstitutional? A Reply to Mayor Jackson." *North Carolina Central Law Journal*, Volume 10, 1979.

———. "Restoring the Balance: The Second Amendment Revisited." *Fordham University Law Journal*, Volume V, 1976.

———. "The Right of the Individual to Bear Arms: A Recent Judicial Trend." *Detroit College of Law Review*, Volume 1982, Issue 4.

———. "Second Amendment: Its Meaning Today." *Gun Week*, May 10, 1974.

'Constitutional Law—National Firearms Act—The Right to Bear Arms." *St. John's Law Review*, Volume 14, 1939.

"Constitutional Limitations on Firearms Regulation." *Duke Law Journal*, Volume 1969, August.

Coke, Edward, *Institutes of the Laws of England*. Philadelphia: Johnson and Warner, and Samuel Fisher, Jr., 1812. 2 Volumes.

Cooley, Thomas M. *A Treatise on the Constitutional Limitations Which Rest upon the Legislative Power of the States of the American Union*. Boston: Little, Brown and Company, 1868.

Cooley, Thomas M. *The General Principles of Constitittional Law in the United States of America*. Boston: Little, Brown and Company, 1880.

Corwin, G. Lester II. "The Right to Keep and Bear Arms: America's Legacy Through the Common Law." A Thesis in Fulfillment of the Law and Liberty Fellowship. Menlo Park, California: Institute of Humane Studies, Summer, 1975.

Critchley, T. A. *The Conquest of Violence*. New York: Schocken Books, 1970.

Cruickshank, C. G. *Elizabeth's Army*. Oxford: At the Clarendon Press, 2nd Edition, 1966.

Cunliffe, Marcus. *Soldiers and Civilians*. Boston: Little, Brown and Company, 1968.

Davidson, Bill R. *To Keep and Bear Arms*. New Rochelle, New York: Arlington House, 1969.

Decision-Making Information, Inc. *Attitudes of the American Electorate Toward Gun Control*. Santa Ana, California: 1978.

Defensor, H. Charles. *Gun Registraton Now—Confiscation Later?* New York: Vantage Press, 1970.

*Documentary History of the Constitution of the United States of America*. Washington, D.C. U.S. Government Printing Office, 3 Volumes, 1894.

*Documents Illustrative of the Formation of the Union of the American States*. 69th Congress, 1st Session. House Document No. 398. Washington: U.S. Government Printing Office, 1927.

Douglas, David C., and George W. Greenaway. *English Historical Documents, Volume II, 1042-1189*. London: Eyre Methuen, and New York: Oxford University Press, 2nd Edition, 1981.

Dowlut, Robert. "The Right to Arms: Does the Constitution or the Predilection of Judges Reign?" *Oklahoma Law Review*, Volume 36, Winter, 1983.

Dowlut, Robert; and Knoop, Janet A. "State Constitutions and the Right to Keep and Bear Arms." *Oklahoma City University Law Review*, Volume 7, No. 2, Summer, 1982.

Draper, Thomas. *The Issue of Gun Control*. The Reference Shelf, Volume 53, No. 1. New York: H. W. Wilson Company, 1981.

Drinan, Robert F. "Gun Control: The Good Outweighs the Evil." *The Civil Liberties Review*, Volume 3, No. 5, August/September, 1976.

Dumbauld, Edward. *The Bill of Rights and What It Means Today*. Norman: University of Oklahoma Press, 1957.

Edwards, James E. *Myths About Guns*. Coral Springs, Florida: Peninsula Press, 1978.

Elliott, Jonathan. *The Debates in the Several State Conventions, on the Adoption of the Federal Constitution*. 5 Volumes. Philadelphia: J. B. Lippincott Company, 2d. ed., 1836.

Emery, Lucilius A. "The Constitutional Right to Keep and Bear Arms." *Harvard Law Review*, Volume XXVIII, 1914-1915.

Erskine, Hazel. "The Polls: Gun Control." *Public Opinion Quarterly*, Volume 36, Fall, 1974.

Euwer, Cary McN. "Taxation – National Firearms Act of 1934." *Georgetown Law Journal*, Volume 28, 1939.

Faiman, Charles. "Does the Fourteenth Amendment Incorporate the Bill of Rights? The Original Understanding." *Stanford Law Review*, Volume 2, December, 1949.

Featherstone, James J. "The Second Amendment to the United States Constitution Guarantees an Individual Right to Keep and Bear Arms." In *The Right to Keep and Bear Arms*, Report of the Subcommittee on the Constitution of the Committee on the Judiciary, United States Senate, 97th Congress, 2d Session, February, 1982.

Feder, Donald. "A Libertarian Looks at Gun Control." *Reason*, March, 1976.

"Federal Regulation of Firearms Sales." *University of Chicago Law Review*, Volume 31, No. 4, Summer, 1964.

Feller, Peter Buck, and Gotting, Karl L. "The Second Amendment: A Second Look." *Northwestern University Law Review*, Volume 61, No. 4, 1966.

Fields, Samuel. "Guns, Crime and the Negligent Gun Owner." *Northern Kentucky Law Review*, Volume 10, No. 1. 1982.

________. "Handgun Prohibition and Social Necessity." *Saint Louis University Law Journal*, Volume 23, No. 1, 1979.

"Firearms: Problems of Control." *Harvard Law Review*, Volume 80, No. 6, April, 1967.

Fletcher, John G. "The Corresponding Duty to the Right of Bearing Arms." *The Florida Bar Journal*, Volume 39, No. 3, March, 1965.

Frederick, Karl T. "Pistol Regulation: Its Principles and History." *American Journal of Police Science*, Part I, September-October, 1931; Part II, January-February, 1932; Part III, August-September, 1932.

Friebun, Eric S. "Banning Handguns: *Quilici v. Village of Morton Grove* and the Second Amendment." *Washington University Law Quarterly*, Volume 60, Fall, 1982.

Freund, Ernest. *The Police Power: Public Policy and Constitutional Rights*. Chicago: Callaghan & Company, 1904. Reprinted, New York: Arno Press, 1976.

Gardiner, Richard E. "To Preserve Liberty—A Look at the Right to Keep and Bear Arms." *Northern Kentucky Law Review*, Volume 10, No. 1, 1982.

Geisel, Martin S.; Roll, Richard, and Wettick R. Stanton, Jr. "The Effectiveness of State and Local Regulation of Handguns: A Statistical Analysis." *Duke Law Journal*, Volume 1969, No. 4, August.

Gottlieb, Alan M. *Gun Owner's Political Action Manual*. Ottawa, Ill.: Green Hill Publishers, Inc., 1976.

———, "Gun Ownership: A Constitutional Right." *Northern Kentucky Law Review*, Volume 10, No. 1, 1982.

———, *The Rights of Gun Owners*. Aurora, Ill.: Caroline House Publishers, Inc., 1981.

Graham, Howard Jay. "The Early Anti-Slavery Backgrounds of the Fourteenth Amendment—I, Genesis, 1833-1835; II, Systematization, 1835-1837," *Wisconsin Law Review*, May and July, 1950.

Graham, Hugh Davis and Gurr, Ted Robert, eds. *Violence in America: Historical and Comparative Perspectives*. Beverly Hills: Sage Publications, revised ed., 1979.

Greenwood, Colin. *Firearms Control: A Study of Armed Crime and Firearms Control in England and Wales*. London: Routledge and Kegan Paul, 1972.

Grotius, Hugo. *De Jure Belli ac Pacis*. Translated by Francis W. Kelsey, with the collaboration of Arthur E. R. Boak, Henry A. Sanders, Jesse S. Reeves, and Herbert F. Wright, with an Introduction by James Brown Scott. 3 Volumes. New York: Oceana Publications, 1964.

Grundeman, Arnold. "Constitutional Limitations on Federal Firearms Control." *Washburn Law Journal*, Volume 8, Winter, 1969.

Haight, George I. "The Right to Keep and Bear Arms." *Bill of Rights Review*, Volume II, 1941.

Halbrook, Stephen P. *That Every Man Be Armed: The Evolution of a Constitutional Right*. Albuquerque: University of New Mexico Press, 1984.

———, "The Fourteenth Amendment and the Right to Keep and Bear Arms: The Intent of the Framers." In *The Right to Keep and Bear Arms*.

Report of the Subcommittee on the Constitution of the Committee on the Judiciary, United States Senate, 97th Congress, 2d Session, February, 1982.

———, "The Jurisprudence of the Second and Fourteenth Amendments." *George Mason University Law Review*, Volume 4, 1981.

———, "To Keep and Bear Their Private Arms: The Adoption of the Second Amendment, 1787-1791." *Northern Kentucky Law Review*, Volume 10, No. 1, 1982.

———, "The Second Amendment as a Phenomenon of Classical Political Philosophy." In Don B. Kates, Jr., ed., *Firearms and Violence: Issues of Public Policy*. San Francisco: Pacific Institute for Public Policy Research, and Ballinger Publishing Company, 1984.

Hamilton, Alexander; Madison, James; and Jay, John. *The Federalist*. With an Introduction by Carl Van Doren. New York: The Heritage Press, 1945.

Hardy, David T. "Firearms Ownership and Regulation: Tackling an Old Problem with Renewed Vigor." *William and Mary Law Review*, Volume 20, No. 2, Winter, 1978.

———, "Historical Basis of the Right to Keep and Bear Arms." In *The Right to Keep and Bear Arms*. Report of the Subcommittee on the Constitution of the Committee on the Judiciary, United States Senate, 97th Congress, 2d Session, February, 1982.

———, "Legal Restriction of Firearm Ownership As An Answer to Violent Crime: What Was the Question?" *Hamline Law Review*, Volume 6, No. 2, July, 1983.

———, "Of Arms and the Law." *Chicago-Kent Law Review*, Volume 51, 1974.

———, "On Turning Citizens Into Criminals." *Law and Liberty*, Volume 4, No. 4, Winter, 1979.

Harrington, Michael. "The Politics of Gun Control." In Phillip Whitten, ed., *Readings in Sociology: Contempoary Perspectives*. New York: Harper and Row, 1979.

Harris, Richard. "Annals of Legislation: If You Love Your Guns." *The New Yorker*, April 20, 1968.

Hawkins, William. *A Treatise of the Pleas of the Crown*. John Curwood Edition. London: C. Rowoth, 1824. 2 Volumes.

Hayes, Stuart R. "The Right to Bear Arms, A Study in Judicial Misinterpretation." *William and Mary Law Review*, Volume 2, 1960.

Hill, Jim Dan. *The Minute Man in Peace and War: A History of the National Guard*. Harrisburg: The Stackpole Company, 1964.

*Hobbes's Leviathan*. Reprinted from the Edition of 1651, with an essay by the late W. G. Pogson Smith. Oxford: At the Clarendon Press, 1967.

Hofstadter, Richard. "America as a Gun Culture." *American Heritage*, Volume XXI, Number 6, October, 1970.

———, and Wallace, Michael, eds. *American Violence: A Documentary History*. New York: Alfred A. Knopf, 1970.

Holdsworth, W. S. *A History of English Law*. London: Methuen & Co., 3 volumes, 1903.

Hollister, C. Warren. *Anglo-Saxon Military Institutions on the Eve of the Norman Conquest*. Oxford: At the Clarendon Press, 1962.

———, *The Military Organization of Norman England*. Oxford: At the Clarendon Press, 1965.

Horowitz, Edward J. "Reflections on Gun Control: Does the Problem Have Solutions or Do the Solutions Have Problems?" *Los Angeles Bar Journal*, November, 1976.

"Impact of State Constitutional Right to Bear Arms Provisions on State Gun Control Legislation." *University of Chicago Law Review*, Volume 38, No. 1, Fall, 1970.

Inbau, Fred E. "Firearms and Legal Doctrine." *Tulane Law Review*, Volume VII, No. 4, June, 1983.

Jackson, Maynard Holbrook, Jr. "Handgun Control: Constitutional and Critically Needed." *North Carolina Central Law Journal*, Volume 8, 1977.

Jacobs, Robert Cooper. "Firearms Control." *St. John's Law Review*, Volume 42, January, 1968.

Jellinek, Georg. *The Declaration of the Rights of Man and of Citizens*. Authorized translation from the German by Max Farrand. New York: Henry Holt, 1901. Hyperion Reprint Edition, Westport, Conn.: 1979.

Josserand, Michel H., and Jan A. Stevenson. *Pistols, Revolvers, and Ammunition*. New York: Crown Publishers, Inc., 1972.

Kane, Jeffrey. "The Case Against Gun Control." *The Forensic Quarterly*, September, 1976.

Kaplan, John. "Controlling Firearms." *Cleveland State Law Review*, Volume 28, 1979.

———, "The Wisdom of Gun Prohibition." *The Annals of the American Academy of Political and Social Science*, Volume 455, May, 1981.

Kates, Don B., Jr. "Against Civil Disarmament: On the Futility of Prohibiting Guns." *Harper's Magazine*, September, 1978.

———, ed., *Firearms and Violence: Issues of Public Policy*. San Francisco: Pacific Institute for Public Policy Research, and Cambridge: Ballinger Publishing Company, 1984.

———, "Handgun Prohibition and the Original Meaning of the Second Amendment," *Michigan Law Review*, Volume 82, No. 2, November, 1983.

———, "Reflections on the Relevancy of Gun Control," *Criminal Law Bul-*

*letin*, Volume 13, April/May, 1977.

_______, ed., *Restricting Handguns: The Liberal Skeptics Speak Out*. North River Press, 1979.

_______, "Some Remarks on the Prohibition of Handguns," *Saint Louis University Law Journal*, Volume 23, no. 1, 1979.

_______, "Why A Civil Libertarian Opposes Gun Control," *The Civil Liberties Review*, Volume 3, No. 2, June, July, 1976.

_______, "Why Gun Control Won't Work," *Commonweal*, Volume CVIII, No. 5, 1976.

Kennedy, Edward M. "The Handgun Crime Control Act of 1981," *Northern Kentucky Law Review*, Volume 10, No. 1. 1982.

_______, "The Need for Gun Control Legislation," *Current History*, Volume 71, No. 418, July/August, 1976.

Kennett, Lee and Anderson, James. *The Gun in America: The Origins of a National Dilemma*. Westport: Greenwood Press, 1975.

Kessler, Raymond G. "Enforcement Problems of Gun Control: A Victimless Crimes Analysis," *Criminal Law Bulletin*, Volume 16, March, April, 1980.

_______, "Gun Control and Political Power," *Law and Policy Quarterly*, Volume 5, No. 3, July, 1983.

Kluin, Kurt F. "Gun Control: Is it a Legal and Effective Means of Controlling Firearms in the United States?" *Washburn Law Journal*, Volume 21, No. 2, Winter, 1982.

Krug, Alan S. *Firearms Registration: Costs v. Benefits*. Riverside, Conn.: National Shooting Sports Foundation, Inc., 1970.

_______, "The Misuse of Firearms in Crime," *Congressional Record*, Volume 114, Part 7, April 2, 1968.

_______, "The Relationship Between Firearms Licensing Laws and Crime Rates," *Congressional Record*, Volume 113, Part 15, July 25, 1967.

_______, "The Relationship Between Firearms Ownership and Crime Rates: A Statistical Analysis," *Congressional Record*, Volume 114, Part 2, January 30, 1968.

Leach, Douglas. "The Military System of Plymouth Colony," *New England Quarterly*, Volume XXIV, No. 3, 1951.

Leff, Carol Skalnik and March H. Leff. "The Politics of Ineffectiveness: Federal Firearms Legislation, 1919-38," *The Annals of the American Academy of Political and Social Science*, May, 1981.

Lester, David. *Gun Control: Issues and Answers*. Springfield: Charles C Thomas, Publisher, 1984.

Levin, John. "The Right to Bear Arms: The Development of the American Experience," *Chicago-Kent Law Review*, Fall-Winter, 1971.

Levine, Ronald B., and Saxe, David B. "The Second Amendment: The

Right to Bear Arms," *Houston Law Review*, Volume 7, No. 1, September, 1969.

Lizotte, Alan J., and Bordua, David J. "Firearms Ownership for Sport and Protection: Two Divergent Models," *American Sociological Review*, Volume 45, April, 1980.

Lyon, Bruce. *A Constitutional and Legal History of Medieval England*. New York: W. W. Norton & Company, 2d edition, 2 volumes, 1980.

McCabe, Michael K. "To Bear or to Ban: Firearms Control and the 'Right to Bear Arms'," *Journal of the Missouri Bar*, Volume 27, July, 1971.

McClain, Paula D. "Firearms Ownership, Gun Control Attitudes, and Neighborhood Environment," *Law and Policy Quarterly*, Volume 5, No. 3, July, 1983.

McClure, James A. "Firearms and Federalism," *Idaho Law Review*, Volume 7, 1970.

McKenna, Daniel J. "The Right to Keep and Bear Arms," *Marquette Law Review*, Volume 12, 1928.

Mahon, John K. *The American Militia: Decade of Decision, 1789-1800*. Gainesville: University of Florida, University of Florida Monographs, Social Sciences, No. 6, Spring, 1960.

Maitland, F. W. *The Constitutional History of England*. Cambridge: Cambridge University Press, 1920.

Malcolm, Joyce Lee. *Disarmed: The Loss of the Right to Bear Arms in Restoration England*. The Mary Ingraham Bunting Institute of Radcliffe College, 1980.

________. "The Right of the People to Keep and Bear Arms: The Common Law Tradition," *Hastings Constitutional Law Quarterly*, Volume 10, 1983.

Mann, James L., II. "The Right to Bear Arms," *South Carolina Law Review*, Volume 19, 1967.

Mereness, Newton D. *Maryland as a Proprietary Province*. New York: The Macmillan Company, 1901.

Millis, Walter. *Arms and Men: A Study in American Military History*. New York: G. P. Putnam's Sons, 1956.

Montague, Willimina. "Case Notes—Constitutional Law—Second Amendment—Firearms Act," *Southern California Law Review*, Volume 13, November, 1939.

Mook, H. Telfer. "Training Day in New England," *New England Quarterly*, Volume XI, December, 1938.

Moore, Mark H., and Kelling, George L. "'To Serve and Protect': Learning from Police History," *The Public Interest*, No. 70, Winter, 1983.

Morison, S. E., ed. *Sources and Documents Illustrating the American Revolution, 1764-1788, and The Formation of the Federal Union*. Oxford: At the Clarendon Press, 2d ed., 1929.

Morton, Louis. "The Origins of American Military Policy," *Military Affairs*, Volume XXII, No. 2, Summer, 1958.

Morrison, Stanley. "Does the Fourteenth Amendment Incorporate the Bill of Rights? The Judicial Interpretation," *Stanford Law Review*, Volume 2, December, 1949.

Mulvihill, Donald J.; Tumin, Melvin M.; and Curtis, Lynn A. *Crimes of Violence*. A Staff Report Submitted to the National Commission on the Causes and Prevention of Violence. Washington, D.C.: U.S. Government Printing Office, 1969. Volumes 11, 12, 13.

Murray, Douglas R. "Handguns, Gun Control Laws, and Firearm Violence," *Social Problems*, Volume 23, No. 1, October, 1975.

Newman, Robert G. "A Farewell to Arms?—An Analysis of Texas Handgun Control Law," *St. Mary's Law Journal*, Volume 13, 1982.

Newton, George D., Jr.; and Zimring, Franklin E. *Firearms and Violence in American Life*. A Staff Report to the National Commission on the Causes and Prevention of Violence. Washington, D.C.: U.S. Government Printing Office, 1969.

"Noncombatant's Guide to the Gun Control Fight," *Changing Times*, August, 1979.

Olds, Nicholas V. "The Second Amendment and the Right to Keep and Bear Arms," *Michigan State Bar Journal*, Volume 46, October, 1967.

Patterson, Bennett B. *The Forgotten Ninth Amendment*. Indianapolis: The Bobbs-Merrill Company, Inc., 1955.

Perry, Richard L., and Cooper, John C., eds. *Sources of Our Liberties: Documentary Origins of Individual Liberties in the United States Constitution and Bill of Rights*. Chicago: American Bar Foundation, 1959.

Peterson, John. "Firearms—A Comparative Analysis of Proposed Federal Controls," *DePaul Law Review*, Volume XV, No. 1, 1965.

Pierce, Darell R. "Second Amendment Survey," *Northern Kentucky Law Review*, Volume 10, 1982.

Pittman, R. Carter. "The Fifth Amendment: Yesterday, Today and Tomorrow," *American Bar Association Journal*, Volume 42, 1956.

Pocock, J. G. A. *The Machiavellian Moment*. Princeton: Princeton University Press, 1975.

Podgers, James. "First Legal Shots Fired Over Handgun Ordinance," *American Bar Association Journal*, Volume 67, August, 1981.

Pollock, Sir Frederick and Maitland, Frederic William. *The History of English Law Before the Time of Edward I*. Cambridge: At the University Press, 2d Edition, 2 Volumes, 1968.

Pound, Roscoe. *The Development of Constitutional Guarantees of Liberty*. Westport: Greenwood Press, Publishers, 1957.

Powicke, Michael Rhys. *Military Obligation in Medieval England*. Westport:

Greenwood Press, Publishers, 1975.

President's Commission on Law Enforcement and Administration of Justice. *The Challenge of Crime in a Free Society*. Washington, D.C.: U.S. Government Printing Office, 1967.

Pufendorf, Samuel. *De Jure Naturae et Gentium*. Translation of the edition of 1688 by C. H. and W. A. Oldfather. New York: Oceana Publications, Inc., and London: Wildy & Sons, Ltd. Reprinted 1964.

R. T. G. "The Federal Firearms Act," *Temple University Law Quarterly*, Volume 17, May, 1943.

Radabaugh, Jack S. "The Militia of Colonial Massachusetts," *Military Affairs*, Volume XVIII, Spring, 1954.

Rawle, William. *A View of the Constitution of the United States of America*. Philadelphia: Philip H. Nicklin, 2d ed., 1829. A Da Capo Press Reprint Edition, New York: Da Capo Press, 1970.

"Regulation of Firearms." *Journal of Criminal Law, Criminology and Police Science*, Volume 17, November, 1926.

"Restrictions on the Right to Bear Arms: State and Federal Firearms Legislation," *University of Pennsylvania Law Review*, Volume 98, 1950.

*Right to Keep and Bear Arms*, Report of the Subcommittee on the Constitution of the Committee on the Judiciary, United States Senate, 97th Congress, 2d Session. Washington, D.C.: U.S. Government Printing Office, February, 1982.

Riker, William H. *Soldiers of the States: The Role of the National Guard in American Democracy*. Washington, D.C.: Public Affairs Press, 1957.

Riley, Robert J. "Shooting to Kill the Handgun: Time to Martyr Another American 'Hero'," *Journal of Urban Law*, Volume 51, Issue 3, February, 1974.

Riseley, Richard F., Jr. "The Right to Keep and Bear Arms: A Necessary Constitutional Guarantee or an Outmoded Provision of the Bill of Rights?" *Albany Law Review*, Volume 31, March/April, 1966.

Rose, Thomas, ed. *Violence in America: A Historical and Contemporary Reader*. New York: Random House, 1969.

Rutland, Robert Allen. *The Birth of the Bill of Rights*. Chapel Hill: University of North Carolina Press, 1955.

Rutman, Darrett Bruce. "A Militant New World, 1607-1640." Ph.D. Dissertation, University of Virginia. 2 Volumes. 1959.

Santee, John C. "The Right to Keep and Bear Arms," *Drake Law Review*, Volume 26, 1976-1977.

Savin, Laura Chauss. "Municipalities and Gun Control: Handgun Bans," *Hamline Law Review*, Volume 6, No. 2, July, 1983.

Schwartz, Bernard, ed. *The Bill of Rights: A Documentary History*. New York: Chelsea House Publishers, in Association with McGraw-Hill Book

Company, 2 Volumes, 1971.

———. *The Great Rights of Mankind: A History of the American Bill of Rights.* New York: Oxford University Press, 1977.

Schwoerer, Lois G. *No Standing Armies*. Baltimore: Johns Hopkins University Press, 1974.

Seitz, Steven Thomas. "Firearms, Homicides and Gun Control Effectiveness," *Law and Society Review*, Volume 6, No. 4, May, 1972.

Shalhope, Robert E. "The Ideological Origins of the Second Amendment," *The Journal of American History*, Volume 69, No. 3, December, 1982.

Sheppard, Edward H. "Control of Firearms," *Missouri Law Review*, Volume 34, 1969.

Shy, John. *A People Numerous and Armed*. New York: Oxford University Press, 1976.

———. *Toward Lexington: The Role of the British Army in the Coming of the American Revolution*. Princeton: Princeton University Press, 1965.

Singletary, Otis A. *Negro Militia and Reconstruction*. Austin: University of Texas Press, 1957.

Smith, H. F. Russell. *Harrington and His Oceana*. New York: Octagon Books, 1971.

Smith, Joseph H., and Barnes, Thomas G. *The English Legal System: Carryover to the Colonies*. Los Angeles: William Andrews Clark Memorial Library, 1975.

Smith, Tom W. "The 75% Solution: An Analysis of the Structure of Attitudes on Gun Control, 1959-1977," *The Journal of Criminal Law and Criminology*, Volume 71, No. 3, Fall, 1980.

Spannaus, Warren. "State Firearms Regulation and the Second Amendment," *Hamline Law Review*, Volume 6, No. 2, July, 1983.

Sprecher, Robert A. "The Lost Amendment," *American Bar Association Journal*, Volume 51, June and July, 1965.

Stern, Frederick Martin. *The Citizen Army*. New York: St. Martin's Press, 1957.

Stevens, Charles Ellis. *Sources of the Constitution of the United States*. New York: Macmillan and Co., 1894.

Story, Joseph. *Commentaries on the Constitution of the United States*. Boston: Hilliar, Gray and Company, Cambridge: Brown, Shattuck, and Co. 3 Volumes. 1833.

Tiedeman, Christopher G. *A Treatise on the Limitations of Police Power in the United States*. St. Louis: The F. H. Thomas Law Book Co., 1886.

Tilly, Charles. *From Mobilization to Revolution*. Reading: Addison-Wesley Publishing Co., 1978.

Tonso, William R. *Gun and Society: The Social and Existential Roots of the American Attachment to Firearms*. Washington, D.C.: University Press of

America, Inc., 1982.

Tribe, Lawrence H. *American Constitutional Law*. Mineola: The Foundation Press, Inc., 1978.

Tucker, Henry St. George. *Commentaries on the Laws of Virginia*. Winchester: Office of the Republican, 2 Volumes, 1837.

Tucker, John Randolph. *The Constitution of the United States*. Chicago: Callaghan & Co., 2 Volumes, 1899.

Tunis, Edwin. *Weapons: A Pictorial History*. Cleveland: The World Publishing Company, 1954.

Turley, Windle. "Manufacturers' and Suppliers' Liability to Handgun Victims," *Northern Kentucky Law Review*, Volume 10, No. 1, 1982.

Turner, J. W. Cecil. *Russel on Crime*. London: Stevens & Sons, 2 Volumes, 1964.

United States Constitution Sesquicentennial Commission. *History of the Formation of the Union under the Constitution, with Liberty Documents and Report of the Commission*. Washington, D.C.: U.S. Government Printing Office, 1946.

Vattel, Emmerich de. *The Law of Nations*. Philadelphia: Abraham Small, 1817.

Vinogradoff, Paul. *English Society in the Eleventh Century*. Oxford: At the Clarendon Press, 1908.

*Violent Crime in the United States*. Washington, D.C.: U.S. Department of Justice, 1981.

Wallitsch, Thomas A. "Right to Bear Arms in Pennsylvania: The Regulation of Possession," *Duquesne Law Review*, Volume 11, Summer, 1973.

Waybright, Roger J. "The Right to Bear Arms," *Florida Law Journal*, Volume XIII, No. 7, July, 1939.

Weatherup, Roy G. "Standing Armies and Armed Citizens: An Historical Analysis of the Second Amendment," *Hastings Constitutional Law Quarterly*, Volume 2, No. 1, Winter, 1975.

Weiss, Jonathan A. "A Reply to Advocates of Gun-Control Law," *Journal of Urban Law*, Volume 52, Issue 3, Winter, 1974.

Weller, Jac. "Irreglar But Effective: Partisan Weapons Tactics in the American Revolution, Southern Theatre," *Military Affairs*, Volume XXI, No. 3, Fall, 1957.

Western, J. R. *The English Militia in the Eighteenth Century*. London: Routledge and Kegan Paul, 1965.

Whisker, James B. *The Citizen Soldier and United States Military Policy*. North River Press, 1979.

———. "Historical Development and Subsequent Erosion of the Right to Keep and Bear Arms," *West Virginia Law Review*, Volume 78, 1976.

———. *Our Vanishing Freedom: The Right to Keep and Bear Arms*. Skokie:

Publisher's Development Corporation, 2d Ed., 1973.

_______. *The Right to Hunt*. North River Press, 1981.

_______. "The Second Amendment: The Right to Keep and Bear Arms." Ph.D. Dissertation, University of Maryland, 1969.

Whitelock, Dorothy, ed. *English Historical Documents c. 500-1042*. Volume I. New York: Oxford University Press, 1955.

Williams, E. N. *A Documentary History of England*. Volume II. Baltimore: Penguin Books, 1965.

Williams, John. *Atlas of Weapons and War*. New York: The John Day Company, 1976.

Wilson, James Q. "Crime and American Culture," *The Public Interest*, No. 70, Winter, 1983.

Wright, James D. "Public Opinion and Gun Control: A Comparison of Results From Two Recent National Surveys," *Annals of the American Academy of Political and Social Science*, Volume 455, May, 1981.

Wright, James D., and Marston, Linda L. "The Ownership of the Means of Destruction: Weapons in the United States," *Social Problems*, Volume 23, No. 1, October, 1975.

Wright, James D.; Rossi, Peter H.; Daly, Kathleen; and Weber-Burdin, Eleanor. *Weapons, Crime and Violence in America: A Literature Review and Research Agenda*. Washington, D.C.: U.S. Department of Justice, National Institute of Justice, 1981.

Wright, Paul B. "The Effect of Federal Firearms Control on Civil Disorder," *Brooklyn Law Review*, Volume 35, Spring, 1969.

Yeager, Matthew G. *Do Mandatory Prison Sentences for Handgun Offenders Curb Violent Crime?* United States Conference of Mayors, 2d. Edition, 1976.

Zimring, Franklin. "Firearms and Federal Law: The Gun Control Act of 1968," *The Journal of Legal Studies*, Volume IV, No. 1, January, 1975.

_______. "Handguns in the Twenty-First Century: Alternative Policy Futures," *The Annals of the American Academy of Political and Social Science*, Volume 455, May, 1981.

_______. "Is Gun Control Likely to Reduce Violent Killings?" *University of Chicago Law Review*, Volume 35, 1968.